Rx.NET in Action

Rx.NET in Action

TAMIR DRESHER

MANNING
SHELTER ISLAND

For online information and ordering of this and other Manning books, please visit
www.manning.com. The publisher offers discounts on this book when ordered in quantity.
For more information, please contact

> Special Sales Department
> Manning Publications Co.
> 20 Baldwin Road
> PO Box 761
> Shelter Island, NY 11964
> Email: orders@manning.com

Manning Publications Co.
20 Baldwin Road
PO Box 761
Shelter Island, NY 11964

Development editor:	Lesley Trites
Review editor:	Donna Clements
Technical development editor:	Michael Lund
Copyeditor:	Sharon Wilkey
Proofreader:	Elizabeth Martin
Technical proofreader:	Cody Sand
Typesetter:	Marija Tudor
Cover designer:	Marija Tudor

ISBN 9781617293061
Printed in the United States of America

To Gabi, my wife and best friend, who made this dream a reality

contents

foreword

This book, *Rx.NET in Action*, does a great job in explaining the details and background that .NET developers need to effectively use Rx. In particular, it explains how to connect the plethora of asynchronous types in .NET to Rx observables, and how to deal with errors, resource allocation, and last but not least, concurrency.

Since its inception, the .NET Framework has emphasized the importance of asynchronous execution and nonblocking I/O. Through delegates, the .NET Framework has emphasized higher-order functional programming from the beginning, and by automatically defining the `BeginInvoke` and `EndInvoke` methods on delegates, developers may call any method asynchronously.

But the `BeginInvoke`/`EndInvoke` pattern for asynchronous operations is tedious and verbose, because it requires converting your code into continuation-passing style. As an alternative, the .NET Framework introduced the event-based asynchronous pattern that uses the built-in support of .NET for events and event handlers. Although the event-based pattern was a big step forward compared to asynchronous delegates, more opportunities remained to streamline the development experience.

For synchronous streams of values, modeled by the standard interfaces of `Enumerable`/`IEnumerator`, the LINQ standard query operators provide a beautiful and elegant algebra for processing streams in a high-level and declarative manner. Wouldn't it be nice if we could use the fact that events are conceptually also streams of values and hence provide a similar LINQ-based programming model for events?

Another disadvantage of using events for asynchronous calls is that this ignores the fact that unlike most other events, such as mouse clicks, the events wired up to asynchronous operations produce at most one value. Wouldn't it be nice if we could use the fact that asynchronous methods return only a single value and hence provide a

xiii

similar imperative programming model that supports regular control-flow-like conditionals, loops, and exception handling for asynchronous methods?

As it turns out, the answer to both questions is a resounding yes! By using the mathematical trick of equalization, we can mechanically convert the `IEnumerable`/`IEnumerator` interfaces for synchronous pull-based streams into the monadic `IObservable`/`IObserver` interfaces for asynchronous push-based streams. The async/await syntax in C# and Visual Basic allows developers to use regular imperative syntax to write both synchronous and asynchronous methods, and the LINQ query comprehensions allow developers to write queries over both synchronous and asynchronous data streams.

This is the heart of Rx. Many languages outside the .NET world have now adopted the magic square of one/many × sync/async, making developers happy and productive no matter what language they're using.

If you're a .NET developer, you'll want to keep a copy of this book handy to put Rx.NET into action!

—ERIK MEIJER
INVENTOR OF RX, FOUNDER OF APPLIED DUALITY

preface

Reactive Extensions (Rx) for .NET was first published in November 2009 under the short description "Rx is a .NET Library that allows programmers to write succinct declarative code to orchestrate and coordinate asynchronous and event-based programs based on familiar .NET idioms and patterns." (See http://mng.bz/gQ31.)

I remember watching the first examples and reading the discussions. I was amazed by the elegance of the solutions and how simple they looked. Unfortunately, when I sat down and tried to use Rx, things were harder than I thought, and the mental change I needed to make toward reactive programming was significant. In those days, there wasn't a lot of material on the subject, and I had to struggle to solve my issues and learn things the hard way with a lot of trial and error.

In 2012, at end of my military service and upon joining CodeValue (www.code-value.net), I had two major projects that enabled me to really appreciate my Rx knowledge. The first was about a cybersecurity application that needed to react to multiple events and coordinate them in order to show the end user the state of various incidents all happening in parallel. The second was a video chat application, running on mobile and PC devices. The video chat application reacted to events such as users logging in and out of the system and receiving messages of various types that had to be dealt with differently. Though these two systems were different, they shared the same problems of writing a flow based on events—a flow that involves filtering of received values, dealing with asynchronicity and concurrency, and identifying patterns of recurring events so that the application could respond efficiently and correctly. I introduced Rx to both of those systems, and it was one of the things that made each a success. We exceeded expectations and preceded our schedule.

Still, even though I had knowledge of Rx, problems still happened from time to time, and little material on Rx, such as books and guides, was available. Many times problems originated because of my colleagues' lack of knowledge or situations that were new to us. Luckily, after I identified the problem source, it would be easy to fix, mostly because of the flexibility of Rx operators. In the following years, I started to blog and speak about Rx and how it made solving complex problems easy. That is when the idea for this book started to grow. My vision was to create a step-by-step guide that holds the pieces needed for the .NET programmer to get the maximum out of the Rx library and the reactive programming paradigm. I also wanted to write about the practices that I acquired over the years, as well as the pitfalls and their solutions.

It took hard and careful work to make sure the book fulfills its aim. Some chapters had to be rewritten, topics were changed, and some material had to be left out in order to concentrate on the important and fundamental features. The result of this hard work is *Rx.NET in Action*, a book that you can read front to back or go directly to a specific chapter to solve a problem or refresh your memory.

Rx is an evolving technology that was also ported to numerous other platforms and languages. It is an open source project and part of the .NET Foundation (www.dotnet-foundation.org). My hope is that Rx will become the de facto way to program, orchestrate, and coordinate asynchronous and event-based programs in .NET and that this book will give you everything you need to be ready for this new and exciting world of Rx.

acknowledgments

I dedicate this book to my marvelous wife Gabriela. Your support, love, and care throughout my writing process is what allowed me to turn this book into a reality. I love you and admire you for your many efforts while I was busy writing.

To my beautiful children Shira and Yonatan, you bring joy and light to my life; I love you dearly. Sitting by you while you fell asleep gave me the inspiration for many chapters.

To my parents Ester and Shlomo, who bought me my first computer and lit the fire of my passion for computer science, I thank you.

To my cousin, Guy, who had an enormous effect on my life and the way I see things today, much of my software capabilities are rooted in what you taught me.

To the rest of my family, who had to put up with me while my mind drifted to the book while I was talking with them, I appreciate everything you've done.

A special thanks to my good friend Dror Helper, who without even knowing gave me advice that contributed to this book.

Thanks also to all my colleagues at CodeValue, who supported me throughout the process.

A special appreciation goes to Erik Meijer for contributing the wonderful foreword to my book and of course for helping to create Rx.

Thank you to the staff at Manning. Everyone who worked with me in editorial, production, and promotion, both directly and behind the scenes, helped to create the best book possible. It was truly a team effort.

Thanks to the many reviewers who provided feedback during the writing and development process: Bruno Sonnino, Bachir Chihani, Carsten Jørgensen, Dror Helper, Edgar Knapp, Fabrizio Cucci, Goetz Heller, Ignacio Rigoni, Jason Hales, Joel

Kotarski, Jorge Branco, Mattias Lundell, Michele Mauro, Oscar Vargas, Rohit Sharma, and Stephen Byrne. Thanks also to Cody Sand, the technical proofreader, who meticulously reviewed the sample code of the final manuscript.

Finally, much gratitude to the Rx team and contributors who built a wonderful technology.

about this book

Rx.NET in Action is a full guide for the Reactive Extensions library for .NET developers. It delivers explanations, best practices, and tips and tricks that will allow you to fully use Rx in your applications.

Who should read this book

Rx.NET in Action is for .NET developers who write event-based and asynchronous applications and need powerful consuming and querying capabilities over events and push-based sources.

Rx.NET in Action is also suitable for developers who are curious about reactive programming and the Rx library techniques, but who may not have an immediate need to use it. Adding Rx know-how to your toolbox is valuable for future projects; reactive programing is a hot topic and will continue to be in the future.

This book primarily uses the .NET version of Rx, and the code examples use the C# language. Readers familiar with C# will be right at home.

This book is suitable for any platform supported by .NET (including .NET Core).

How this book is organized

The book's 11 chapters are divided into two sections.

Part 1 provides an introduction to reactive programming and to the .NET skills you need in order to understand the functional aspects of the library.

- Chapter 1 explores the reactive programming paradigm and Reactive Manifesto concepts. The chapter introduces the building blocks of Rx and explains when and why it should be used.

- Chapter 2 is where you really meet Rx and the steps needed to incorporate it into your application. It shows a simple case-study of using Rx inside an application and compares two versions of the same application, before and after Rx is used.
- Chapter 3 provides an overview of the functional programming concepts and techniques that Rx uses and how they're provided with the .NET Framework and the C# language.

Part 2 dives into each of the tasks you'll do with Rx—from creating observables and observers, to controlling their lifetimes and reacting to queries you create on top of them.

- Chapter 4 teaches ways to create observable sequences and it shows how synchronous observables can be created from enumerables and built-in creation operators.
- Chapter 5 explains the way Rx handles asynchronous code and how to bridge the native .NET asynchronous types into observables. This chapter also discusses the importance of asynchronous code in the modern application and how to add periodic behavior to your programs.
- Chapter 6 concentrates on the observable-observer relationship and how to control it. In this chapter, I explain the best way to create observers for various scenarios and how to limit the lifetime of the observer subscription.
- Chapter 7 explains the differences between hot and cold observables and introduces Rx subjects. This chapter teaches you how to control the state of the observable when observers subscribe to it and how to share emissions between the observers.
- Chapter 8 provides a catalog of the basic query operators provided in the Rx library. Rx is often referred to as *LINQ to Events*, and knowing the details of the Rx operators will help you build powerful queries that will save you time and effort.
- Chapter 9 continues where chapter 8 leaves off and shows advanced ways to partition and combine observables. You'll learn how to group elements by condition or by coincidence and how to react to correlations between observables.
- Chapter 10 delves deep into the Rx concurrency model and synchronization. I introduce the concept of schedulers and explain the schedulers Rx has to offer. Then I explain how to control the time and computation location of your Rx queries.
- Chapter 11 teaches you to protect your Rx queries from faults and to react to errors that might happen in the query processing. This chapter also covers ways to manage resources that are consumed by the observables and the Rx queries.

The book also has three appendices:

- Appendix A summarizes the concepts of asynchronous programming in .NET.

- Appendix B presents the Rx Disposables library and explains how to use the utilities it provides.
- Appendix C explains how to test Rx operators and queries.

The book is intended to be used as a guide and as a reference. If you're new to Rx, I recommend reading from the beginning. If you're already familiar with Rx concepts, you might find it useful to read a specific chapter based on the task you're trying to accomplish.

About the code

This book contains many examples of source code both in numbered listings and inline with normal text. In both cases, source code is formatted in a `fixed-width font like this` to separate it from ordinary text. Sometimes code is also **in bold** to highlight code that has changed from previous steps in the chapter, such as when a new feature adds to an existing line of code.

In many cases, the original source code has been reformatted; we've added line breaks and reworked indentation to accommodate the available page space in the book. In rare cases, even this was not enough, and listings include line-continuation markers (⟼). Additionally, comments in the source code have often been removed from the listings when the code is described in the text. Code annotations accompany many of the listings, highlighting important concepts.

The source code for this book is available to download from the publisher's website (www.manning.com/books/rx-dot-net-in-action) and from GitHub (https://github.com/tamirdresher/RxInAction). Instructions for using this code are provided in the README file included in the repository root.

In the e-book, color is used in some listings and code snippets. Blue is used for primitive types and saved keywords. Aqua highlights user-defined types, and red is used for string literals. Brown is used for string parameters placeholders, and green is for comments. As always, black is user code.

Author Online

Purchase of *Rx.NET in Action* includes free access to a private web forum run by Manning Publications, where you can make comments about the book, ask technical questions, and receive help from the author and from other users. To access the forum and subscribe to it, point your web browser at www.manning.com/books/rx-dot-net-in-action. This page provides information on how to get on the forum after you're registered, the kinds of help available, and the rules of conduct on the forum.

Manning's commitment to our readers is to provide a venue where a meaningful dialogue between individual readers and between readers and the author can take place. It's not a commitment to any specific amount of participation on the part of the author, whose contribution to the Author Online forum remains voluntary (and unpaid). We suggest you try asking him some challenging questions, lest his interest stray! The Author Online forum and the archives of previous discussions will be accessible from the publisher's website as long as the book is in print.

Other online resources

If you're interested in Rx, you may also want to check out the Rx portal http://reactivex.io, which provides a Developer Center. It contains the most recent information about the library and its ports.

Rx.NET is an open source project, and you can find the full code and discussions at https://github.com/Reactive-Extensions/Rx.NET.

If you want to ask a question about Rx, you can visit the gitter channel (https://gitter.im/Reactive-Extensions/Rx.NET) or the slack #rx channel, which requires you to subscribe through the sign-up page for the .NET Core Slack Channel (http://tattoocoder.com/aspnet-slack-sign-up/).

about the author

 TAMIR DRESHER is a senior software architect working as a consultant at CodeValue in Israel. As a prominent member of the Microsoft programming community, Tamir frequently speaks on software development topics at developers conferences, and as a lecturer for software engineering at the Ruppin Academic Center.

As an expert in .NET Framework and software craftsmanship, Tamir has trained hundreds of developers and helped many high-profile clients in the commercial and public sector.

Tamir has used Rx since it was released and fell in love instantly. Being one of the early adopters helped Tamir understand the Rx library internals, and he has the passion to explain it to other developers and help them enhance their programming skills with the power of the reactive programming paradigm.

Tamir writes about his coding adventures at his blog, www.tamirdresher.com.

about the cover illustration

The figure on the cover of *Rx.NET in Action* is captioned "Habit of a Bonza or Priest in China." The illustration is taken from publisher Thomas Jefferys' *A Collection of the Dresses of Different Nations, Ancient and Modern* (four volumes), London, published between 1757 and 1772. The title page states that these are hand-colored copperplate engravings, heightened with gum arabic. Thomas Jefferys (1719–1771) was called "Geographer to King George III." An English cartographer, he was the leading map supplier of his day. He engraved and printed maps for government and other official bodies and produced a wide range of commercial maps and atlases, especially of North America. His work as a mapmaker sparked an interest in local dress customs of the lands he surveyed and mapped, which are brilliantly displayed in this collection.

Fascination with faraway lands and travel for pleasure were relatively new phenomena in the late 18th century, and collections such as this one were popular, introducing both the tourist as well as the armchair traveler to the inhabitants of other countries. The diversity of the drawings in Jefferys' volumes speaks vividly of the uniqueness and individuality of the world's nations some 200 years ago. Dress codes have changed since then, and the diversity by region and country, so rich at the time, has faded away. It's now often hard to tell the inhabitant of one continent from another. Perhaps, trying to view it optimistically, we've traded a cultural and visual diversity for a more varied personal life. Or a more varied and interesting intellectual and technical life.

At a time when it's hard to tell one computer book from another, Manning celebrates the inventiveness and initiative of the computer business with book covers based on the rich diversity of regional life of two centuries ago, brought back to life by Jefferys' pictures.

Part 1

Getting started with Reactive Extensions

What are reactive applications? What are they good for? How does programming with Reactive Extensions (Rx) change the way you write code? What should you do before you start working with Rx? And why is Rx better than traditional event-driven programming? These are the questions we'll begin to address in these first three chapters.

You'll learn what reactive systems and applications are, and why you should care. You'll see a real example of creating an application that uses Rx and what you need to do to create your own Rx applications. You'll also look at the functional programming foundations that Rx is based on, to make it easier to understand the rest of the concepts that this book introduces.

Reactive programming

This chapter covers

- Being reactive
- Thinking about events as streams
- Introducing Reactive Extensions (Rx)

The reactive programming paradigm has gained increasing popularity in recent years as a model that aims to simplify the implementation of event-driven applications and the execution of asynchronous code. Reactive programming concentrates on the propagation of changes and their effects—simply put, how to react to changes and create data flows that depend on them.[1]

With the rise of applications such as Facebook and Twitter, every change happening on one side of the ocean (for example, a status update) is immediately observed on the other side, and a chain of reactions occurs instantly inside the application. It shouldn't come as a surprise that a simplified model to express this reaction chain is needed. Today, modern applications are highly driven by changes happening in the outside environment (such as in GPS location, battery and power management, and social networking messages) as well as by changes inside the

---

[1] This book is about reactive programming and not about functional reactive programming (FRP). FRP can operate on continuous time, whereas Rx can operate only on discrete points of time. More info can be found at the FRP creator's keynote, http://mng.bz/TcB6.

3

application (such as web call responses, file reading and writing, and timers). To all of those events, the applications are reacting accordingly—for instance, by changing the displayed view or modifying stored data.

We see the necessity for a simplified model for reacting to events in many types of applications: robotics, mobile apps, health care, and more. Reacting to events in a classic imperative way leads to cumbersome, hard-to-understand, and error-prone code, because the poor programmer who is responsible for coordinating events and data changes has to work manually with isolated islands of code that can change that same data. These changes might happen in an unpredictable order or even at the same time. Reactive programming provides abstractions to events and to states that change over time so that we can free ourselves from managing the dependencies between those values when we create the chains of execution that run when those events occur.

Reactive Extensions (Rx) is a library that provides the reactive programming model for .NET applications. Rx makes event-handling code simpler and more expressive by using declarative operations (in LINQ style) to create queries over a single sequence of events. Rx also provides methods called *combinators* (combining operations) that enable you to join sequences of events in order to handle patterns of event occurrences or the correlations between them. At the time of this writing, more than 600 operations (with overloads) are in the Rx library. Each one encapsulates recurring event-processing code that otherwise you'd have to write yourself.

This book's purpose is to teach you why you should embrace the reactive programming way of thinking and how to use Rx to build event-driven applications with ease and, most important, fun. The book will teach you step by step about the various layers that Rx is built upon, from the building blocks that allow you to create reactive data and event streams, through the rich query capabilities that Rx provides, and the Rx concurrency model that allows you to control the asynchronicity of your code and the processing of your reactive handlers. But first you need to understand what being reactive means, and the difference between traditional imperative programming and the reactive way of working with events.

1.1   *Being reactive*

As changes happen in an application, your code needs to react to them; that's what being *reactive* means. Changes come in many forms. The simplest one is a change of a variable value that we're so accustomed to in our day-to-day programming. The variable holds a value that can be changed at a particular time by a certain operation. For instance, in C# you can write something like this:

```
int a = 2;
int b = 3;
int c = a + b;
Console.WriteLine("before: the value of c is {0}",c);

a=7;
b=2;
Console.WriteLine("after: the value of c is {0}",c);
```

The output is

```
before: the value of c is 5
after: the value of c is 5
```

In this small program, both printouts show the same value for the c variable. In our imperative programming model, the value of c is 5, and it will stay 5 unless you override it explicitly.

Sometimes you want c to be updated the moment a or b changes. Reactive programming introduces a different type of variable that's *time varying*: this variable isn't fixed to its assigned value, but rather the value varies by reacting to changes that happen over time.

Look again at our little program; when it's running in a reactive programming model, the output is

```
before: the value of c is 5
after: the value of c is 9
```

"Magically" the value of c has changed. This is due to the change that happened to its dependencies. This process works just like a machine that's fed from two parallel conveyers and produces an item from the input on either side, as shown in figure 1.1.

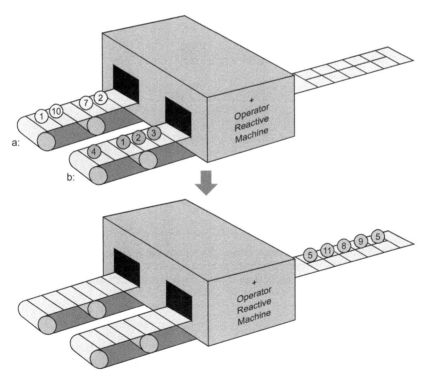

Figure 1.1 A reactive representation of the function c = a + b. As the values of a and b are changing, c's value is changing as well. When a is 7 and b is 2, c automatically changes to 9. When b changes to 1, c becomes 8 because a's value is still 7.

You might find it surprising, but you've probably worked with reactive applications for years. This concept of reactiveness is what makes your favorite spreadsheet application so easy and fun to use. When you create this type of equation in a spreadsheet cell, each time you change the value in cells that feed into the equation, the result in the final cell changes automatically.

1.1.1 Reactiveness in your application

In a real-world application, you can spot possible time-variant variables in many circumstances—for instance, GPS location, temperature, mouse coordinates, or even text-box content. All of these hold a value that's changing over time, to which the application reacts, and are, therefore, time variant. It's also worth mentioning that time itself is a time variant; its value is changing all the time. In an imperative programming model such as C#, you'd use events to create the mechanism of reacting to change, but that can lead to hard-to-maintain code because events are scattered among various code fragments.

Imagine a mobile application that helps users find discounts and specials in shops located in their surrounding area. Let's call it *Shoppy*. Figure 1.2 describes the Shoppy architecture.

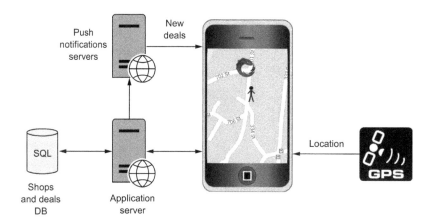

Figure 1.2   The Shoppy application architecture. The mobile app receives the current location from the GPS and can query about shops and deals via the application service. When a new deal is available, the application service sends a push notification through the push notifications server.

One of the great features you want from Shoppy is to make the size of the shop icon bigger on the map as the user gets closer (from a certain minimal radius), as shown in figure 1.3. You also want the system to push new deals to the application when updates are available.

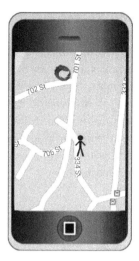 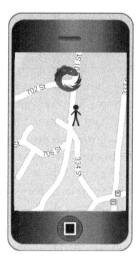

Figure 1.3 The Shoppy application view of the map. When the user is far from the Rx shop, the icon is small (on the left), and as the user gets closer, the icon gets bigger (on the right).

In this scenario, you could say that the `store.Location`, `myLocation`, and `iconSize` variables are time variant. For each store, the icon size could be written:

```
distance = store.Location - myLocation;
iconSize = (MINIMAL_RADIUS / distance)*MinIconSize
```

Because you've used time-variant variables, each time a change occurs in the `myLocation` variable, a change is triggered in the `distance` variable. The application will eventually react by making the store icon appear bigger or smaller, depending on the distance from the store. Note that for simplicity, I didn't handle the boundary check on the minimum allowed icon size, and that distance might be 0 or close to it.

This is a simple example, but as you'll see, the great power of using the reactive programming model lies in its ability to combine and join, as well as to partition and split the *stream* of values that each time-variant variable is pushing. This is because reactive programming lets you focus on what you're trying to achieve rather than on the technical details of making it work. This leads to simple and readable code and eliminates most boilerplate code (such as change tracking or state management) that distracts you from the intent of your code logic. When the code is short and focused, it's less buggy and easier to grasp.

We can now stop talking theoretically so you can see how to bring reactive programming into action in .NET with the help of Rx.

1.2 *Introducing Reactive Extensions*

Now that we've covered reactive programming, it's time to get to know our star: Reactive Extensions, which is often shortened to Rx. Microsoft developed the Reactive Extensions library to make it easy to work with streams of events and data. In a way, a time-variant value is by itself a stream of events; each value change is a type of event that you subscribe to and that updates the values that depend on it.

Rx facilitates working with streams of events by abstracting them as observable sequences, which is also the way Rx represents time-variant values. *Observable* means that you as a user can observe the values that the sequence carries, and *sequence* means an order exists to what's carried. Rx was architected by Erik Meijer and Brian Beckman and drew its inspiration from the functional programming style. In Rx, a stream is represented by *observables* that you can create from .NET events, tasks, or collections, or can create by yourself from another source. Using Rx, you can query the observables with LINQ operators and control the concurrency with schedulers;[2] that's why Rx is often defined in the Rx.NET sources as Rx = Observables + LINQ + Schedulers.[3] The layers of Rx.NET are shown in figure 1.4.

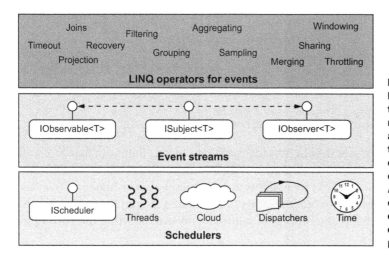

Figure 1.4   The Rx layers. In the middle are the key interfaces that represent event streams and on the bottom are the schedulers that control the concurrency of the stream processing. Above all is the powerful operators library that enables you to create an event-processing pipeline in LINQ style.

You'll explore each component of the Rx layers as well as their interactions throughout this book, but first let's look at a short history of Rx origins.

1.2.1   Rx history

I believe that to get full control of something (especially technology), you should know the history and the details behind the scenes. Let's start with the Rx logo which features an electric eel, shown in figure 1.5; this eel was Microsoft Live Labs' Volta project logo.

Figure 1.5   The Rx electric eel logo, inspired from the Volta project

---

[2]   A *scheduler* is a unit that holds an internal clock and is used to determine when and where (thread, task, and even machine) notifications are emitted.

[3]   Reactive-Extensions/Rx.Net github repository, https://github.com/Reactive-Extensions/Rx.NET.

The Volta project was an experimental developer toolset for creating multitier applications for the cloud, before the term *cloud* was formally defined. Using Volta, you could specify which portion of your application needed to run in the cloud (server) and which on the client (desktop, JavaScript, or Silverlight), and the Volta compiler would do the hard work for you. Soon it became apparent that a gap existed in transferring events arising from the server to the clients. Because .NET events aren't first-class citizens, they couldn't be serialized and pushed to the clients, so the observable and observer pair was formed (though it wasn't called that at the time).

Rx isn't the only technology that came out of project Volta. An intermediate language (IL) to the JavaScript compiler was also invented and is the origin of Microsoft TypeScript. The same team that worked on Volta is the one that brought Rx to life.

Since its release in 2010, Rx has been a success story that's been adopted by many companies. Its success was seen in other communities outside .NET, and it was soon being ported to other languages and technologies. Netflix, for example, uses Rx extensively in its service layer and is responsible for the RxJava port.[4] Microsoft also uses Rx internally to run Cortana—the intelligent personal assistant that's hosted inside every Windows Phone device; when you create an event, an observable is created in the background.

At the time of this writing, Rx is supported in more than 10 languages, including JavaScript, C++, Python, and Swift. Reactive Extensions is now a collection of open source projects. You can find information about them as well as documentation and news at http://reactivex.io/. Reactive Extensions for .NET is hosted under the GitHub repo at https://github.com/Reactive-Extensions/Rx.NET.

Now that we've covered a bit of the history and survived to tell about it, let's start exploring the Rx internals.

1.2.2 Rx on the client and server

Rx is a good fit with event-driven applications. This makes sense because events (as you saw earlier) are the imperative way to create time-variant values. Historically, event-driven programming was seen mainly in client-side technologies because of the user interaction that was implemented as events. For example, you may have worked with OnMouseMove or OnKeyPressed events. For that reason, it's no wonder that you see many client applications using Rx. Furthermore, some client frameworks are based on Rx, such as ReactiveUI (http://reactiveui.net).

But let me assure you that Rx isn't client-side-only technology. On the contrary, many scenarios exist for server-side code that Rx will fit perfectly. In addition, as I said before, Rx is used for large applications such as Microsoft Cortana, Netflix, and complex event processing (CEP) using Microsoft StreamInsight. Rx is an excellent library for dealing with messages that the application receives, and it doesn't matter whether it's running on a service layer or a client layer.

---

[4] See "Reactive Programming in the Netflix API with RxJava" by Ben Christensen and Jafar Husain (http://techblog.netflix.com/2013/02/rxjava-netflix-api.html) for details.

1.2.3   *Observables*

Observables are used to implement time-variant values (which we defined as observable sequences) in Rx. They represent the *push model*, in which new data is pushed to (or notifies) the observers.

Observables are defined as the source of the events (or notifications) or, if you prefer, the publishers of a stream of data. And the push model means that instead of having the observers fetch data from the source and always checking whether there's new data that wasn't already taken (the *pull model*), the data is delivered to the observers when it's available.

Observables implement the `IObservable<T>` interface that has resided in the `System` namespace since version 4.0 of the .NET Framework.

Listing 1.1   The `IObservable` interface

```
public interface IObservable<T>
{
    IDisposable Subscribe(IObserver<T> observer);      ◁──── Subscribes an observer to
}                                                             the observable sequence
```

The `IObservable<T>` interface has only one method, `Subscribe`, that allows observers to be subscribed for notifications. The `Subscribe` method returns an `IDisposable` object that represents the subscription and allows the observer to unsubscribe at any time by calling the `Dispose` method. Observables hold the collection of subscribed observers and notify them when there's something worth notifying. This is done using the `IObserver<T>` interface, which also has resided in the `System` namespace since version 4.0 of the .NET Framework, as shown here.

Listing 1.2   The `IObserver` interface

```
public interface IObserver<T>
{
    void OnNext(T value);        ◁──── Notifies the observer of a new
    void OnError(Exception error);      element in the observable sequence
    void OnCompleted();
}                               ◁──── Notifies the observer that the observable
                                      sequence has completed and no more
                                      notifications will be emitted
```

Notifies the observer that an exception has occurred

The basic flow of using `IObservable` and `IObserver` is shown in figure 1.6. Observables don't always complete; they can be providers of a potentially unbounded number of sequenced elements (such as an infinite collection). An observable also can be "quiet," meaning it never pushed any element and never will. Observables can also fail; the failure can occur after the observable has already pushed elements or it can happen without any element ever being pushed.

This observable algebra is formalized in the following expression (where * indicates zero or more times, ? indicates zero or one time, and | is an OR operator):

OnNext(t)* (OnCompleted() | OnError(e))?

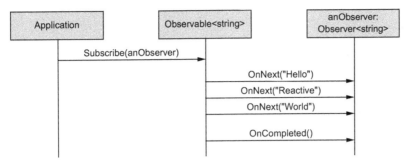

Figure 1.6 A sequence diagram of the happy path of the observable and observer flow of interaction. In this scenario, an observer is subscribed to the observable by the application; the observable "pushes" three messages to the observers (only one in this case), and then notifies the observers that it has completed.

When failing, the observers will be notified using the `OnError` method, and the exception object will be delivered to the observers to be inspected and handled (see figure 1.7). After an error (as well as after completion), no more messages will be pushed to the observers. The default strategy Rx uses when the observer doesn't provide an error handler is to escalate the exception and cause a crash. You'll learn about the ways to handle errors gracefully in chapter 10.

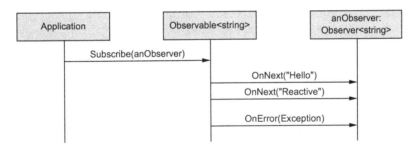

Figure 1.7 In the case of an error in the observable, the observers will be notified through the `OnError` method with the exception object of the failure.

The Observer design pattern

In certain programming languages, events are sometimes offered as first-class citizens, meaning that you can define and register events with the language-provided keywords and types and even pass events as parameters to functions.

For languages that don't support events as first-class citizens, the Observer pattern is a useful design pattern that allows you to add event-like support to your application. Furthermore, the .NET implementation of events is based on this pattern.

(continued)

The Observer pattern was introduced by the Gang of Four (GoF) in *Design Patterns: Elements of Reusable Object-Oriented Software* (Addison-Wesley Professional, 1994). The pattern defines two components: subject and observer (not to be confused with `IObserver` of Rx). The *observer* is the participant that's interested in an event and subscribes itself to the subject that raises the events. This is how it looks in a Unified Modeling Language (UML) class diagram:

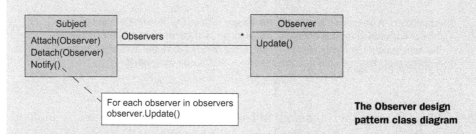

The Observer design pattern class diagram

The observer pattern is useful but has several problems. The observer has only one method to accept the event. If you want to attach to more than one subject or more than one event, you need to implement more update methods. Another problem is that the pattern doesn't specify the best way to handle errors, and it's up to the developer to find a way to notify of errors, if at all. Last but not least is the problem of how to know when the subject is done, meaning that there will be no more notifications, which might be crucial for correct resource management. The Rx `IObservable` and `IObserver` are based on the Observer design pattern but extend it to solve these shortcomings.

1.2.4 Operators

Reactive Extensions also brings a rich set of operators. In Rx, an *operator* is a nice way to say *operation*, but with the addition that it's also part of a domain-specific language (DSL) that describes event processing in a declarative way. The Rx operators allow you to take the observables and observers and create pipelines of querying, transformation, projections, and other event processors you may know from LINQ. The Rx library also includes time-based operations and Rx-specific operations for queries, synchronization, error handling, and so on.

For example, this is how you subscribe to an observable sequence of strings that will show only strings that begin with *A* and will transform them to uppercase:

```
IObservable<string> strings= ... ◄───  Observable of strings
                                        that will push strings
                                        to observers

IDisposable subscription =                          ◄──── Saving the subscription
    strings.Where(str => str.StartsWith("A")) ◄───        enables you to
                                                          unsubscribe later.

                                     Allows only strings that start with
                                     A to be passed to the observer
```

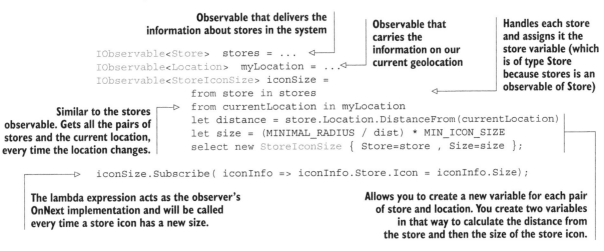

String is transformed to uppercase before continuing.

```
                    .Select(str => str.ToUpper())
                    .Subscribe(...);

//Rest of the code
:
subscription.Dispose();
```

Observer is subscribed to receive strings that passed through the filtering and transformation.

Dispose of the subscription when you no longer want to receive the strings.

NOTE Don't be scared if you don't understand all the syntax or the meaning of each keyword. I explain all of them in the next chapters.

In this simple example, you can see the declarative style of the Rx operators—say what you want and not how you want it—and so the code reads like a story. Because I want to focus on the querying operators in this example, I don't show how the observable is created. You can create observables in many ways: from events, enumerables, asynchronous types, and more. Those are discussed in chapters 4 and 5. For now, you can assume that the observables were created for you behind the scenes.

The operators and combinators (operators that combine multiple observables) can help you create even more complex scenarios that involve multiple observables. To achieve the resizable icon for the shops in the Shoppy example, you can write the following Rx expressions:

Observable that delivers the information about stores in the system

Observable that carries the information on our current geolocation

Handles each store and assigns it the store variable (which is of type Store because stores is an observable of Store)

```
IObservable<Store> stores = ...
IObservable<Location> myLocation = ...
IObservable<StoreIconSize> iconSize =
                from store in stores
                from currentLocation in myLocation
                let distance = store.Location.DistanceFrom(currentLocation)
                let size = (MINIMAL_RADIUS / dist) * MIN_ICON_SIZE
                select new StoreIconSize { Store=store , Size=size };

iconSize.Subscribe( iconInfo => iconInfo.Store.Icon = iconInfo.Size);
```

Similar to the stores observable. Gets all the pairs of stores and the current location, every time the location changes.

The lambda expression acts as the observer's OnNext implementation and will be called every time a store icon has a new size.

Allows you to create a new variable for each pair of store and location. You create two variables in that way to calculate the distance from the store and then the size of the store icon.

Even without knowing all the fine details of Reactive Extensions, you can see that the amount of code needed to implement this feature in the Shoppy application is small, and it's easy to read. All the boilerplate of combining the various streams of data was done by Rx and saved you the burden of writing the isolated code fragments required to handle the events of data change.

1.2.5 *The composable nature of Rx operators*

Most Rx operators have the following format:

```
IObservable<T> OperatorName(arguments)
```

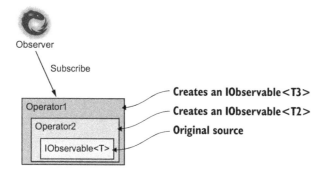

Creates an IObservable<T3>

Creates an IObservable<T2>

Original source

Figure 1.8   The composable nature of Rx operators allows you to encapsulate what happens to the notification since it was emitted from the original source.

Note that the return type is an observable. This allows the composable nature of Rx operators; you can add operators to the observable pipeline, and each one produces an observable that encapsulates the behavior that's been applied to the notification from the moment it was emitted from the original source.

Another important takeaway is that from the observer point of view, an observable with or without operators that are added to it is still an observable, as shown in figure 1.8.

Because you can add operators to the pipeline not only when the observable is created, but also when the observer is subscribed, it gives you the power to control the observable even if you don't have access to the code that created it.

1.2.6   *Marble diagrams*

A picture is worth a thousand words. That's why, when explaining reactive programming and Rx in particular, it's important to show the execution pipeline of the observable sequences. In this book, I use marble diagrams to help you understand the operations and their relationships.

Marble diagrams use a horizontal axis to represent the observable sequence. Each notification that's carried on the observable is marked with a symbol, usually a circle (although other symbols are used from time to time), to distinguish between values. The value of the notification is written inside the symbol or as a note above it, as shown in figure 1.9.

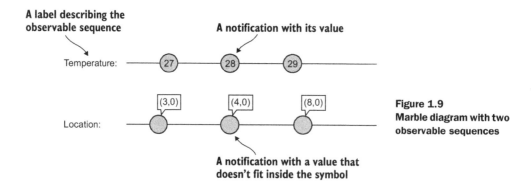

A label describing the observable sequence

A notification with its value

Temperature: (27)   (28)   (29)

Location: (3,0) (4,0) (8,0)

A notification with a value that doesn't fit inside the symbol

Figure 1.9 Marble diagram with two observable sequences

In the marble diagram, time goes from left to right, and the distance between the symbols shows the amount of time that has passed between the two events. The longer the distance, the more time has passed, but only in a relative way. There's no way to know whether the time is in seconds, hours, or another measurement unit. If this information is important, it'll be written as a note.

To show that the observable has completed, you use the | symbol. To show that an error occurred (which also ends the observable), you use X. Figure 1.10 shows examples.

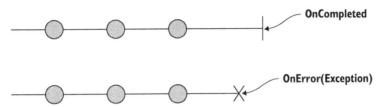

Figure 1.10 An observable can end because it has completed or because an error occurred.

To show the output of an operator (or multiple operators) on an observable, you can use an arrow that indicates the relationship between the source event and the result. Remember that each operator (at least the vast majority of operators) returns observables of its own, so in the diagram I'm writing the operator that's part of the pipeline on the left side and the line that represents the observable returned from it on the right side. Figure 1.11 shows a marble diagram for the previous example of an observable sequence of strings that shows only the strings that begin with A and transforms them to uppercase.

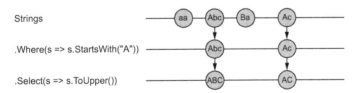

Figure 1.11 Marble diagram that shows the output of various operators on the observable

Marble diagrams are used in this book to show the effects of operators as well as examples of combining operators to create observable pipelines. At this point, you might be wondering how observable sequences relate to nonobservable sequences. The answer is next.

1.2.7 *Pull model vs. push model*

Nonobservable sequences are what we normally call *enumerables* (or *collections*), which implement the `IEnumerable` interface and return an iterator that implements the

`IEnumerator` interface. When using enumerables, you pull values out of the collection, usually with a loop. Rx observables behave differently: instead of pulling, the values are pushed to the observer. Tables 1.1 and 1.2 show how the pull and push models correspond to each other. This relationship between the two is called the *duality principle.*[5]

Table 1.1   How `IEnumerator` and `IObserver` correspond to each other

IEnumerator	IObserver
MoveNext—when false	OnCompleted
MoveNext—when exception	OnError(Exception exception)
Current	OnNext(T)

Table 1.2   How `IEnumerable` and `IObservable` correspond to each other

IEnumerable	IObservable
IEnumerator GetEnumerator(void)	IDisposable Subscribe(IObserver)[a]

[a] There's one exception to the duality here, because the twin of the `GetEnumerator` parameter (which is void) should have been transformed to the `Subscribe` method return type (and stay void), but instead `IDisposable` was used.

Observables and observers fill the gap .NET had when dealing with an asynchronous operation that needs to return a sequence of values in a push model (pushing each item in the sequence). Unlike `Task<T>` that provides a single value asynchronously, or `IEnumerable` that gives multiple values but in a synchronous pull model, observables emit a sequence of values asynchronously. This is summarized in table 1.3.

Table 1.3   Push model and pull model data types

	Single value	Multiple values
Pull/Synchronous/Interactive	T	IEnumerable<T>
Push/Asynchronous/Reactive	Task<T>	IObservable<T>

Because a reverse correspondence exists between observables and enumerables (the duality), you can move from one representation of a sequence of values to the other. A fixed collection, such as `List<T>`, can be transformed to an observable that emits all its values by pushing them to the observers. The more surprising fact is that observables can be transformed to pull-based collections. You'll dive into the details of how and when to make those transformations in later chapters. For now, the important

---

[5] This observation was made by Erik Meijer; see http://mng.bz/0jO4.

thing to understand is that because you can transform one model into the other, everything you can do with a pull-based model can also be done with the push-based model. So when you face a problem, you can solve it in the easiest model and then transform the result if needed.

The last point I'll make here is that because you can look at a single value as if it were a collection of one item, you can by the same logic take the asynchronous single item—the `Task<T>`—and look at it as an observable of one item, and vice versa. Keep that in mind, because it's an important point in understanding that "everything is an observable."

1.3 Working with reactive systems and the Reactive Manifesto

So far, we've discussed how Rx adds reactiveness to an application. Many applications aren't standalone, but rather part of a whole system that's composed of more applications (desktop, mobile, web), servers, databases, queues, service buses, and other components that you need to connect in order to create a working organism. The reactive programming model (and Rx as an implementation of that model) simplifies the way an application handles the propagation of changes and the consumption of events, thus making the application reactive. But how can you make a whole system reactive?

As a system, *reactiveness* is defined by being responsive, resilient, elastic, and message-driven. These four traits of reactive systems are defined in the *Reactive Manifesto* (www.reactivemanifesto.org), a collaborative effort of the software community to define the best architectural style for building a reactive system. You can join the effort of raising awareness about reactive systems by signing the manifesto and spreading the word.

It's important to understand that the Reactive Manifesto didn't invent anything new; reactive applications existed long before it was published. An example is the telephone system that has existed for decades. This type of distributed system needs to react to a dynamic amount of load (the calls), recover from failures, and stay available and responsive to the caller and the callee 24/7, and all this by passing signals (messages) from one operator to the other.

The manifesto is here to put the reactive systems term on the map and to collect the best practices of creating such a system. Let's drill into those concepts.

1.3.1 Responsiveness

When you go to your favorite browser and enter a URL, you expect that the page you were browsing to will load in a short time. When the loading time is longer than a few milliseconds, you get a bad feeling (and may even get angry). You might decide to leave that site and browse to another. If you're the website owner, you've lost a customer because your website wasn't responsive.

Responsiveness of a system is determined by the time it takes for the system to respond to the request it received. Obviously, a shorter time to respond means that the system is more responsive. A response from a system can be a positive result, such as the page you tried to load or the data you tried to get from a web service or the chart you wanted to see in the financial client application. A response can also be negative, such as an error message specifying that one of the values you gave as input was invalid.

In either case, if the time that it takes the system to respond is reasonable, you can say that the application is *responsive*. But a reasonable time is a problematic thing to define, because it depends on the context and on the system you're measuring. For a client application that has a button, it's assumed that the time it takes the application to respond to the button click will be a few milliseconds. For a web service that needs to make a heavy calculation, one or two seconds might also be reasonable. When you're designing your application, you need to analyze the operations you have and define the bounds of the time it should take for an operation to complete and respond. Being responsive is a goal that reactive systems are trying to achieve.

1.3.2 Resiliency

Every once in a while, your system might face failures. Networks disconnect, hard drives fail, electricity shuts down, or an inner component experiences an exceptional situation. A *resilient* system is one that stays responsive in the case of a failure. In other words, when you write your application, you want to handle failures in a way that doesn't prevent the user from getting a response.

The way you add resiliency to an application is different from one application to another. One application might catch an exception and return the application to a consistent state. Another application might add more servers so that if one server crashes, another one will compensate and handle the request. A good principle you should follow to increase the resiliency of your system is to avoid a single point of failure. This can be done by making each part of your application isolated from the other parts; you might separate parts into different AppDomains, different processes, different containers, or different machines. By isolating the parts, you reduce the risk that the system will be unavailable as a whole.

1.3.3 Elasticity

The application that you're writing will be used by a number of users—hopefully, a large number of users. Each user will make requests to your system that may result in a high load that your system will need to deal with. Each component in your system has a limit on the load level it can deal with, and when the load goes above that limit, requests will start failing and the component itself may crash. This situation of increasing load can also be caused by a distributed denial of service (DDoS) attack that your system is experiencing.

To overcome the causes of overload, your system needs to be *elastic*: it needs to span instances as the load increases and remove instances as the load decreases. This kind of automatic behavior has been much more apparent since the cloud entered our lives. When running on the cloud, you get the illusion of infinite resources; with a few simple configurations, you can set your application to scale up or down, depending on the threshold you define. You need to remember only that a cost is associated with running extra servers.

1.3.4 Message driven

At this point, you can say that responsiveness is your goal, resiliency is the way to ensure that you keep being responsive, and elasticity is one method for being resilient. The missing piece of the puzzle of reactive systems is the way that the parts of a system communicate with each other to allow for the type of reactiveness we've explored.

Asynchronous message passing is the communication process that best suits our needs, because it allows us to control the load level on each component without limiting producers—normally with an intermediate channel such as a queue or service bus. It allows routing of messages to the right destination and resending of failing messages in case a component crashes. It also adds transparency to the inner system components, because users don't need to know the internal system structure except the type of messages it can handle. Being *message driven* is what makes all the other reactive concepts possible. Figure 1.12 shows how the message-driven approach using a message queue helps level the rate of message processing in the system and enables resiliency and elasticity.

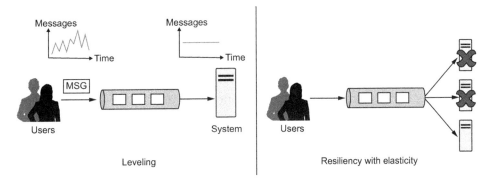

Figure 1.12 The relationship of a message-driven approach to load leveling and elasticity. On the left, messages are arriving at a high frequency, but system processing is leveled to a constant rate, and the queue is filling faster than it's emptied. On the right, even if the processing worker role has crashed, users can still fill the queue; and when the system recovers and adds a new worker, the processing continues.

In the figure, the participants are communicating in a message-driven approach through the message queue. The client sends a message that's later retrieved by the server. This asynchronous communication model provides greater control over the processing in the system—controlling the rate and dealing with failures. Many implementations for message queuing exist, with different feature sets. Some allow the persistence of the messages, which provides durability, and some also give a "transactional" delivery mode that locks the message until the consumer signals that the processing completed successfully. No matter which message queue (or message-driven platform) you choose, you'll need to somehow get ahold of the messages that were sent and start processing them. This is where Rx fits in.

1.3.5   *Where is Rx?*

The Reactive Extensions library comes into play inside the applications that compose a reactive system, and it relates to the message-driven concept. Rx isn't the mechanism to move messages between applications or servers, but rather it's the mechanism that's responsible for handling the messages when they arrive and passing them along the chain of execution inside the application. It's important to state that working with Rx is something you can do even if you're not developing a full system with many components. Even a single application can find Rx useful for reacting to events and the types of messages that the application may want to process. The relationships between all the Reactive Manifesto concepts and Rx are captured in figure 1.13.

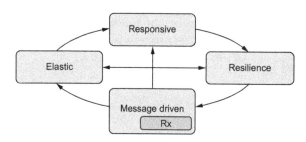

Figure 1.13   The relationships between the Reactive Manifesto core concepts. Rx is positioned inside the message-driven concept, because Rx provides abstractions to handle messages as they enter the application.

To get a fully reactive system, all the concepts in the diagram must exist. Each one can be implemented differently in different systems. Rx is one way to allow easier consumption of messages, so it's shown as part of the message-driven block. Rx was introduced as a way to handle asynchronous and event-based programs, as in the case of messages, so it's important that I explain what it means to be asynchronous and why it's important.

1.4   *Understanding asynchronicity*

Asynchronous message passing is a key trait of a reactive system. But what exactly is asynchronicity, and why is it so important to a reactive application? Our lives are made up of many asynchronous tasks. You may not be aware of it, but your everyday activities would be annoying if they weren't asynchronous by nature. To understand what asynchronicity is, you first need to understand nonasynchronous execution, or synchronous execution.

> **DEFINITION**   *Synchronous*: Happening, existing, or arising at precisely the same time

Synchronous execution means that you have to wait for a task to complete before you can continue to the next task. A real-life example of synchronous execution takes place at a fast-food restaurant: you approach the staff at the counter, decide what to order while the clerk waits, order your food, and wait until the meal is ready. The clerk waits until you hand over the payment and then gives you the food. Only then you can continue the next task of going to your table to eat. This sequence is shown in figure 1.14.

This type of sequence feels like a waste of time (or, better said, a waste of resources), so imagine how your applications feel when you do the same for them. The next section demonstrates this.

Figure 1.14 Synchronous food order in which every step must be completed before going to the next one

1.4.1 It's all about resource use

Imagine what your life would be like if you had to wait for every single operation to complete before you could do something else. Think of the resources that would be waiting and used at that time. The same issues are also relevant in computer science:

```
writeResult = LongDiskWrite();
response = LongWebRequest();
entities = LongDatabaseQuery();
```

In this synchronous code fragment, `LongDatabaseQuery` won't start execution until `LongWebRequest` and `LongDiskWrite` complete. During the time that each method is executed, the calling thread is blocked and the resources it holds are practically wasted and can't be used to serve other requests or handle other events. If this were happening on the UI thread, the application would look frozen until the execution finishes. If this were happening on a server application, at some point you might run out of free threads and requests would start being rejected. In both cases, the application stops being responsive.

The total time it takes to run the preceding code fragment is as follows:

$$total\_time = LongDiskWrite_{time} + LongWebRequest_{time} + LongDatabaseQuery_{time}$$

The total completion time is the sum of the completion time of its components. If you could start an operation without waiting for a previous operation to complete, you could use your resources much better. This is what asynchronous execution is for.

Asynchronous execution means that an operation is started, but its execution is happening in the background and the caller isn't blocked. Instead, the caller is notified when the operation is completed. In that time, the caller can continue to do useful work.

In the food-ordering example, an asynchronous approach would be similar to sitting at the table and being served by a waiter. First, you sit at the table, and the waiter comes to hand you the menu and leaves. While you're deciding what to order, the waiter is still available to other customers. When you've decided what meal you want, the waiter comes back and takes your order. While the food is being prepared, you're free to chat, use your phone, or enjoy the view. You're not blocked (and neither is the waiter). When the food is ready, the waiter brings it to your table and goes back to serve other customers until you request the bill and pay.

This model is asynchronous: tasks are executed concurrently, and the time of execution is different from the time of the request. This way, the resources (such as the waiter) are free to handle more requests.

Where does the asynchronous execution happen?

In a computer program, we can differentiate between two types of asynchronous operations: CPU-based and I/O-based.

In a CPU-based operation, the asynchronous code runs on another thread, and the result is returned when the execution on the other thread finishes.

In an I/O-based operation, the operation is made on an I/O device such as a hard drive or network. On a network, a request is made to another machine (by using TCP or UDP or another network protocol), and when the OS on your machine gets a signal from the network hardware by an interrupt that the result came back, then the operation will be completed.

In both cases, the calling thread is free to execute other tasks and handle other requests and events.

There's more than one way to run code asynchronously, and it depends on the language that's used. Appendix A shows the ways this can be done in C# and dives deeper into bits and bytes of each one. For now, let's look at one example of doing asynchronous work by using the .NET implementation of futures—the `Task` class:

The asynchronous version of the preceding code fragment looks like the following:

```
taskA = LongDiskWriteAsync();
taskB = LongWebRequestAsync();
taskC = LongDatabaseQueryAsync();

Task.WaitAll(taskA, taskB, taskC);
```

In this version, each method returns `Task<T>`. This class represents an operation that's being executed in the background. When each method is called, the calling thread isn't blocked, and the method returns immediately. Then the next method is called while the previous method is still executing. When all the methods are called, you wait for their completion by using the `Task.WaitAll` method that gets a collection of tasks and blocks until all of them are completed. Another way to write this is as follows:

```
taskA = LongDiskWriteAsync();
taskB = LongWebRequestAsync();
taskC = LongDatabaseQueryAsync();

taskA.Wait();
taskB.Wait();
taskC.Wait();
```

This way, you get the same result; you wait for each task to complete (while they're still running in the background). If a task is already completed when you call the `Wait` method, it will return immediately.

The total time it takes to run the asynchronous version of the code fragment is as follows:

$$total\_time = MAX(LongDiskWrite_{time}, LongWebRequest_{time}, LongDatabaseQuery_{time})$$

Because all of the methods are running concurrently (and maybe even in parallel), the time it takes to run the code will be the time of the longest operation.

1.4.2 Asynchronicity and Rx

Asynchronous execution isn't limited to being handled only by using `Task<T>`. In appendix A, you'll be introduced to other patterns used inside the .NET Framework to provide asynchronous execution.

Looking back at `IObservable<T>`, the Rx representation of a time-variant variable, you can use it to represent any asynchronous pattern, so when the asynchronous execution completes (successfully or with an error), the chain of execution will run and the dependencies will be evaluated. Rx provides methods for transforming the various types of asynchronous execution (such as `Task<T>`) to `IObservable<T>`.

For example, in the Shoppy app, you want to get new discounts not only when your location changes, but also when your connectivity state changes to online—for example, if your phone loses its signal for a short time and then reconnects. The call to the Shoppy web service is done in an asynchronous way, and when it completes, you want to update your view to show the new items:

```
IObservable<Connectivity> myConnectivity=...
IObservable<IEnumerable<Discount>> newDiscounts =
    from connectivity in myConnectivity               GetDiscounts returns a Task
    where connectivity == Connectivity.Online         that's implicitly converted
    from discounts in GetDiscounts()            ◁──── to an observable.
    select discounts;
                                                              RefreshView
                                                              displays
newDiscounts.Subscribe(discounts => RefreshView(discounts));  ◁── the discounts.
private Task<IEnumerable<Discount>> GetDiscounts()
```

```
{
    //Sends request to the server and receives the collection of discounts
}
```

In this example, you're reacting to the connectivity changes that are carried on the `myConnectivity` observable. Each time a change in connectivity occurs, you check to see whether it's because you're online, and if so, you call the asynchronous `Get-Discounts` method. When the method execution is complete, you select the result that was returned. This result is what will be pushed to the observers of the `new-Discounts` observable that was created from your code.

1.5   *Understanding events and streams*

In a software system, an *event* is a type of message that's used to indicate that something has happened. The event might represent a technical occurrence—for example, in a GUI application you might see events on each key that was pressed or each mouse movement. The event can also represent a business occurrence, such as a money transaction that was completed in a financial system.

An event is raised by an *event source* and consumed by an *event handler*. As you've seen, events are one way to represent time-variant values. And in Rx, the event source can be represented by the observable, and an event handler can be represented by the observer. But what about the simple data that our application is using, such as data sitting in a database or fetched from a web server. Does it have a place in the reactive world?

1.5.1   *Everything is a stream*

The application you write will ultimately deal with some kind of data, as shown in figure 1.15. Data can be of two types: data at rest and data in motion. *Data at rest* is stored

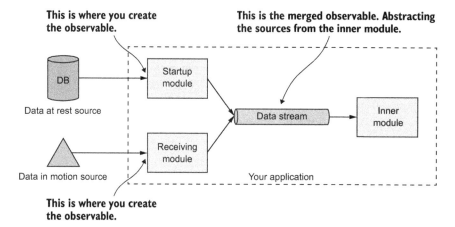

Figure 1.15   Data in motion and data at rest as one data stream. The connection points from the outside environment are a perfect fit for creating observables. Those observables can be merged easily with Rx to create a merged observable that the inner module can subscribe to without knowing the exact source of a data element.

in a digital format, and you usually read it from persisted storage such as a database or files. *Data in motion* is moving on the network (or other medium) and is being pushed to your application or pulled by your application from any external source.

No matter what type of data you use in your application, it's time to understand that everything can be observed as a stream, even data at rest and data that looks static to your application. For example, configuration data is perceived as static, but even configuration changes at some point, either after a long time or short time. From your application's perspective, it doesn't matter; you want to be *reactive* and handle those changes as they happen. When you look at the data at rest as another data stream, you can more easily combine both types of data. For your application, it doesn't matter where the data came from.

For example, application startup usually loads data from its persisted storage to restore its state (the one that was saved before the application was closed). This state can, of course, change during the application run. The inner parts of your application that care about the state can look at the data stream that carries it. When the application starts, the stream will deliver the data that was loaded, and when the state changes, the stream will carry the updates.

A nice analogy I like to use for explaining streams is a water hose, but this hose has data packets going through it, just like the one you see in figure 1.16. When using a water hose, you can do many things with it. You can put filters at the end. You can add different hose heads that give different functionality. You can add pressure monitors to help you regulate the flow. You can do the same things with your data stream. You'll want to build a pipeline that lets the information flow through it, to eventually give an end result that suits your logic; this includes filtering, transformations, grouping, merging, and so on.

The data and event streams are a perfect fit for **Rx** observables. Abstracting them with an `IObservable` enables you to make a composition of the operators and create a complex pipeline of execution. This is similar to what you did with the Shoppy example, where a call to a server obtained the discounts as part of a more complex pipeline of execution that also used filtering (on the connectivity) and eventually refreshed the view (like a sprinkler splashing water).

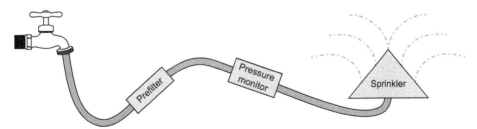

Figure 1.16 A data stream is like a hose: every drop of water is a data packet that needs to go through stations until it reaches the end. Your data also needs to be filtered and transformed until it gets to the real handler that does something useful with it.

1.6   *Summary*

This chapter covered what being reactive means and how you can use Rx to implement reactive programming in your applications.

- In reactive programming, you use time-variant variables that hold values that change by reacting to changes happening to their dependencies. You saw examples of these variables in the Shoppy example: `location`, `connectivity`, `iconSize`, and so on.
- Rx is a library developed by Microsoft to implement reactive programming in .NET applications.
- In Rx, time-variant variables are abstracted by observable sequences that implement the `IObservable<T>` interface.
- The observable is a producer of notifications, and observers subscribe to it to receive those notifications.
- Each observer subscription is represented as `IDisposable` that allows unsubscribing at any time.
- Observers implement the `IObserver<T>` interface.
- Observables can emit a notification with a payload, notify on its completion, and notify on an error.
- After an observable notifies an observer on its completions or about an error, no more notifications will be emitted.
- Observables don't always complete; they can be providers of potentially unbounded notifications.
- Observables can be "quiet," meaning they have never pushed any element and never will.
- Rx provides operators that are used to create pipelines of querying, transformation, projections, and more in the same syntax that LINQ uses.
- Marble diagrams are used to visualize the Rx pipelines.
- Reactive systems are defined as being responsive, resilient, elastic, and message driven. These traits of reactive systems are defined in the Reactive Manifesto.
- In a reactive system, Rx is placed in the message-driven slot, as the way you want to handle the messages the application is receiving.
- Asynchronicity is one of the most important parts of being reactive, because it allows you to better use your resources and thus makes the application more responsive.
- "Everything is a stream" explains why Rx makes it easy to work with any source, even if it's a data source such as a database.

In the next chapter, you'll get the chance to build your first Rx application, and you'll compare it with writing the same application in the traditional event-handling way. You'll see for yourself how awesome Rx is.

Hello, Rx

This chapter covers

- Working without Rx
- Adding Rx to a project
- Creating your first Rx application

The goal of Rx is to coordinate and orchestrate event-based and asynchronous computations that come from various sources, such as social networks, sensors, UI events, and others. For instance, security cameras around a building, together with movement sensors that trigger when someone might be near the building, send us photos from the closest camera. Rx can also count tweets that contain the names of election candidates to estimate a candidate's popularity. This is done by calling an external web service in an asynchronous way. For those scenarios and other similar ones, the orchestrations tend to lead to complex programs, and Rx definitely eases that effort, as you'll see.

In this chapter, you'll look at an example to see how working with and without Rx makes a difference in how the application is structured, how readable it is, and how easy it is to extend and evolve. Imagine you receive a letter from Mr. Penny, the well-known chief technology officer of the Stocks R Us company. *Stocks R Us* is a stock-trading company that advises its clients where to invest their money and collect interest from earnings. This is why it's important to the company to react quickly to changes in the stock market. Recently, Stocks R Us found out that it can save money by using a system that provides alerts about stocks that have experienced—as Mr. Penny calls it—a *drastic change*. Mr. Penny's definition of a drastic change is a price change of more than 10%. When these changes happen, Stocks R Us wants to know as fast as possible so it can react by selling or buying the stock.

Mr. Penny comes to you because he knows he can count on you to deliver a high-quality application quickly. Your job (and the target of this chapter) is to create an application that notifies users about stocks that experience a drastic change. A drastic change occurs when the value of the stock increases or decreases by a certain threshold (10% in this case) between two readings. When this happens, you want to notify users by sending a push notification to their mobile phones or displaying an alert on the screen of an application, showing a red flashing bar, for example.

In the first part of the chapter, you'll explore the steps that usually occur when creating an application with the traditional .NET events approach. We'll then analyze the solution and discuss its weaknesses.

The second part of this chapter introduces **Rx** into your application. You'll first add the libraries to the project and then work step by step to make the application for Stocks R Us in the Rx style.

2.1   *Working with traditional .NET events*

Stock information comes from a stock-trading source, and many services provide this information. Each has its own API and data formats, and several of those sources are free, such as Yahoo Finance (http://finance.yahoo.com) and Google Finance (www.google.com/finance). For your application, the most important properties are the stock's quote symbol and price. The stock's quote symbol is a series of characters that uniquely identifies traded shares or stock (for example, *MSFT* is the Microsoft stock symbol).

The flowchart in figure 2.1 describes the logical flow of the application.

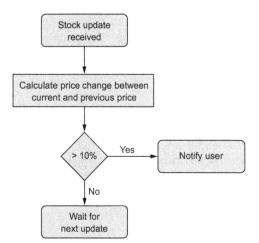

Figure 2.1   Flowchart of the Stock R Us application logic. We notify the user of drastic change—a change of more than 10% in price.

For each piece of stock information the application receives, it calculates the price difference of the stock as a change ratio between the new price and the previous price. Say you receive an update that the price of MSFT has changed from $50 to $40, a change of 20%. This is considered a drastic change and causes an alert to be shown in the application.

In real life, the ticks arrive at a variable rate. For now, to keep from confusing you, you can assume that the ticks arrive at a constant rate; you'll deal with time aspects later.

To keep the source of the stock information abstract, it's exposed through the class `StockTicker`. The class exposes only an event about a `StockTick` that's raised every time new information about a stock is available.

Listing 2.1   StockTicker class

```
class StockTicker
{
    public event EventHandler<StockTick> StockTick;
}
```

The `StockTick` class holds the information about the stock, such as its quote symbol and price.

Listing 2.2   StockTick class

```
class StockTick
{
    public string QuoteSymbol { get; set; }
    public decimal Price { get; set; }

    //other properties
}
```

You'll usually see traditional .NET events in these types of scenarios. When notifications need to be provided to an application, .NET is a standard way of delivering data into an application. To work with the stock ticks, you'll create a `StockMonitor` class that will listen to stock changes by hooking up to the `StockTick` event via the `+=` operator.

Listing 2.3   StockMonitor class

```
class StockMonitor
{
    public StockMonitor(StockTicker ticker)
    {
        ticker.StockTick += OnStockTick;    ◁──┐  The OnStockTick method is
    }                                           called each time the
    . . .                                       event is raised.
        //rest of the code
}
```

The core of the example is in the `OnStockTick` method. This is where you'll check for each stock tick if you already have its previous tick so that you can compare the new price with the old price. For this, you need a container to hold all the information about previous ticks. Because each tick contains the `QuoteSymbol`, it makes sense to use a dictionary to hold that information, with `QuoteSymbol` as the key. To hold the information about the previous ticks, you define a new class with the name `StockInfo` (listing 2.4), and then you can declare the dictionary member in your `StockMonitor` class (listing 2.5).

Listing 2.4   `StockInfo` class

```
class StockInfo
{
    public StockInfo(string symbol, decimal price)
    {
        Symbol = symbol;
        PrevPrice = price;
    }
    public string Symbol { get; set; }
    public decimal PrevPrice { get; set; }
}
```

Every time `OnStockTick` is called with a new tick, the application needs to check whether an old price has already been saved to the dictionary. You use the `TryGet-Value` method that returns `true` if the key you're looking for exists in the dictionary, and then you set the `out` parameter with the value stored under that key.

Listing 2.5   `OnStockTick` event handler checking the existence of a stock

```
Dictionary<string,StockInfo> _stockInfos=new Dictionary<string, StockInfo>();

void OnStockTick(object sender, StockTick stockTick)
{
    StockInfo stockInfo ;
    var quoteSymbol = stockTick.QuoteSymbol;
    var stockInfoExists = _stockInfos.TryGetValue(quoteSymbol, out stockInfo);
...
}
```

If the stock info exists, you can check the stock's current and previous prices, as shown in the following listing, to see whether the change was bigger than the threshold defining a drastic change.

Listing 2.6   `OnStockTick` event handler handling drastic price change

```
const decimal maxChangeRatio = 0.1m;
...
var quoteSymbol = stockTick.QuoteSymbol;
var stockInfoExists = _stockInfos.TryGetValue(quoteSymbol, out stockInfo);
```

```
          if (stockInfoExists)
          {
              var priceDiff = stockTick.Price-stockInfo.PrevPrice;
              var changeRatio = Math.Abs(priceDiff/stockInfo.PrevPrice);
              if (changeRatio > maxChangeRatio)
              {
                  //Do something with the stock - notify users or display on screen
                  Console.WriteLine("Stock:{0} has changed with {1} ratio,
                                     Old Price:{2} New Price:{3}",
                          quoteSymbol,
                          changeRatio,
                          stockInfo.PrevPrice,
                          stockTick.Price);
              }
              _stockInfos[quoteSymbol].PrevPrice = stockTick.Price;
          }
```

The percentage of change → `var changeRatio = Math.Abs(priceDiff/stockInfo.PrevPrice);`

stockInfo variable holds the information about the stock; because stockInfoExists is true, you know for sure that stockInfo isn't null.

Save the price for the next event. → `_stockInfos[quoteSymbol].PrevPrice = stockTick.Price;`

If the stock info isn't in the dictionary (because this is the first time you got a tick about it), you need to add it to the dictionary with

```
_stockInfos[quoteSymbol]=new StockInfo(quoteSymbol,stockTick.Price);
```

When no more updates are required (for example, when the user decides to stop receiving notifications or closes the page), you need to unregister from the event by using the -= operator. But where should you do that? One option is to create a method in the StockMonitor class that you can call when you want to stop. But luckily, .NET provides a mechanism for handling this type of "cleanup" by implementing the IDisposable interface that includes the single method Dispose for freeing resources. This is how it looks in StockMonitor:

```
public void Dispose()
{
    _ticker.StockTick -= OnStockTick;
    _stockInfos.Clear();
}
```

The full code is shown in listing 2.7. I ran it on the following series:

```
Symbol: "MSFT" Price: 100
Symbol: "INTC" Price: 150
Symbol: "MSFT" Price: 170
Symbol: "MSFT" Price: 195
```

and I got these results:

```
Stock:MSFT has changed with 0.7 ratio, Old Price:100 New Price:170
Stock:MSFT has changed with 0.15 ratio, Old Price:170 New Price:195.5
```

Listing 2.7 StockMonitor full code

```
class StockMonitor : IDisposable
{
    private readonly StockTicker _ticker;
```

```
Dictionary<string, StockInfo> _stockInfos =
                new Dictionary<string, StockInfo>();
public StockMonitor(StockTicker ticker)
{
    _ticker = ticker;
    ticker.StockTick += OnStockTick;        ◁────  Registration to the
}                                                  stock update notification


void OnStockTick(object sender, StockTick stockTick)
{
    const decimal maxChangeRatio = 0.1m;                    Checking whether the stock
    StockInfo stockInfo;                                    price information already
    var quoteSymbol = stockTick.QuoteSymbol;               exists in the application
    var stockInfoExists =
    _stockInfos.TryGetValue(quoteSymbol, out stockInfo);
    if (stockInfoExists)
    {
        var priceDiff = stockTick.Price - stockInfo.PrevPrice;
        var changeRatio = Math.Abs(priceDiff / stockInfo.PrevPrice);
        if (changeRatio > maxChangeRatio)
        {
            Debug.WriteLine("Stock:{0} has changed with {1} ratio
                            OldPrice:{2} newPrice:{3}",
                quoteSymbol,
                changeRatio,
                stockInfo.PrevPrice,
                stockTick.Price);
        }
        _stockInfos[quoteSymbol].PrevPrice = stockTick.Price;  ◁──  Storing the new
    }                                                               stock price
    else
    {                                                          ◁
      _stockInfos[quoteSymbol] =                                  If this is the first
                new StockInfo(quoteSymbol, stockTick.Price);  ◁   time you get
    }                                                             information on the
}                                                             ◁   stock, you store it.

public void Dispose()
{                                      Disposing of the resources and
    _ticker.StockTick -= OnStockTick;  unregistering from the event. You
    _stockInfos.Clear();               won't get any more notifications
}                                      from this point forward.
}
```

Calculating the price change in percentages to see whether it's more than 10%

Mr. Penny is satisfied, Stock R Us staff is using the application, and the effects are already shown in their reports. The application receives the stock updates, can calculate the difference ratio between the old and the new price, and sends an alert to the user.

Like everything in life, change is inevitable, and Stocks R Us decides to change its stock information source. Luckily, you abstracted the source with your StockTicker class so the StockTicker is the only class that needs to be changed.

After the source change, you start to receive complaints on crashes and other bugs such as missing alerts or unnecessary alerts. And so you start to investigate the problem and find it has something to do with concurrency.

2.1.1 Dealing with concurrency

It may not seem obvious, but the code hides a problem: concurrency. Nothing in the `StockTicker` interface promises anything about the thread in which the tick event will be raised, and nothing guarantees that a tick won't be raised while another one is processed by your `StockMonitor`, as shown in figure 2.2.

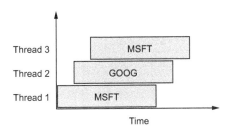

Figure 2.2 Multiple threads executing the event-handler code at the same time. Each box represents the execution time of a stock. While the first thread is running the code for MSFT, the second thread starts executing for the GOOG stock. Then the third thread starts for the same stock symbol as the first thread.

The `StockMonitor` class you wrote uses a dictionary to keep the information about the stocks, but the dictionary you're using isn't thread-safe.

Thread safety

Thread safety of a code portion means that the code works correctly when called from more than one thread, no matter the order in which those threads execute the code and without any need for synchronization of the calling code.

A class is called thread-safe if any one of its methods is thread-safe, even if different methods are called from different threads simultaneously. This usually means the inner data structures are protected from modifications at the same time.

The dictionary you're using does support multiple readers at the same time, but if the dictionary is read while it's being modified, an exception is thrown. This situation is illustrated in table 2.1. `Thread1` (on the left) reaches the marked code, where it tries to get the `StockInfo` for a stock with the symbol `symbol1`. At the same time, `Thread2` (on the right) reaches the line of code that adds a new `StockInfo` (with a `symbol2` symbol) to the dictionary. Both the reading and the mutating of the dictionary is happening at the same time and leads to an exception.

Table 2.1   Reading and modifying the dictionary at the same time from two threads

Thread 1	Thread 2

:
:
 	
`var stockInfoExists =`
`_stockInfos.TryGetValue(symbol1,`
`out stockInfo);`
`if (stockInfoExists)`
`{`
    `:`
    `:`
`}`
`else`
`{`
    `_stockInfos[symbol1] = new`
`StockInfo(symbol1, price);`
`}`
	:
	:
	
	`var stockInfoExists =`
	`_stockInfos.TryGetValue(symbol2,out`
	`stockInfo);`
	`if (stockInfoExists)`
	`{`
	    `:`
	    `:`
	`}`
	`else`
	`{`
	    `_stockInfos[symbol2] = new`
	`StockInfo(symbol2, price);`
	`}`

You can overcome this problem by using the .NET `ConcurrentDictionary`. This lock-free collection internally synchronizes the readers and writers so no exception will be thrown.

Unfortunately, `ConcurrentDictionary` isn't enough, because the ticks aren't synchronized by `StockTicker`. If you handle two (or more) ticks of the same stock at the same time, what's the value of the `PrevPrice` property? There's a nondeterministic answer to that question: the last one wins. But the last one isn't necessarily the last tick that was raised, because the order in which the threads are running is determined by the OS and isn't deterministic.[1] This makes your code unreliable, because the end user could be notified on an incorrect conclusion that your code makes. The `OnStockTick` event handler holds a *critical section*, and the way to protect it is by using a lock.

Listing 2.8   Locked version of `OnStockTick`

```
object _stockTickLocker = new object();          ◁──  An object that acts as a
void OnStockTick(object sender, StockTick stockTick)  mutual-exclusion lock that
{                                                     you'll use in the lock statement
    const decimal maxChangeRatio = 0.1m;
    StockInfo stockInfo;
    var quoteSymbol = stockTick.QuoteSymbol;
    lock (_stockTickLocker)                       ◁──  Ensures that one
    {                                                  thread doesn't enter a
        var stockInfoExists =                          critical section of code
            _stockInfos.TryGetValue(quoteSymbol, out stockInfo);  while another thread
        if (stockInfoExists)                           is there. If another
        {                                              thread tries to enter
            var priceDiff = stockTick.Price - stockInfo.PrevPrice;  a locked code, it will
            var changeRatio =                          block until the
                Math.Abs(priceDiff/stockInfo.PrevPrice);  object is released.
```

[1]   *Deterministic* means that no randomness is involved in the development of future states of the system.

```
        if (changeRatio > maxChangeRatio)
        {
            Debug.WriteLine("Stock:{0} has changed with {1} ratio
                            OldPrice:{2} newPrice:{3}",
                quoteSymbol,
                changeRatio,
                stockInfo.PrevPrice,
                stockTick.Price);
        }
        _stockInfos[quoteSymbol].PrevPrice = stockTick.Price;
    }
    else
    {
        _stockInfos[quoteSymbol] =
                new StockInfo(quoteSymbol, stockTick.Price);
    }
  }
}
```

Using locks is a perfect solution for many cases. But when you start to add locks in various places in an application, you can end up with a performance hit, because locks can increase execution time as well as the time that threads wait for the critical section to become available. The harder problem is that locks can cause your application to get into a deadlock, as shown in figure 2.3. Each thread is holding a resource that another thread needs, while at the same time they each are waiting for a resource that the other holds.

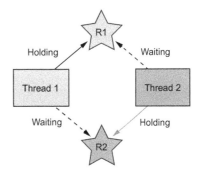

Figure 2.3 A deadlock: Thread 1 is holding the resource R1 and waiting for the resource R2 to be available. At the same time, Thread 2 is holding resource R2 and waiting for resource R1. Both threads will remain locked forever if no external intervention occurs.

Working with multithreaded applications is difficult, and no magic solution exists. The only reasonable thing to do is to make the code that will run multithreaded easier to understand, and make going into the trap of working with concurrent code more difficult.

Rx provides operators to run concurrent code, as you'll see later in this chapter. For now, let's step back, look at what you've created, and analyze it to see whether you can do better.

2.1.2 Retrospective on the solution and looking at the future

Thus far, our code gives a solution to the requirements Mr. Penny described at the beginning of the chapter. Functionally, the code does everything it needs to do. But what's your feeling about it? Is it readable? Does it seem to be maintainable? Is it easy to extend? I'd like to point your attention to a few things.

CODE SCATTERING

Let's start with the scattering of the code. It's a well-known fact that scattered code makes a program harder to maintain, review, and test. In our example, the main logic of the program is in the OnStockTick event handler that's "far" from the registration of the event:

```csharp
class StockMonitor
{
    public StockMonitor(StockTicker ticker)
    {
        ...
        ticker.StockTick += OnStockTick;      ◁────┐  Register
    }                                                │  the event.

    void OnStockTick(object sender, StockTick stockTick)   ◁───┐
    {                                                            │  Handle the event.
        ...                                               ◁───┤
    }                                                     ◁───┘

    public void Dispose()
    {                           │  Unregister and clean up.
        ...                     │
    }
}
```

It's common to see classes that handle more than one event (or even many more), with each one in its own event handler, and you can start to lose sight of what's related to what:

```csharp
class SomeClass
{
    public SomeClass(StockTicker ticker)
    {
        ...
        eventSource.event1 += OnEvent1;   ◁───┐
        ...                                     │  Register events and
        eventSource.event2 += OnEvent2;   ◁───┤  initialize the object.
        ...                                     │
        eventSource.event3 += OnEvent3;   ◁───┘
        ...

    }

    void OnEvent1(object sender, EventArgs args)   ◁───┐
    {                                                    │  An event handler for each event;
        ...                                       ◁───┤  several might need to do
    }                                             ◁───┤  something related to another
                                                         │  event. Methods that deal with class
    //Other methods                                      │  logic, with or without a connection
                                                         │  to the events, might be present.
    void OnEvent2(object sender, EventArgs args)   ◁───┘
    {
```

```
         . . .
    }

//Other methods

    void OnEvent2(object sender, EventArgs args)
    {
         . . .
    }

//Other methods

    public void Dispose()
    {
         . . .
    }
}
```

An event handler for each event; several might need to do something related to another event. Methods that deal with class logic, with or without a connection to the events, might be present.

Unregister and clean up the class, with or without a relation to the events.

Many times developers choose to change the event-handler registration to a lambda expression such as

```
anObject.SomeEvent += (sender, eventArgs)=>{...};
```

Although you moved the event-handler logic to the registration, you added a bug to your resource cleaning. How do you unregister? The `-=` operator expects you to unregister the same delegate that you registered. A lambda expression can be unregistered only as follows:

```
eventHandler = (sender, eventArgs)=>{...};
anObject.SomeEvent += eventHandler;
:
anObject.SomeEvent -= eventHandler;
```

This looks unclean, so now you need to save the `eventHandler` as a member if you need to unregister from it, which leads me to the next point.

RESOURCE HANDLING

The unregistration from the event and the rest of the resources cleanup that you added to support your code (such as the dictionary) took place in the `Dispose` method. This is a well-used pattern, but more frequently than not, developers forget to free the resources that their code uses. Even though C# and .NET as a whole are managed and use garbage collection, many times you'll still need to properly free resources to avoid memory leaks and other types of bugs. Events are often left registered, which is one of the main causes of memory leaks. The reason (at least for some) is that the way we unregister doesn't feel natural for many developers, and deciding the correct place and time to unregister isn't always straightforward—especially because many developers prefer to use the lambda style of registering events, as I stated previously. Beside the event itself, you added code and state management (such as our dictionary) to support your logic. Many more types of applications handle the same scenarios, such as filtering, grouping, buffering, and, of course, the cleaning of what they bring. This brings us to the next point.

REPEATABILITY AND COMPOSABILITY

To me, our logic also feels repeatable. I swear I wrote this code (or similar code) in a past application, saving a previous state by a key and updating it each time an update comes in, and I bet you feel the same. Moreover, I also feel that this code isn't composable, and the more conditions you have, the more inner `if` statements you'll see and the less readable your code will be. It's common to see this kind of code in an application, and with its arrowhead-like structure, it's becoming harder to understand and follow what it does:

```
if (some condition)
{
    if (another condition)
    {
            if (another inner condition)
            {
                    //some code
            }
    }
}
else
{
    if (one more condition)
    {
        //some code
    }
    else
    {
        //some code
    }
}
```

Composition
Composition is the ability to compose a complex structure from simpler constructs.

This definition is similar to that in mathematics, where you can compose a complex expression from a set of other functions: $f(x) = x^2 + sin(x)$

Composition also allows us to use a function as the argument of another function:

$g(x) = x + 1$
$f(g(x)) = (x + 1)^2 + sin(x + 1)$

In computer science, we use composition to express complex code with simpler functions. This allows us to make higher abstractions and concentrate on the purpose of the code and less on the details, making it easier to grasp.

If you were given new requirements to your code, such as calculating the change ratio by looking at more than two consecutive events, your code would have to change dramatically. The change would be even more dramatic if the new requirement was time based, such as looking at the change ratio in a time interval.

SYNCHRONIZATION

Synchronization is another thing that developers tend to forget, resulting in the same problems that we had: unreliable code due to improperly calculated values, and crashes that might occur when working with non-thread-safe classes. Synchronization is all about making sure that if multiple threads reach the same code at the same time (virtually, not necessarily in parallel, because a context switch might be involved), then only one thread will get access. Locks are one way to implement synchronization, but other ways exist and do require knowledge and care.

It's easy to write code that isn't thread-safe, but it's even easier to write code with locks that lead to deadlocks or starvation. The main issue with those types of bugs is that they're hard to find. Your code could run for ages (literally), until you run into a crash or other error.

With so many points from such a small program, it's no wonder people say that programming is hard. It's time to see the greatness of Rx and how it makes the issues we've discussed easier to overcome. Let's see the Rx way and start adding Rx to your application.

2.2 Creating your first Rx application

In this section, the Rx example uses the same `StockTicker` that you saw in the previous section, but this time you won't work with the traditional standard .NET event. Instead you'll use `IObservable<T>`, which you'll create, and then write your event-processing flow around it. You'll go slowly and add layer after layer to the solution until you have a fully running application that's easier to read and extend.

Every journey starts with the first step. You'll begin this journey by creating a new project (a console application will do) and adding the Rx libraries.

2.2.1 Selecting Rx packages

The first step in working with Reactive Extensions is adding the library to your project. No matter whether you write a Windows Presentation Foundation (WPF) application, ASP.NET website, Windows Communication Foundation (WCF) service, or a simple console application, Rx can be used inside your code to benefit you. But you do need to select the correct libraries to reference from your project.

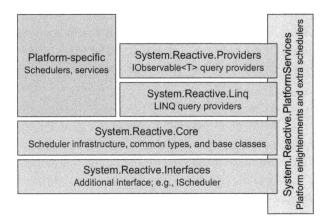

Figure 2.4   Rx assemblies are a set of portable class libraries (middle and bottom) and platform-specific libraries (top left). The `PlatformServices` assembly holds the platform enlightments that are the glue between the two.

The Rx library is deployed as a set of a portable class libraries (PCLs)[2] and platform-specific providers that you install depending on your project platform. This is shown in figure 2.4.

To add the necessary references to your project, you need to select the appropriate packages from NuGet, a .NET package manager from which you can easily search and install packages (which usually contain libraries). Table 2.2 describes the Rx packages you can choose from at the time of this writing and figure 2.5 shows the NuGet package manager.

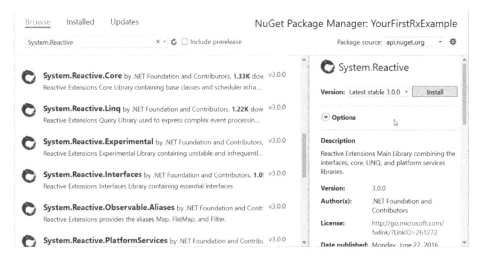

Figure 2.5   Reactive Extensions NuGet packages. Many packages add things on top of Rx to identify the Rx.NET-specific libraries. Look for a package ID with the prefix System.Reactive and make sure the publisher is Microsoft.

---

[2]   The Portable Class Library project enables you to build assemblies that work on more than one .NET Framework platform. For details, see http://mng.bz/upA5.

NOTE Rx 3.0, published in June 2016, added Rx support to the .NET Core and Universal Windows Platform (UWP). Rx.NET also joined the .NET Foundation (www.dotnetfoundation.org/projects). To conform with the naming convention used by .NET Core, the Rx packages were renamed to match their library names, and the previous Rx packages are now hidden in the NuGet gallery.

Table 2.2 Rx packages

Package name	Description
`System.Reactive.Interfaces` (Rx-Interfaces prior to Rx 3.0)	Installs the `System.Reactive.Interfaces` assembly that holds only interfaces that other Rx packages depend on.
`System.Reactive.Core` (Rx-Core prior to Rx 3.0)	Installs the `System.Reactive.Core` assembly that includes portable implementations of schedulers, disposables, and others.
`System.Reactive.Linq` (Rx-Linq prior to Rx 3.0)	Installs the `System.Reactive.Linq` assembly. This is where the query operators are implemented.
`System.Reactive.PlatformServices` (Rx-PlatformServices prior to Rx 3.0)	Installs the `System.Reactive.PlatformServices` assembly. This is the glue between the portable and nonportable Rx packages.
`System.Reactive` (Rx-Main prior to Rx 3.0)	This is the main package of Rx and what you'll install in most cases. It includes `System.Reactive.Interfaces`, `System.Reactive.Core`, `System.Reactive.Linq`, and `System.Reactive.PlatformServices` (the specific enlightenments provider that will be used depends on the project platform).
`System.Reactive.Providers` (Rx-Providers prior to Rx 3.0)	Installs `System.Reactive.Providers` together with the `System.Reactive.Core` package. This package adds the `IQbservable` LINQ API operators that allow creating the expression tree on the event tree so that the query provider can translate to a target query language. This is the Rx `IQueryable` counterpart.
`System.Reactive.Windows.Threading` (Rx-Xaml prior to Rx 3.0)	Installs the `System.Reactive.Windows.Threading` assembly together with the `System.Reactive.Core` package. Use this package when you need to add UI synchronization classes for any platform that supports the XAML dispatcher (WPF, Silverlight, Windows Phone, and Windows Store apps).
`System.Reactive.Runtime.Remoting` (Rx-Remoting prior to Rx 3.0)	Installs `System.Reactive.Runtime.Remoting` together with the `System.Reactive.Core` package. Use this package to add extensions to .NET Remoting and expose it as an observable sequence.

Table 2.2   Rx packages *(continued)*

Package name	Description
`System.Reactive.Windows.Forms /` `System.Reactive.WindowsRuntime` (Rx-WPF/Rx-Silverlight/Rx-WindowsStore/ Rx-WinForms prior to Rx 3.0)	Subset of packages that's specific to the platform. Add UI synchronization classes and Rx utilities for the platform types (such as `IAsyncAction` and `IAsyncOperationWithProgress` in WinRT).
`Microsoft.Reactive.Testing` (Rx-Testing prior to Rx 3.0)	The Rx testing library that enables writing reactive unit tests. Appendix C includes explanations and examples of reactive unit tests.
`System.Reactive.Observable.Aliases` (Rx-Aliases prior to Rx 3.0)	Provides aliases for some of the query operators such as `Map`, `FlatMap`, and `Filter`.

Most of the time, you'll add the `System.Reactive` package to your project because it contains the types that are most used. When you're writing to a specific platform or technology, you'll add the complementary package.[3]

2.2.2   *Installing from NuGet*

After you decide which package you need, you can install it from the Package Manager dialog box or the Package Manager console. To use the Package Manager console, choose Tools > NuGet Package Manager > Package Manager Console. In the console, select the destination project from the Default Project drop-down list, shown in figure 2.6.

In the console, write the installation command of the package you need:

```
Install-Package  [Package Name]
```

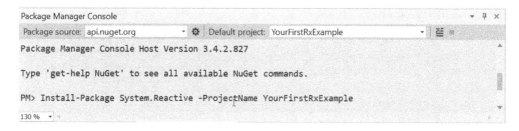

Figure 2.6   Installing the Rx libraries through the Package Manager console. Make sure you select the correct project for installation from the Default Project drop-down list. You can also define the project by typing `-ProjectName [project name]`**.**

---

[3] Although the examples in the book are in C#, you can use Rx with other .NET languages. Also, if you're using F#, look at http://fsprojects.github.io/FSharp.Control.Reactive, which provides F# wrappers for Rx.

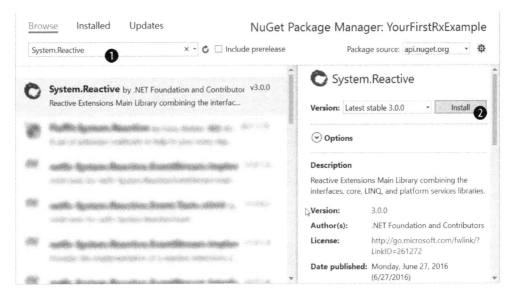

Figure 2.7 NuGet Package Manager from VS 2015. Search for the package you want by typing its name ❶ and then select the package and click Install ❷.

Another option for installing the packages is through the Package Manager dialog box, shown in figure 2.7. This UI enables you to search for packages and see their information in a more user-friendly way. Right-click your project and choose Manage NuGet Packages. Type in the package name, select the package you want to install from the drop-down list, and then click Install.

After the NuGet package is installed, you can write the Rx version of `Stock-Monitor`. You can find the entire code at the book's source code in the GitHub repository: http://mng.bz/18Pr.

Instructions for running the examples with .NET Core

Microsoft recently announced that the format I describe here is deprecated (but will be supported in the transition time). Microsoft recommends using the normal csproj file with the new MSBuild additions (PackageReference for example). To use .NET Core, you first need to install the latest version from www.microsoft .com/net/core. Then, create a new project in your favorite tool, such as Visual Studio 2015 or Visual Studio Code (https://code.visualstudio.com/docs/runtimes/dotnet).

Add a reference to the `System.Reactive` NuGet package by updating the `dependencies` section inside the project.json file, as shown here:

```
{
  "version": "1.0.0-*",
  "buildOptions": {
    "debugType": "portable",
    "emitEntryPoint": true
```

```
(continued)
    },
    "dependencies": { "System.Reactive": "3.0.0" },
    "frameworks": {
      "netcoreapp1.0": {
        "dependencies": {
          "Microsoft.NETCore.App": {
            "type": "platform",
            "version": "1.0.0"
          },
        },
        "imports": "dnxcore50"
      }
    }
}
```

Finally, run the dotnet restore command at the command prompt. You now have a configured Rx project.

2.3   *Writing the event-processing flow*

After you install the Rx package that adds the needed references to the Rx libraries, you can start building your application around it. To start creating the event-processing flow, you need the source of the events. In Rx, the source of events (the publisher, if you prefer) is the object that implements the IObservable<T> interface.

To recap, the IObservable<T> interface defines the single method Subscribe that allows observers to subscribe to notifications. Observers implement the IObserver interface that defines the methods that will be called by the observable when there are notifications.

Rx provides all kinds of tools to convert various types of sources to IObservable<T>, and the most fundamental tool that's included is the one that converts a standard .NET event into an observable.

In our example of creating an application that provides notifications of drastic stock changes, you'll continue to work with the StockTick event. You'll see how to make it into an observable that you can use to do magic.

2.3.1   *Subscribing to the event*

StockTicker exposes the event StockTick that's raised each time an update occurs on a stock. But to work with Rx, you need to convert this event into an observable. Luckily, Rx provides the FromEventPattern method that enables you to do just that:

```
IObservable<EventPattern<StockTick>> ticks =
      Observable.FromEventPattern<EventHandler<StockTick>, StockTick>(
    h => ticker.StockTick += h,
    h => ticker.StockTick -= h)
```

Attaching
the Rx event
handler

Detaching the
Rx event
handler

In most cases, you'd use
var instead of the full
variable type name.

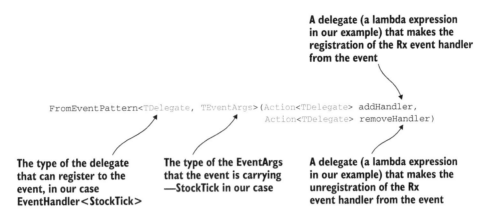

Figure 2.8 `FromEventPattern` **method signature**

The `FromEventPattern` method has a couple of overloads. The one you're using here takes two generic parameters and two method parameters. Figure 2.8 shows the method signature explanation.

The `addHandler` and `removeHandler` parameters register and unregister the Rx handler to the event; the Rx handler will be called by the event and then will call the `OnNext` method of the observers.

UNWRAPPING THE EVENTARGS

The `ticks` variable now holds an observable of type `IObservable<EventPattern<StockTick>>`. Each time the event is raised, the Rx handler is called and wraps the event-args and the event source into an object of `EventPattern` type that will be delivered to the observers through the `OnNext` method. Because you care only for the `StockTick` (the `EventArgs` in the `EventPattern` type) of each notification, you can add the `Select` operator that will transform the notification and unwrap the `EventArgs` so that only the `StockTick` will be pushed down the stream:

```
var ticks = Observable.FromEventPattern<EventHandler<StockTick>, StockTick>(
    h => ticker.StockTick += h,
    h => ticker.StockTick -= h)
    .Select(tickEvent => tickEvent.EventArgs)
```

Select gets a delegate (such as a lambda expression) that takes the input notification and returns the value you're interested in—EventArgs in this case.

2.3.2 Grouping stocks by symbol

Now that you have an observable that carries the ticks (updates on the stocks), you can start writing your query around it. The first thing to do is to group the ticks by their symbols so you can handle each group (stock) separately. With Rx, this is an easy task, as shown in figure 2.9.

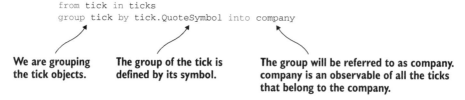

Figure 2.9   A simple grouping of the stock ticks by the quote symbol

This expression creates an observable that provides the groups. Each group represents a company and is an observable that will push only the ticks of that group. Each tick from the `ticks` source observable is routed to the correct observable group by its symbol. This is shown in figure 2.10.

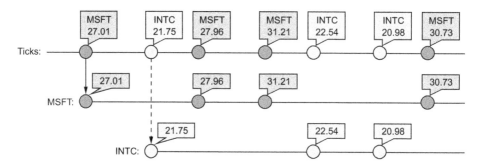

Figure 2.10   The `ticks` observable is grouped into two company groups, each one for a different symbol. As the notifications are pushed on the `ticks` observable, they're routed to their group observable. If it's the first time the symbol appears, a new observable is created for the group.

This grouping is written with a query expression. Query expressions are written in a declarative *query syntax* but are a sugar syntax that the compiler turns into a real chain of method calls. This is the same expression written in a method syntax:

```
ticks.GroupBy(tick => tick.QuoteSymbol);
```

2.3.3   *Finding the difference between ticks*

The next step on your way to finding any drastic changes is to compare two consecutive ticks to see whether the difference between them is higher than a particular ratio. For this, you need a way to batch the ticks inside a group so you can get two ticks together. The batching should be done in such a way that two consecutive batches will include a shared tick; the last tick in a batch will be the first one in the next batch. Figure 2.11 shows an example of this batching.

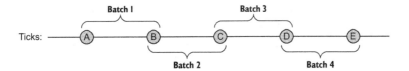

Figure 2.11 Ticks are batched together. Each batch has two items; two consecutive batches have a shared item.

To create batches on an observable sequence, you use the `Buffer` operator. `Buffer` gets as parameters the number of items you want in a batch—two, in this case—and the number of items to skip before opening a new batch. You need to skip one item before opening a new batch, thus making one item shared between two batches. You need to apply the `Buffer` method to each group by writing the following:

```
company.Buffer(2, 1)
```

The `Buffer` method outputs an array that holds the two consecutive ticks, as shown in figure 2.12. This enables you to calculate the difference between the two ticks to see whether it's in the allowed threshold.

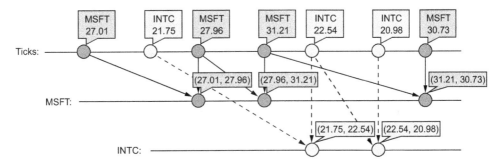

Figure 2.12 After applying the `Buffer(…)` method on each group, you a get new type of notification that holds an array of the two consecutive ticks.

By using the `Let` keyword, Rx allows you to keep the calculation in a variable that will be carried on the observable:

```
from tick in ticks
group tick by tick.QuoteSymbol into company
from tickPair in company.Buffer(2, 1)
let changeRatio = Math.Abs((tickPair[1].Price - tickPair[0].Price) /
    tickPair[0].Price)
```

This code fragment includes all your steps until now. Applying the buffering on the company observable creates a new observable that pushes the buffers of two ticks. You observe its notifications by using the `from … in …` statement. Each notification is represented by the `tickPair` variable.

You then introduce the `changeRatio` variable that holds the ratio of change between the two ticks; this variable will be carried on the observable to the rest of your query, as shown in figure 2.13.

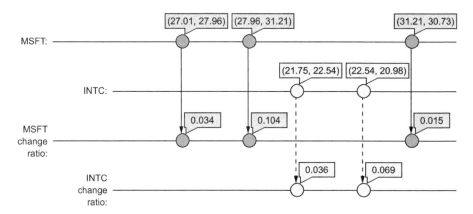

Figure 2.13   From each pair of consecutive ticks per company group, you calculate the ratio of difference.

Now that you know the change ratio, all that's left is filtering out all the notifications that aren't interesting (not a drastic change) and keeping only those that are above your wanted ratio by applying the `Where (…)` operator:

```
var drasticChanges =
    from tick in ticks
    group tick by tick.QuoteSymbol
    into company
    from tickPair in company.Buffer(2, 1)
    let changeRatio = Math.Abs((tickPair[1].Price - tickPair[0].Price)/
      tickPair[0].Price)
    where changeRatio > maxChangeRatio
    select new DrasticChange()
    {
        Symbol = company.Key,
        ChangeRatio = changeRatio,
        OldPrice = tickPair[0].Price,
        NewPrice = tickPair[1].Price
    };
```

> Write the condition that the notification needs to fulfill inside the where operator.

> Create an object from every notification that's a drastic change. This type includes the properties that you will use to render a screen alert.

The `drasticChanges` variable is an observable that pushes notifications only for ticks that represent a change in a stock price that's higher than `maxChangeRatio`. In figure 2.14, the maximum change ratio is 10%.

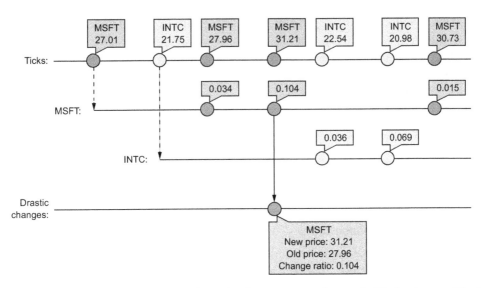

Figure 2.14 **After filtering the notifications with the** `Where` **operator, you find that only one notification is a drastic change.**

To consume the drastic change notifications, you need to subscribe to the `drastic-Change` observable. Then you can notify the user by printing it to the screen.

> Every notification of a drastic change is delivered to the lambda expression written in the Subscribe method. The notification is represented by the change parameter.

```
_subscription =
    drasticChanges.Subscribe(change =>
    {
        Console.WriteLine($"Stock:{change.Symbol} has changed with
                          {change.ChangeRatio} ratio,
                          Old Price:{change.OldPrice}
                          New Price:{change.NewPrice}");
    },
    ex => { /* code that handles errors */},
    () => {/* code that handles the observable completeness */});
```

The subscription to the observable that allows you to unregister

> If something goes wrong and an exception is thrown, or when the sequence is done, this is where you handle those cases.

2.3.4 Cleaning resources

If the user doesn't want to receive any more notifications about drastic changes, you need to dispose of the subscription to the `drasticChanges` observable. When you subscribed to the observable, the subscription was returned to you, and you stored it in the `_subscription` class member.

As before, the `StockMonitor Dispose` method (which is provided because you implemented the `IDisposable` interface) makes a perfect fit. The only thing you need to do in your `Dispose` method is to call to `Dispose` method of the subscription object:

```
public void Dispose()
{
    _subscription.Dispose();
}
```

Notice that you don't need to write anything about delegates involved in the processing of your query, and you don't need to clean up any data structures related to the storage of the previous ticks data. All of those are kept in the Rx internal operators implementation, and when you dispose of the subscription, a chain of disposals happen, causing all the internal data structures to be disposed of as well.

2.3.5   *Dealing with concurrency*

In the traditional events version, you needed to add code to handle the critical section in your application. This critical section enabled two threads to reach the event handler simultaneously and read and modify your collection of past ticks at the same time, leading to an exception and miscalculation of the change ratio. You added a lock to synchronize the access to the critical section, which is one way to provide synchronization between threads.

With Rx, adding synchronization to the execution flow is much more declarative. Add the `Synchronize` operator to where you want to start synchronizing, and Rx will take care of the rest. In this case, you can add synchronization from the beginning, so you add the `Synchronize` operator when creating the observable itself:

```
var ticks = Observable.FromEventPattern<EventHandler<StockTick>, StockTick>(
    h => ticker.StockTick += h,
    h => ticker.StockTick -= h)
    .Select(tickEvent => tickEvent.EventArgs)
    .Synchronize()
```

From here on, the execution will be synchronized. Notification will be pushed only after the previous one completes.

It doesn't get any simpler than that, but as before, you need to remember that every time you add synchronization of any kind, you risk adding a probable deadlock. Rx doesn't fix that, so developer caution is still needed. Rx only gives you tools to make the introduction of synchronization easier and more visible. When things are easy, explicit, and readable, chances increase that you'll make it right, but making sure you do it correctly is still your job as a developer.

2.3.6   *Wrapping up*

Listing 2.9 shows the entire code of the Rx version. The main difference from the traditional events example is that the code tells the story about what you're trying to achieve rather than how you're trying to achieve it. This is the declarative programming model that Rx is based on.

Listing 2.9 Locked version of `OnStockTick`

```
class RxStockMonitor : IDisposable
{
    private IDisposable _subscription;

    public RxStockMonitor(StockTicker ticker)
    {
        const decimal maxChangeRatio = 0.1m;

        var ticks =
            Observable.FromEventPattern<EventHandler<StockTick>, StockTick>(
            h => ticker.StockTick += h,
            h => ticker.StockTick -= h)
            .Select(tickEvent => tickEvent.EventArgs)
            .Synchronize();

        var drasticChanges =
            from tick in ticks
            group tick by tick.QuoteSymbol
            into company
            from tickPair in company.Buffer(2, 1)
            let changeRatio = Math.Abs((tickPair[1].Price -
            ➥ tickPair[0].Price)/tickPair[0].Price)
            where changeRatio > maxChangeRatio
            select new
            {
                Symbol = company.Key,
                ChangeRatio = changeRatio,
                OldPrice = tickPair[0].Price,
                NewPrice = tickPair[1].Price
            };

        _subscription =
            drasticChanges.Subscribe(change =>
                {
                    Console.WriteLine("Stock:{change.Symbol} has changed
                                        with {change.ChangeRatio} ratio,
                                        Old Price: {change.OldPrice}
                                        New Price: {change.NewPrice}");
                },
                ex => { /* code that handles errors */},
                () =>{/* code that handles the observable completeness */});
    }

    public void Dispose()
    {
        _subscription.Dispose();
    }
}
```

Creates a synchronized observable that pushes the stock ticks from the StockTick event.

Groups ticks and checks whether the difference between two consecutive ticks is above a threshold.

Subscribes to the observable of drastic change, showing an alert on the screen. Also handles the error cases and when the observable sequence is complete.

It's now a good time to compare the Rx and events versions.

KEEPING THE CODE CLOSE

In the Rx example, all the code that relates to the logic of finding the drastic changes is close together, in the same place—from the event conversion to the observable to the subscription that displays the notifications onscreen. It's all sitting in the same method, which makes navigating around the solution easier. This is a small example, and even though all the code sits together, it doesn't create a huge method. In contrast, the traditional events version scattered the code and its data structures in the class.

PROVIDING BETTER AND LESS RESOURCE HANDLING

The Rx version is almost free of any resource handling, and those resources that you do want to free were freed explicitly by calling `Dispose`. You're unaware of the real resources that the Rx pipeline creates because they were well encapsulated in the operators' implementation. The fewer resources you need to manage, the better your code will be in managing resources. This is the opposite of the traditional events version, in which you needed to add every resource that was involved and had to manage its lifetime, making the code error prone.

USING COMPOSABLE OPERATORS

One of the hardest computer science problems is naming things—methods, classes, and so on. But when you give a good name to something, it makes the process of using it later easy and fluid. This is exactly what you get with the Rx operators. The Rx operators are a recurring named code pattern that reduces the repeatability in your code that otherwise you'd have to write by yourself—meaning now you can write less code and reuse existing code. With each step of building your query on the observable, you added a new operator on the previously built expression; this is composability at its best. Composability makes it easy to extend the query in the future and make adjustments while you're building it. This is contrary to the traditional events version, in which no clear separation exists between the code fragments that handled each step when building the whole process to find the drastic change.

PERFORMING SYNCHRONIZATION

Rx has a few operators dedicated specifically to concurrency management. In this example, you used only the `Synchronize` operator that, as generally stated before about Rx operators, saved you from making the incorrect use of a lock by yourself. By default, Rx doesn't perform any synchronization between threads—the same as regular events. But when the time calls for action, Rx makes it simple for the developer to add the synchronization and spares the use of the low-level synchronization primitives, which makes the code more attractive.

2.4   *Summary*

This chapter presented a simple yet powerful example of something you've probably done in the past (or might find yourself doing in the future) and solved it in two ways: the traditional events style and the Rx style of event-processing flow.

- Writing an event-driven application in .NET is very intuitive but holds caveats regarding resource cleanup and code readability.

- To use the Rx library, you need to install the Rx packages. Most often you'll install the `System.Reactive` package.
- You can use Rx in any type of application WPF desktop client, an ASP.NET website, or a simple console application and others.
- Traditional .NET events can be converted into observables.
- Rx allows you to write query expression on top of the observable.
- Rx provides many query operators such as filtering with the `Where` operator, transformation with `Select` operator, and others.

This doesn't end here, of course. This is only the beginning of your journey. To use Rx correctly in your application and to use all the rich operators, you need to learn about them and techniques for putting them together, which is what this book is all about. In the next chapter, you'll learn about the functional way of thinking that, together with the core concepts inside .NET, allowed Rx to evolve.

Functional thinking in C#

This chapter covers

- Blending C# with functional techniques
- Using delegates and lambda expressions
- Querying collections by using LINQ

The object-oriented paradigm offers great productivity in application development. It makes projects more manageable by decomposing complex systems into classes, and objects are silos that you can concentrate on separately. Yet other paradigms have gathered attention in recent years, especially the functional programming paradigm. Functional programming languages, together with a functional way of thinking, greatly influenced the way Rx was designed and used. Specifically, the functional programming concepts of anonymous types, first-order functions, and function composition are an integral part of Rx that you'll see used heavily throughout the book and in your everyday work with Rx.

Some of the attention functional programming is receiving arises from functional languages being good for multithreaded applications. Rx excels in creating asynchronous and concurrent processing pipelines, which were also inspired by functional thinking. Although C# is considered an object-oriented language, it has evolved over the years and added aspects that exist in functional programming.

.NET even has a functional programming language of its own, named F#, which runs on top of the Common Language Runtime (CLR) in the same way C# does. Using functional programming techniques can make your code cleaner and easier to read and can change the way you think when writing code, eventually making you more productive. Rx is highly influenced by the functional way of thinking, so it's good to understand those concepts in order to more easily adopt the Rx way of thinking.

The concepts in this chapter may not be new to you. You can skip to the next chapter if you wish, but I encourage you to at least briefly review the concepts to refresh your memory.

3.1 The advantages of thinking functionally

As computer science evolves, new languages appear with new concepts and techniques. All these languages share the same underlying purpose: improving developer productivity and program robustness. Productivity and robustness have many faces: shorter code, readable statements, internal resource management, and so on. Functional programming languages also try to achieve those goals. Although many types of functional programming languages exist, each with unique characteristics, we can see their similarities:

- *Declarative style of programming*—This is based on the concept of "Tell what, not how."
- *Immutability*—Values can't be modified; instead, new values are created.
- *First-class functions*—Functions are the primary building block used.

With object-oriented languages, developers think about programs as a collection of objects that interact with each other. This allows you to create modular code by encapsulating data and behavior that relates to the data in an object. This modularity, again, improves the productivity of the developer and makes your program more robust because it's easier for the developer to understand the code (less detail to remember) and concentrate effort on a specific module when writing new code or changing (or fixing) existing ones.

3.1.1 Declarative programming style

In the first two chapters, you saw examples of the declarative programming style. In this style, you write your program statements as a description of what you want to achieve as the result instead of specifying how you want this to be done. It's up to the environment to figure out how to do it best. Consider this example of an English statement in an imperative style (the *how*) and declarative style (the *what*):

- *Imperative*—For each customer in the list of customers, take the location and print the city name.
- *Declarative*—Print the city name of every customer in the list.

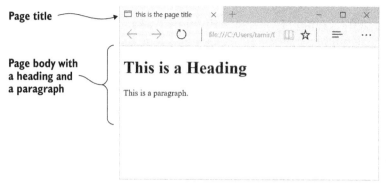

Page title

Page body with a heading and a paragraph

Figure 3.1   A simple web page that has a title, a heading, and a paragraph

A declarative style makes it easier to grasp the code you write, which leads to better productivity and usually makes your code less error prone. The next code block shows another example of the declarative programming style, this time using HTML that produces what you see in figure 3.1.

To create this page, you don't have to write the rendering logic or the layout management and set the position for each element. Instead, all you have to do is to write this short HTML script:

```
<html>
<head>
    <title>this is the page title</title>
</head>
<body>
    <h1>This is a Heading</h1>
    <p>This is a paragraph.</p>
</body>
</html>
```

Even if you don't know HTML, it's easy to see that this example only declares the outcome you want to see and doesn't deal with the technical details of making the browser do it. With a declarative language such as HTML, you can create a complex page with little effort. You want to attain the same results with the C# code you write, and you'll see examples of that in the rest of this chapter. One thing you need to pay attention to is that because you're indicating the *what* and not the *how*, how can you know what will happen to the system? Could there be side effects? It turns out that functional programming solves this problem from the start, as you'll see next.

3.1.2   *Immutability and side effects*

Consider this method, which prints a message to the console:

```
public static void WriteRedMessage(string message)
{
    Console.ForegroundColor = ConsoleColor.Red;
    Console.WriteLine(message);
}
```

This short method causes a side effect to the program: the method changes a shared state in the system, the console color in this case. Side effects can come in different flavors and are sometimes hidden inside the code. If you change the method signature and remove the word *Red* from the method name, as shown in the following code sample, the side effect still happens:

```
public static void WriteMessage(string message)
```

But now it's far more difficult to predict that this method will cause the side effect of changing the color of the console output. Side effects aren't limited to console color, of course; they also include changes to a shared object state, such as a list of items that's modified (as you saw in the previous chapter). Side effects can cause all kinds of bugs in your code—for example, in concurrent execution the code is reached from two places (like threads) at the same time and leads to race conditions. Side effects can also cause your code to be harder to track and predict, thus making it harder to maintain.

Functional programming languages solve the side-effect problem by preventing it in the first place. In functional programming, every object is immutable. You can't modify the object state. After the value is set, it never changes; instead, new objects are created. This concept of immutability shouldn't be new to you. Immutability exists in C# as well, such as in the type `string`. For example, try to answer what this next program will print:

```
string bookTitle = "Rx.NET in Action";
bookTitle.ToUpper();
Console.WriteLine("Book Title: {0}", bookTitle);
```

If your answer is *Rx.NET in Action*, you're correct. In C#, strings are immutable. All the methods that transform a string's content don't really change it; instead, they create a new string instance with the modifications. The previous example should've been written like this:

```
string bookTitle = "Rx.NET in Action";
string uppercaseTitle = bookTitle.ToUpper();
Console.WriteLine("Book Title: {0}", uppercaseTitle);
```

This version of the code stores the result of the `ToUpper` call in a new variable. This variable holds a different string instance with the uppercase value of the book title.

The immutability implies that calling a function ends only with the function computing its result, without any other effect that the programmer needs to worry about. This takes away a major source of bugs and makes the functions idempotent—calling a function with the same input always ends with the same result, no matter whether it was applied once or multiple times.

A WORD ABOUT CONCURRENCY

The idempotency that you get from the immutability makes the program deterministic and predictable and makes the order in which execution happens irrelevant, making it a perfect fit for concurrent execution.

Writing concurrent code is hard, as you saw in the previous chapter. When you take sequential code and try to run it in parallel, you could find yourself facing bugs. With side effect-free and immutable code, this problem doesn't exist. Running the code from different threads won't cause any synchronization issues, because you have nothing to synchronize. Knowing that using functional programming languages makes writing concurrent applications easier, it's no wonder that functional programming languages started to gain more interest in recent years and became the de facto community choice for building large-scale concurrent applications. Just to name a few, companies such as Twitter, LinkedIn, and AT&T are known to use functional programming in their systems.

3.1.3   *First-class functions*

The name *functional programming* is used because a function is the basic construct that you work with. It's one of the language primitives, like an int or a string, and similar to other primitive types, the function is a first-class citizen, which means it can be passed as an argument and be returned from a function. Here's an example in F# (a functional programming language that's part of .NET):

```
let square x = x * x
let applyAndAdd f x y = f(x) + f(y)
```

Here we define a function, square, that calculates the square of its argument. We then define a new function, applyAndAdd, that takes three arguments: the first argument is a function that's applied to the two other arguments, and then the results are summed.

> **NOTE** If you find this confusing, don't worry. Read the rest of the chapter and then come back and read this short section again.

When you call the applyAndAdd function and pass the square function as the first argument together with two numbers as the other arguments, you get the sum of two squares. For example, applyAndAdd square 5 3 outputs the number 34, as shown in figure 3.2.

Functions that receive functions as their arguments or return functions as their return values are called *higher-order functions*. With higher-order functions, you can compose new functions and add new behaviors to existing functions by changing the inner function they use, as you did in the applyAndAdd

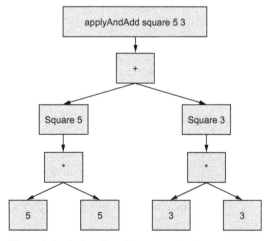

Figure 3.2 In functional programming languages, functions can be passed as arguments. This is the expression tree of the call to applyAndAdd f x y **with** f: **square,** x: **5,** y: **3.**

example. This way, you can extend the "language" that your code uses and adapt it to your domain.

3.1.4 *Being concise*

The core functional programming concepts mentioned earlier in the chapter serve the same purpose that makes functional thinking a powerful tool you should embrace: making your code concise and short.

Writing declaratively means that you can hide the complexity required to achieve a result and instead focus on the result that you want to achieve. This is done using the compositional nature of first-class and higher-order functions that create the glue between the various parts of your code. The expressiveness of your program is better achieved when you know that no side effects will arise and cause uncertainty in the outcome of the execution. Working with an immutable data structure enables you to be certain that the function will always end the same predictable way.

Writing code that's concise makes you more productive when creating new code or when changing existing code, even if it's new to you. Figure 3.3 displays the key elements for productivity.

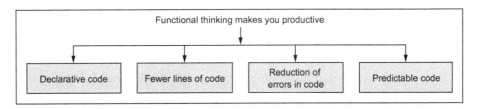

Figure 3.3   The key benefit of functional programming is that it makes you more productive. The key elements for productivity are illustrated here.

The key elements shown in figure 3.3 are where the true benefits of functional programming lie. It's important for you to know that so you can achieve the same advantages when writing programs in C#.

3.2   *First-class and higher-order functions using delegates and lambdas*

When C# was introduced in 2002, it was possible to make "function pointers" that you could pass as arguments and hold as class members. These function pointers are known as *delegates*. Over the years, C# became a multi-paradigm language that supports not only object-oriented programming but also event-driven programming or simple procedural programming. Functional programming also started to influence language as the years went by, and delegates became the underlying mechanism to support functions as first-class citizens in the language.

3.2.1   *Delegates*

In C#, a *delegate* is a type that represents references to methods. Delegates are most commonly used with .NET events, but in this chapter, you'll see how to use them to spice up code with functional programming techniques.

The delegate type is defined with the exact signature of the methods you want the delegate to reference. For example, if you want to create a reference to methods that receive two string parameters and return a `bool`, figure 3.4 shows how to define the delegate type.

Figure 3.4   Declaration of a delegate type for methods that receive two strings and return an integer

After creating the delegate type, you can reference methods with the same signature by creating a new instance of the delegate and passing the method you want to reference:

```
ComparisonTest delegateInstance = new ComparisonTest( <the method> );
```

Say you have a class that holds different methods that compare strings:

```
class StringComparators
{
    public static bool CompareLength(string first, string second)
    {
        return first.Length == second.Length;
    }
    public bool CompareContent(string first, string second)
    {
        return first == second;
    }
}
```

You can then use your delegate type to reference the comparison methods:

```
string s1 = "Hello";
string s2 = "World";

var comparators = new StringComparators();
ComparisonTest test = new ComparisonTest(comparators.CompareContent);
Console.WriteLine("CompareContent returned: {0}", test(s1, s2));

test = new ComparisonTest(StringComparators.CompareLength);
Console.WriteLine("CompareLength returned: {0}", test(s1, s2));
```

The delegate type can reference instance methods that have the same signature as the delegate definition.

The delegate type can also reference static methods.

The sample output from the previous code is as follows:

```
CompareContent returned: False
CompareLength returned: True
```

Beginning with C# 2.0 it's much easier to create delegates. You can simply assign the method to the delegate variable (or parameter):

```
ComparisonTest test2 = comparators.CompareContent;
```

With delegates, you can make something similar to the higher-order functions that functional programming languages have. The next method checks whether two string arrays are similar by traversing the items in both collections and checking them against each other using a comparison function that was passed to a delegate reference.

Listing 3.1 `AreSimilar` method uses a delegate as a parameter type

```
bool AreSimilar(string[] leftItems, string[] rightItems, ComparisonTest
    tester)
{
    if (leftItems.Length != rightItems.Length)        The two arrays aren't similar if they
        return false;                                  have different numbers of items.

    for (int i = 0; i < leftItems.Length; i++)
    {
        if (tester(leftItems[i],rightItems[i]) == false)    ◁──┐ Checks the two strings.
        {                                                         If it returns false, the
            return false;                                         arrays aren't similar.
        }                              If you get here, all the items
    }                                  are similar in both arrays,
    return true;                    ◁─┘ so you return true.
}
```

The method receives the two arrays and calls the `tester` on every two corresponding items to check whether they're similar. The `tester` is referencing a method that was sent as an argument. Here you're calling the `AreSimilar` method and passing the `CompareLength` method as an argument:

```
string[] cities = new[] { "London", "Madrid", "TelAviv" };
string[] friends = new[] { "Minnie", "Goofey", "MickeyM" };
Console.WriteLine("Are friends and cities similar? {0}",
        AreSimilar(friends,cities, StringComparators.CompareLength));
```

The output result for this sample is as follows:

```
Are friend and cities similar? True
```

3.2.2 *Anonymous methods*

The problem with delegates as you've seen them so far is that they force you to write a method in a class—this is called a *named method*. This burden slows you down and therefore hurts your productivity. *Anonymous methods* are a feature in C# that enable you to pass a code block as a delegate value:

```
ComparisonTest lengthComparer = delegate (string first, string second)
{
    return first.Length == second.Length;
};
Console.WriteLine("anonymous method returned: {0}",
                    lengthComparer("Hello", "World"));
```

The anonymous method can also send the code block as an argument:

```
AreSimilar(friends, cities,
            delegate (string s1, string s2) { return s1 == s2; });
```

Anonymous methods make it far easier to create higher-order functions in your C# program and reuse existing code, as with the `AreSimilar` method in the previous example. You can use the method over and over and pass different comparison methods, improving the extendibility of your program.

CLOSURES (CAPTURED VARIABLES)

Anonymous methods are created within a scope, such as a method scope or a class scope. The code block of your anonymous method can access anything that's visible to it in that scope—variables, methods, and types, to name a few. An an example:

```
int moduloBase = 2;
var similarByMod=AreSimilar(friends, cities, delegate (string s1, string s2)
{
    return ((str1.Length % moduloBase) == (str2.Length % moduloBase));
});
```

Here the anonymous method uses a variable that's declared in the outer scope. The variable `moduloBase` is called a *captured variable*, and its lifetime now spans the lifetime of the anonymous method that uses it.

The anonymous method that uses captured variables is called a *closure*. Closures can use the captured variable even after the scope that created it has completed:

```
ComparisonTest comparer;          Creating an inner scope—every
                                  variable declared in this scope
{                          ◄───── is visible only under it.         Changing the value of the
    int moduloBase = 2;                                             variable the anonymous
    comparer = delegate (string s1, string s2)                     method uses affects the value
    {                                                               that the method sees.
        Console.WriteLine("the modulo base is: {0}", moduloBase);
        return ((s1.Length % moduloBase) == (s2.Length % moduloBase));
    };
    moduloBase = 3;                                         ◄───────
}
var similarByMod = AreSimilar(new[] { "AB" }, new[] { "ABCD" }, comparer);

Console.WriteLine("Similar by modulo: {0}", similarByMod);
```

When running this example, you get this interesting output

```
the modulo base is: 3
Similar by modulo: False
```

The anonymous method was created in a scope that's different from the scope that uses it, but the anonymous method still has access to a variable declared in that scope. Not only that, but the value that the anonymous method sees is the last one that the variable was holding. This leads to a powerful observation:

> The value of a captured variable that a closure uses is evaluated at the time of the method execution and not at the time of declaration.

Captured variables can cause confusion from time to time, so consider this example and try to determine what will print:

```
public delegate void ActionDelegate();    ⟵── Defines a delegate for methods that
                                              get no parameters and return void

var actions = new List<ActionDelegate>();
for (var i = 0; i < 5; i++)                         Adds a new
{                                                   anonymous method
    actions.Add(delegate () { Console.WriteLine(i); });  ⟵── to the list of actions
}
foreach (var act in actions) act();    ⟵┐  Executes every action in the collection.
                                          Each action prints to the screen.
```

The output of this example might not be what you expected. Instead of printing the numbers 0 to 4, this code prints the number 5 five times. This is because when each action is executed, it reads the value of i, and the value of i is the value it received in the last iteration of the loop, which is 4.

3.2.3 Lambda expressions

To make it even simpler to create anonymous methods, you can use the lambda expression syntax introduced in C# 3.0. Lambda expressions enable you to create anonymous methods that are more concise and more closely resemble the functional style.

Here's an example of an anonymous method written as both anonymous method syntax and with lambda expressions:

```
                                         The semicolon closes the assignment and
                                         isn't for the inner statement. The value of
                                         the expression is implicitly returned.
ComparisonTest x = (s1,s2) => s1==s2 ;    ⟵
ComparisonTest y = delegate (string s1,string s2) { return s1 == s2; };
```

The lambda expression is written as a parameter list, followed by =>, which is followed by an expression or a block of statements.

If the lambda expression receives only one parameter, you can omit the parentheses:

```
x => Console.WriteLine(x);
```

The lambda expression also uses type inference of the parameters. You can, however, write the types of the parameters explicitly:

```
ComparisonTest x = (string s1, string s2) => s1==s2 ;
```

Typically, you want your lambda expression to be short and concise, but it's not always possible to have only one statement in your lambda expression. If your lambda contains more than one expression, you need to use curly braces and write the `return` statement explicitly in case it needs to return a value:

```
() =>                              ◄────────────┐  Lambda expression with no parameters
{                                                │  that contain multiple expressions
    Console.WriteLine("Hello");
    Console.WriteLine("Lambdas");
    return true;          ◄──────────┐  To return a value, you must write
};                                    │  the return statement explicitly.
```

Lambda expressions are used heavily with Rx because they make your processing pipeline short and expressive, which is cool! But you still have the requirement to create new delegate types each time you want to specify a method signature for the method types to which you want to receive a reference, which is far from ideal. That's why you usually won't create new delegate types but instead use `Action` and `Func`.

3.2.4   *Func and Action*

A delegate type is a way to enforce the method signatures you want to receive as a parameter or set as a variable. Most of the time, you're not interested in creating a new type of delegate to enforce that constraint; you only want to state what you're expecting. For example, the following two delegate types are the same except for the names used:

```
public delegate bool NameValidator(string name);
public delegate bool EmailValidator(string email);
```

Because the two delegate types definitions are the same, you can set both to the same lambda expression:

```
NameValidator nameValidator = (name) => name.Length > 3;
EmailValidator emailValidator = (email) => email.Length > 3;
```

You name the two delegate types after the functionality that the assigned code needs to have—checking the validity of a name and of an email address. You could've changed the name to reflect the signature:

```
public delegate bool OneParameterReturnsBoolean(string parameter);
```

Now you have a delegate type that's reusable, but only to code that has access to your definition, which cries for a standard implementation. The .NET Framework contains reusable delegate type definitions named `Func<...>` and `Action<...>`:

- Func is a delegate type that returns a value and can receive parameters.
- Action is a delegate type that can receive parameters but returns no value.

The .NET Framework contains 17 definitions of Func and Action, each for different numbers of parameters that the referenced method receives. The Func and Action types are located under the System namespace in the mscorlib assembly.

To reference a method that has no parameters and doesn't return a value, you use the following definition of Action:

```
public delegate void Action();
```

and for a method that has two parameters and doesn't return a value, you use this definition of Action:

```
public delegate void Action<in T1, in T2>(T1 arg1, T2 arg2);
```

To use the Action delegate, you need to specify the types of parameters. Here's an example of a method that traverses a collection and makes an operation on each item by using an Action of an integer:

```
public static void ForEachInt(IEnumerable<int> collection,
                              Action<int> action)
{
    foreach (var item in collection)
    {
        action(item);
    }
}
```

Now you can call the ForEachInt method from your code like this:

```
var oddNumbers = new[] { 1, 3, 5, 7, 9 };
ForEachInt(oddNumbers, n => Console.WriteLine(n));
```

This code prints all the numbers in the oddNumbers collection. You can use the ForEachInt method with a different collection and different option. Because the Action delegate is generic, you can use that and create your generic version of ForEach:

```
public static void ForEach<T>(IEnumerable<T> collection, Action<T> action)
{
    foreach (var item in collection)
    {
        action(item);
    }
}
```

Now you can use ForEach with any collection:

```
ForEach(new[] { 1, 2, 3 }, n => Console.WriteLine(n));
ForEach(new[] { "a", "b", "c" }, n => Console.WriteLine(n));
ForEach(new[] { ConsoleColor.Red, ConsoleColor.Green, ConsoleColor.Blue},
        n => Console.WriteLine(n));
```

> The CLR uses type inference to conclude that the generic parameter T of ForEach is int.

Because `Console.WriteLine` is a method that can accept any number of parameters, you can write the previous example this way too:

```
ForEach(new[] { 1, 2, 3 }, Console.WriteLine);
ForEach(new[] { "a", "b", "c" }, Console.WriteLine);
ForEach(new[] { ConsoleColor.Red, ConsoleColor.Green, ConsoleColor.Blue},
        Console.WriteLine));
```

Whenever you need to create a delegate for methods that return a value, you should use the type `Func`. This type (like `Action`) receives a variable number of generic parameters corresponding to the types of parameters that the method referenced by the delegate can receive. Unlike `Action`, in the `Func` definition the last generic parameter is the type of return value:

```
public delegate TResult Func<in T1,…,T16, out TResult>(T1 arg,…,T16 arg16);
```

and there's a definition for a `Func` that gets no parameters:

```
public delegate TResult Func<out TResult>();
```

Using `Func`, you can extend your implementation of the `ForEach` method so that it'll accept a filter (also known as a *predicate*). The filter is a method that accepts an item and returns a Boolean indicating whether it's valid:

```
public static void ForEach<T>(IEnumerable<T> collection, Action<T> action,
                              Func<T, bool> predicate)          ◁─────  A delegate to a method
{                                                                       that accepts an item and
    foreach (var item in collection)                                    returns true or false
    {
        if (predicate(item))          ◁─────  If the predicate returns
        {                                      true, the item is valid.
            action(item);
        }
    }
}
```

The filtering you added to the `ForEach` method can be exploited to act only on certain items in a collection—for instance, printing only even numbers:

```
var numbers = Enumerable.Range(1,10);                    ◁───── The items 1-10
ForEach(numbers, n => Console.WriteLine(n), n => (n % 2 == 0));
```

With `Action` and `Func`, you can build classes and methods that can be extended without modifying their code. This is a nice implementation of the Open Close Principle (OCP) that says a type should be open for extension but closed to modifications. Following design principles such as the OCP can improve your code and make it more maintainable.

3.2.5   *Using it all together*

It's nice to see that known design patterns such as Strategy, Command, and Factory (to name a few) can be expressed differently with `Func` and `Action` and demand less code from the developer.

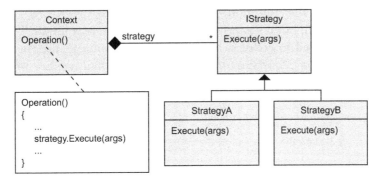

Figure 3.5   The Strategy pattern class diagram. The context's operation can be extended by providing different implementations of the strategy.

Take, for example, the Strategy pattern, whose purpose is to allow extension of an algorithm by encapsulating an operation inside an object. Figure 3.5 shows the Strategy design pattern class diagram. In this design pattern, you have a Context class that performs an operation. This operation depends on an external part that contains a specific algorithm. The algorithm is implemented by a class that implements the IStrategy interface.

The Strategy design pattern is useful when you want to allow extension points in a workflow and give the user of your code the power to control it. The pattern is used in many applications and even in the .NET Framework itself, such as in the case of the IComparer<T> interface.

The IComparer<T> interface is part of the System.Collections.Generic namespace and is used to compare two objects of the same type. A typical use of the IComparer<T> interface is in the Sort method of List<T>, so if you want to sort a list of strings by their length (and by lexicographical order), this is how you do it. First, you create a new IComparer derived class:

```
class LengthComparer : IComparer<string>        IComparer declares a single
{                                                method to implement a
    public int Compare(string x, string y)      comparison between two objects.
    {
        if (x.Length == y.Length)           The method should return 0 if the
        {                                    objects are equal, or a negative
            return 0;                        number if x is less than y . . .
        }
        return (x.Length > y.Length) ? 1 : -1;     . . . and a positive number
    }                                               if x is greater than y.
}
```

You run the sort like this:

```
var words = new List<string> { "ab", "a", "aabb", "abc" };
words.Sort(new LengthComparer());
Console.WriteLine(string.Join(", ", words));
```

The output of this sort is the collection { "a", "ab"," abc", "aabb" };.

This works pretty well, but it's annoying, because each time you want a new comparison method, you need to create a new class. Instead, you can use the power of Func and create a generic IComparer that you can tune to your needs:

```
class GenericComparer<T> : IComparer<T>
{
    private Func<T, T, int> CompareFunc { get; set; }

    public GenericComparer(Func<T,T,int> compareFunc)
    {
        CompareFunc = compareFunc;
    }

    public int Compare(T x, T y)
    {
        return CompareFunc(x,y);
    }
}
```

> In the constructor, you receive the Func that knows how to compare the two objects.

> The Compare method executes the Func you got in the constructor.

This is somehow an adapter between the IComparer and Func. To use it, you pass the required comparison code as a lambda expression (or delegate):

```
var words = new List<string> { "ab", "a", "aabb", "abc" };
words.Sort(new GenericComparer<string>((x, y) =>
    (x.Length == y.Length)
        ? 0
        : (x.Length > y.Length) ? 1 : -1));
```

> If the two strings' lengths are the same, return 0.

> If the lengths aren't the same, return 1 if x is greater than y; -1 otherwise.

With the generic version of IComparer, you can create new comparison code quickly and keep it close to where it's used so it's ready to read and is much more concise.

USING FUNC AS A FACTORY

Another pattern that the Func style can make shorter and more fun is the lazy-loading pattern in which Func is used as a factory (an object creator). *Lazy loading* means that instead of creating something in advance, you'll create it just in time, when it's used.

HeavyClass can take a long time to create or holds many resources so that you want to delay the time they take from the system. Next is an example of a heavy class that's used in another class. You want the object of the heavy class created only when something in the code is trying to use it:

```
class HeavyClass
{
    //This is a heavy class that takes long time to create
}

class ThinClass
{
    private HeavyClass _heavy;
    public HeavyClass TheHeavy
    {
```

```
        get
        {
            if (_heavy == null)
            {
                _heavy = new HeavyClass();
            }
            return _heavy;
        }
    }

    public void SomeMethod()
    {
        var myHeavy = TheHeavy;

        //Rest of code the use myHeavy
    }
}
```

Created only the first time something is trying to reach the heavy object

When SomeMethod is called, the call to the property that holds the heavy object occurs, so you can delay the creation until this point (if it ever happens).

This code has a couple of issues. First, it's repeatable; if you have 10 lazy-loaded types, you need to create the same if-create-return sequence 10 times, and duplication of code can be error prone and boring. Second, you forgot about concurrency and synchronization again (and many do forget, so don't feel bad). It'd be much better if someone else took care of those things for you, and luckily a tool exists for this.

Inside the System namespace you find the Lazy<T> class, whose purpose is to verify whether an instance was already created and, if not, to create it (once and only once). In our example, you could use Lazy<T> as shown here:

```
class ClassWithLazy
{
    Lazy<HeavyClass> _lazyHeavyClass = new Lazy<HeavyClass>();

    public void SomeMethod()
    {
        var myHeavy = _lazyHeavyClass.Value;

        //Rest of code that uses myHeavy
    }
}
```

But what if the HeavyClass constructor needs an argument or if the process of creating it is more complex? For that, you can pass a Func that performs the creation of the object and returns it:

```
Lazy<HeavyClass> _lazyHeavyClass = new Lazy<HeavyClass>(() =>
{
    var heavy = new HeavyClass(...);
    ...
    return heavy;
});
```

The heavy object is created with arguments and code that initializes it.

Delegates are a powerful feature of C#. For many years, their main use was when dealing with events, but since Action and Func were introduced, you can see how to use them to replace classic patterns by providing shorter, more readable, and concise code.

Still, something was missing. When you added new methods such as `ForEach`, it felt a bit like procedural code. You created a method that was exposed as a static from a class and when used, it didn't feel like the natural object-oriented style. You'd prefer to use a regular method on the object you wanted to run it on. This is exactly the point of extension methods.

3.3   Method chaining with extension methods

One of the things that allows functional programming to be concise and declarative is the use of function composition and chaining, where functions are called one after the other such that the output of the first function becomes the input of the next one. Because the functions are first-class citizens, the output of a function can be a function by itself. The queries you write with Rx are written in the same compositional way and make the query look as if it's a sentence in English, which makes it appealing to use. To understand how to add this kind of chaining behavior in your C# code, you first need to understand extension methods.

3.3.1   Extending type behavior with extension methods

In object-oriented programming, you create classes that contain both states (fields, properties, and so forth) and methods. After you create your class and compile it, you can't extend it and add more methods or members unless you change its code and recompile it. At times, however, you'll want to add methods that work on a class you already have—whether it's a class you created or a class that you have access to, such as the types from the .NET Framework. To add those methods, you can create a new class and add methods that accept the class you want to extend as a parameter that resembles the programming style of procedural languages.

Extension methods, a feature added to .NET, enable you to "add" methods to a type. Adding a method to a type doesn't mean you're changing the type; instead, extension methods allow you to use the same syntax of calling a method on an object but let the compiler convert it to a call on an external method. Let's revise our implementation of `ForEach`:

```
static class Tools
{
    public static void ForEach<T>(IEnumerable<T> collection,
                                  Action<T> action)
    {
        //ForEach implementation
    }
}
```

To use the `ForEach` method, you need to pass the collection on which you want to iterate as a parameter. With extension methods, the call for `ForEach` looks like the following example. Note that this won't compile just yet, because you haven't defined an extension method:

```
var numbers = Enumerable.Range(1,10);
numbers.ForEach(x=>Console.WriteLine(x));
```

At compile time, the compiler changes the given call to the regular static method call. To create extension methods, this is what you need to do:

1 Create a static class.
2 Create a public or internal static method.
3 Add the word this before the first parameter.

The type of the first parameter in your method is the type that the extension method can work against. Let's change the ForEach method to be an extension method:

```
public static void ForEach<T>(this IEnumerable<T> collection,
                                Action<T> action)
{
    //ForEach implementation
}
```

Now you can run the ForEach method on every type that implements the IEnumerable<T> interface.

Extension methods are regular methods at their base, and as such, they can receive parameters and return values. Test yourself to see if you can create an extension method that checks whether an integer is even. Here's my solution:

```
namespace ExtensionMethodsExample
{
    static class IntExtensions
    {
        public static bool IsEven(this int number)
        {
            return number % 2 == 0;
        }
    }
}
```

As a convention, classes that hold extension methods are named with a suffix of Extensions (such as StringExtensions and CollectionExtensions).

To use the extension method you created, you must add the namespace in which the extension class is declared to the using statements where the calling code is (unless they're in the same namespace):

```
using ExtensionMethodsExample;
namespace ProgramNamespace
{
    class Program
    {
        static void Main(string[] args)
        {
            int meaningOfLife = 42;
            Console.WriteLine("is the meaning of life even:{0}",
                            meaningOfLife.IsEven());
        }
    }
}
```

WORKING WITH NULL

Because extension methods are regular methods, they can work even on null values. Let me show you what I mean. To check whether a string is null or empty, you can use the static method IsNullOrEmpty of String:

```
string str = "";
Console.WriteLine("is str empty: {0}", string.IsNullOrEmpty(str));
```

You can create a new extension method that performs the same check on the object itself:

```
static class StringExtensions
{
    public static bool IsNullOrEmpty(this string str)
    {
        return string.IsNullOrEmpty(str);
    }
}
```

Now you can use it like this:

```
string str = "";
Console.WriteLine("is str empty: {0}", str.IsNullOrEmpty());
```

Note that the call is on the variable str itself. Now think about what will happen in this case:

```
string str = null;
Console.WriteLine("is str empty: {0}", str.IsNullOrEmpty());
```

The code won't crash, and you can see this message printed:

```
is str empty: True
```

That's pretty neat, even though you execute the IsNullOrEmpty like an instance method, it still runs correctly if there's no instance. Let's take this a step further and discuss the way extension methods can help you create fluent interfaces.

3.3.2 *Fluent interfaces and method chaining*

The term *fluent interface* was introduced by Eric Evans and Martin Fowler to describe a style of interface that allows subsequent calls of methods. The System.Text.String-Builder class, for example, provides an interface such as the following:

```
StringBuilder sbuilder = new StringBuilder();
var result = sbuilder
    .AppendLine("Fluent")
    .AppendLine("Interfaces")
    .AppendLine("Are")
    .AppendLine("Awesome")
    .ToString();
```

StringBuilder offers an efficient way to build strings and provide methods for appending and inserting the substrings into the end result. In the previous code sample, you can keep calling methods on the string builder without adding the variable name until you reach a method that ends the sequence of calls—in this case, ToString. This sequence of calls is also known as *method chaining.*

With fluent interfaces, you get much more fluid code that feels natural and readable. StringBuilder allows you to create the method chains, because this is how it's defined. If you look at its methods signature, you'll see that it returns the type StringBuilder:

```
public StringBuilder AppendLine(string value);
public StringBuilder Insert(int index, string value, int count);
:
public StringBuilder AppendFormat(string format, params object[] args);
```

What's returned from the StringBuilder methods is StringBuilder itself—the same instance. StringBuilder acts as a container of the final string, and every operation changes the internal data structure that forms the final string. Returning the same instance of StringBuilder from the methods allows continuation of the calls.

That's all good, and we should thank the .NET team for creating such a nice interface, but what happens if the class you need to deal with doesn't provide such an interface? And what happens if you don't have access to the source code, and you can't change it? This is where extension methods come in handy. Let's look at List<T> as an example.

List<T> provides a method to add items into it:

```
public class List<T> : IList<T>,...
{
    . . .
    public void Add(T item);
    . . .
}
```

The list's Add method accepts the item you want to add and returns void, so to add items, you have to write it as shown here:

```
var words = new List<string>();
words.Add("This");
words.Add("Feels");
words.Add("Weird");
```

You can also omit the variable name to reduce your typing and save energy. First, you'll create an extension method on the type of List<T> that executes the Add but returns the list afterward:

```
public static class ListExtensions
{
    public static List<T> AddItem<T>(this List<T> list, T item)
    {
        list.Add(item);
        return list;
    }
}
```

Now you can add to the list in the fluent way:

```
var words = new List<string>();
words.AddItem("This")
    .AddItem("Feels")
    .AddItem("Weird");
```

This looks much cleaner, and if you change the `this` parameter to be more abstract, your extension method will be applicable to more types. You can change the `AddItem` extension method so you can run it on all collection types that implement the `ICollection<T>` interface:

```
public static ICollection<T> AddItem<T>(this ICollection<T> list, T item)
```

This ability to add methods on abstract types is interesting, because in object-oriented languages, you can't add method implementation in an interface. If you want all types that implement an interface (such as `ICollection`) to have a method (such as `AddItem`), you have to either implement the method yourself in every one of the subtypes or create a shared base-class from which they all inherit. Both alternatives aren't ideal and sometimes aren't possible, because you don't have multiple class inheritance in .NET.[1] Not having multiple inheritance means that if you implement multiple interfaces, each with one or more methods, and you want to share an implementation between all subtypes, you couldn't make a base class from each interface and inherit from them all. It's not possible.

The extension methods, on the other hand, make this ability possible. When you make an extension method on an interface, it's available on all the types that implement the interface, and if the type implements more interfaces and they have extension methods of their own, the subtype will provide all those methods as well—a kind of virtual multiple inheritance.

It's important to emphasize that to create a fluent interface, you don't have to return the same instance or even the same type that the method chain started from. Each method call can return a different type, and the next method call will operate on it.

As you add more and more extension methods on concrete and abstract types, you can use them to create your own language, as you'll see next.

3.3.3   Creating a language

The extension methods allow you to add new methods on existing types without opening the type code and modifying it. Together with the technique of method chaining, you can build methods that express what you're trying to achieve in a language that describes your domain.

---

[1] A class can implement multiple interfaces even though it can derive from only a single direct base class.

Take the way you write your assertion in unit tests, for example. A *unit test* is a piece of code that executes code and then asserts that the result was as expected. Here's a simple test you can write with MSTest to check a string result:

```
[TestMethod]
public void NonFluentTest()
{
    ...
    string actual = "ABCDEFGHI";

    Assert.IsTrue(actual.StartsWith("AB"));
    Assert.IsTrue(actual.EndsWith("HI"));
    Assert.IsTrue(actual.Contains("EF"));
    Assert.AreEqual(9,actual.Length);
}
```

actual holds the result of the operation you're testing. You want to make sure it holds the result you expected.

Each assert checks a single condition. In this unit test, you want to verify that the result string fulfills all the conditions.

The assertions you use are technical and generic, and you can improve them by using a more fluent interface, such as the one provided by the excellent FluentAssertions library (www.fluentassertions.com). This is the same test after you add FluentAssertion syntax:

```
[TestMethod]
public void FluentTest()
{
    ...
    string actual = "ABCDEFGHI";
    actual.Should().StartWith("AB")
            .And.EndWith("HI")
            .And.Contain("EF")
            .And.HaveLength(9);
}
```

This version of the test checks the same conditions, but uses a much more sentence-like syntax because of the fluent interface. The FluentAssertions library added a DSL for assertions. It does that by adding an extension method for the string type that returns an object with a fluent interface that acts as an assertion builder.

```
public static StringAssertions Should(this string actualValue);
```

When the `Should` method is called, an object of type `StringAssertion` is created and the string you're checking is passed to it. From that point, all the assertions are maintained by the `StringAssertion`.

A DSL, like the one used here for assertions, makes the code concise and declarative. Another important and powerful DSL is the one provided by LINQ that provides generic querying capabilities for collections in .NET.

3.4 Querying collections with LINQ

Extension methods, together with the method-chaining technique, enable you to create DSLs for various domains, even if the original types don't implement the fluent interface themselves. An area for which a domain language existed for a long time is relational database querying. In relational databases, you can use SQL to query tables in a short and declarative way. Here's an example of SQL that fetches all the employees who live in the United States, sorted by their last name:

```
SELECT * --
FROM Employees
WHERE Country='USA'
ORDER BY LastName
```

◁——— **In SQL, * means you want to fetch all the fields from the table.**

As you can see, the syntax used in SQL is short and declarative; you state the desired result and let the database perform the process of fetching the wanted result for you. Wouldn't it be great if .NET had the same capability? It does.

LINQ is a set of standard operators that can be used on any data source to make queries. The data source can be an XML document, a database, a string, or any .NET collection. As long as the data source is a class that implements the `IEnumerable` interface, you can query it using LINQ.

IQueryable

`IEnumerable` isn't the only interface that LINQ is targeting. `IQueryable` is a special interface that makes it possible to evaluate the query against the data source directly so that LINQ queries performed against a database will be translated to SQL.

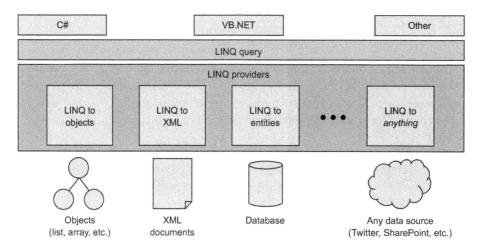

Figure 3.6   LINQ architecture: for each type of data source, a LINQ provider translates the LINQ query to a query language that best fits the source.

Figure 3.6 shows the LINQ architecture and its support for various data sources. The way the LINQ architecture is layered makes it possible to write a query once and run it over different sources without any change. The right query "translation" will depend on what the collection really is, but because the collection is abstracted by `IEnumerable`, you don't need to know the source that the collection is mapped to.

3.4.1 What does LINQ look like?

LINQ is made out of extension methods that operate on the source to build a query. Those methods are generally referred to as *operators*. Here's a simple program that uses a LINQ query against a list of integers to find all the odd numbers that are larger than 10 and returns them sorted and without repetitions after adding the value 2 to each one:

```
using System;
using System.Collections.Generic;
using System.Linq;

namespace LINQExamples
{
    class Program
    {
        static void Main(string[] args)
        {
            var numbers = new List<int> { 1, 35, 22, 6, 10, 11 };
            var result = numbers.Where(x => x % 2 == 1)
                .Where(x => x > 10)
                .Select(x => x+2)
                .Distinct()
                .OrderBy(x => x);

            foreach (var number in result)
            {
                Console.Write("{0}", number);
            }
            Console.WriteLine();
        }
    }
}
```

Adds the using statement for the LINQ namespace to import all LINQ operators.

Performs projection of the collection items by applying a Func that returns the transformation of the item. In this case, the value plus 2.

Checks a condition which is received as a parameter against each item in the collection.

Returns distinct items based on the default equals operator.

Sorts the elements in the result based on a key; the key is determined by the Func that OrderBy receives. In this case, each item is compared based on its value.

The query is performed by creating a method chain of operators, so that each item goes through the operators in the chain one by one and is collected in the final result. The final result is printed as 1337 in our case, because only 35 and 11 will survive the filters and then will be sorted after they're transformed to 37 and 13. The composability nature of creating the method chains in LINQ is described in the query flow that you see in figure 3.7.

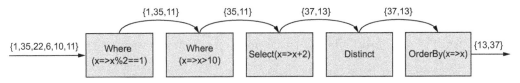

Figure 3.7 Composability of LINQ queries. LINQ is structured as a set of pipes and filters. Conceptually, the output of each operator becomes the input of the next one until you reach the end result.

Using the LINQ operators to create method chains is powerful but not always clear and intuitive. Instead, you can use *query expression syntax* that provides a declarative syntax resembling the SQL structure. The following example shows the same query from earlier in the chapter, only this time as a query expression:

```
using System;
using System.Collections.Generic;
using System.Linq;

namespace LINQExamples
{
    class Program
    {
        static void Main(string[] args)
        {
            var numbers = new List<int> { 1, 35, 22, 6, 10, 11 };
            var result =
                from number in numbers
                where number % 2 == 1
                where number > 10
                orderby number
                select number+2;

            var distinct = result.Distinct();

            foreach (var number in distinct)
            {
                Console.Write("{0}", number);
            }
        }
    }
}
```

> The LINQ query expression begins with from … in, helping IntelliSense know the type the query is working on.

> The select keyword specifies the elements in the end result and must be located at the end of the query syntax.

> LINQ operators that can't be embedded (such as Distinct) should be used as a regular extension method.

Note a few things in the example. First, it starts with the `from . . . in` clause and finishes with `select`; this is the standard structure. Second, not all operators can be embedded in the query expression syntax like `Distinct`. You'll need to add them as method calls inside or outside the query expression. Generally, you can call any method inside the query expression. Eventually, the query expression is syntactic sugar provided by the compiler, but using it makes things much simpler, such as in the case of nested queries and joins.

3.4.2   *Nested queries and joins*

The query expression syntax enables you to easily create readable nested queries and joins between two collections. Suppose you create a program that takes a collection of books and a collection of authors and displays the name of each author next to the name of that author's book. This is how you could do it with LINQ:

```
var authors = new[] {
                new Author(1, "Tamir Dresher"),
                new Author(2, "John Skeet")
};
```

```
var books = new[] {
                    new Book("Rx.NET in Action", 1),
                    new Book("C# in Depth", 2),
                    new Book("Real-World Functional Programming", 2)
};

var authorsBooks =
    from author in authors          Secondary from ... in clauses are the
    from book in books              same as making nested foreach loops.
    where book.AuthorID == author.ID
    select author.Name + " wrote the book: " + book.Name;

foreach (var authorBooks in authorsBooks)
{
    Console.WriteLine(authorBooks);
}
```

The query checks each author from the author's collection against each book in the book collection, similar to a Cartesian product. If the book's author ID is the same as the author ID, you select a string that says that. The output of this program is as follows:

```
Tamir Dresher wrote the book: Rx.NET in Action
John Skeet wrote the book: C# in Depth
John Skeet wrote the book: Real-World Functional Programming
```

What you did here is a type of grouping, and for that you can use the group operator of LINQ, but that's beyond the scope of this chapter.

Selecting a string isn't always what you want; another option is to select the author together with the book inside a new object. But do you need to create a new type each time you want to encapsulate properties together to make simple queries? The answer is no. For that you can use anonymous types.

3.4.3 *Anonymous types*

One of the great features added to C# as part of the support for LINQ was the ability to create anonymous types. An *anonymous type* is a type that's defined in place in your code when its object is created and in advance. The type is generated by the compiler based on the properties you assign to the object. Figure 3.8 shows how to create an anonymous type with two properties, a `string` and a `DateTime`.

The anonymous type is generated by the compiler, and you can't use it by yourself. The compiler is smart enough to know that if two anonymous types are generated

Figure 3.8   Anonymous type with two properties

with the same properties, they're the same type. In our example of finding the authors' books, you created a string for each author and book pair; instead you can create an object that encapsulates the two properties together:

```
var authors = new[] {
                    new Author(1, "Tamir Dresher"),
                    new Author(2, "John Skeet"),
};
var books = new[] {
                new Book("Rx.NET in Action", 1),
                new Book("C# in Depth", 2),
                new Book("Real-World Functional Programming", 2),
};

var authorsBooks =
    from author in authors
    from book in books
    where book.AuthorID == author.ID
    select new {author, book};

foreach (var authorBook in authorsBooks)
{
    Console.WriteLine("{0} wrote the book: {1}" ,
                    authorBook.author.Name,
                    authorBook.book.Name);

}
```

Creates an anonymous type that holds the author and the book as two properties. Without explicit names, the compiler will generate the name to be the same as the variables' names.

Because you're in the scope as the definition of the anonymous type, the IntelliSense and the compiler give access to the inner properties.

The anonymous type is visible only in the scope in which it was created, so you can't return it from a method or send it to another method as an argument unless you cast it to its only base class: object.

Anonymous types are one of the main reasons for the keyword `var` that's used to create implicitly typed local variables. Because the anonymous type is generated by the compiler, you can't create variables of that type; `var` allows you to make those variables and let the compiler deduce the type, as you see in figure 3.9.

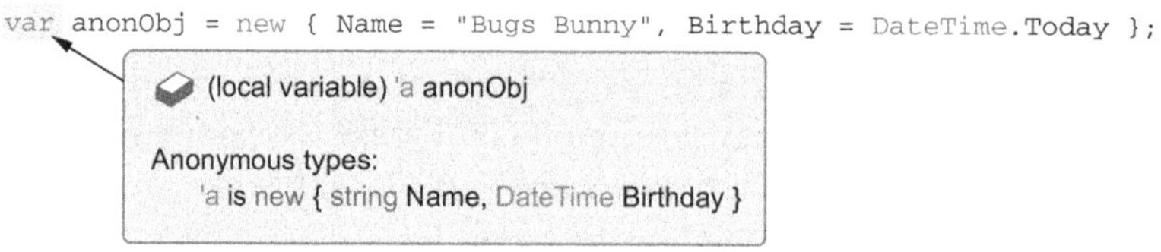

```
var anonObj = new { Name = "Bugs Bunny", Birthday = DateTime.Today };
```

> (local variable) 'a anonObj
>
> Anonymous types:
>   'a is new { string Name, DateTime Birthday }

Figure 3.9   Using `var` on an anonymous type. The compiler and IntelliSense know how to deduce the real type generated.

Anonymous type vs. Tuple

.NET offers another type that can be used to create bags of properties (which are referred to as *items*) on the fly: the `Tuple<>` class. The .NET Framework supports a tuple of up to seven elements, but you can pass eight elements as a tuple so you can get an infinite number of items.

This is how to create a tuple that has two items: a `string` and a `DateTime`:

```
Tuple<string, DateTime> tuple = Tuple.Create("Bugs Bunny", DateTime.Today);
```

The `Tuple.Create` factory method can receive arguments as the number of items you wish to have in the tuple.

As with the anonymous type, the `Tuple` data structure is a generic way to create new types on the fly, but unlike the anonymous type, the access to the `Tuple` items is based on the position of the item. To read the value on the `Tuple` you created previously, you need to know that it's the second item in the tuple:

```
var theDateTime = tuple.Item2;
```

This makes the tuple less readable and error prone.

Unlike the anonymous type, `Tuple` can be returned from a method or passed as an argument, but I advise you to avoid doing so. The better approach in this case is to create a class to serve that purpose and make your code type-safe, readable, and less buggy.

3.4.4   LINQ operators

LINQ operators give LINQ its power and make it attractive. Most of the operators work on collections that implement the `IEnumerable<T>` interface, which makes it broad and generic. The number of standard query operators is large. It would take more than a chapter to cover them all, so this section presents several of the most commonly used operators. If you find this subject interesting, I recommend that you look at the 101 LINQ Sample on the MSDN site (https://code.msdn.microsoft.com/101-LINQ-Samples-3fb9811b). Rx has always been referred to as *LINQ to Events*, and, in fact, the LINQ operators were adapted to support observables, so you can expect to see and learn more about those operators in the rest of the book. Table 3.1 presents the ones that I believe are important, clustered by categories that describe their purpose.

Table 3.1   The most used LINQ query operators

Category	Query operator	Description
Aggregation	`Count`	Returns the number of items in the collection
	`Max`	Returns the maximal item in the collection
	`Min`	Returns the minimal item in the collection
Element operations	`First`	Returns the first item in the collection and throws an error if the collection is empty

Table 3.1   The most used LINQ query operators *(continued)*

Category	Query operator	Description
Element operations	`FirstOrDefault`	Returns the first item in the collection or the default value if the collection is empty
	`Single`	Returns the single item that exists in the collection and throws an error if the collection is empty or if more than one item exists
	`SingleOrDefault`	Returns the single item that exists in the collection and throws an error if more than one item exists. If the collection is empty, the default value will be returned.
Filtering	`OfType<TResult>`	Returns the items in the collection that can be cast to `TResult`
	`Where`	Filters the list based on the condition that's provided as an argument
Grouping data	`GroupBy`	Groups the items according to a specified key selector function
Join	`Join`	Joins two collections based on a key
	`GroupJoin`	Joins two sequences by key, groups the result by matching key, and then returns the collection of grouped result and key
Partitioning	`Skip<TSource>`	Skips the number of items specified; the resulting collection contains the items without those skipped
	`Take<TSource>`	The result contains only the first items in the collection, filtered by the number of items specified
Projection	`Select`	Projects the items in the collection in the form specified in the passed `Func` parameter
	`SelectMany`	Projects each item to the collection and flattens all the returned collections to one
Quantifier operations	`All<TSource>`	Determines whether all elements of a collection satisfy a condition
	`Any`	Determines whether any element in the collection satisfies a condition
	`Contains`	Determines whether the collection contains an item
Set operations	`Distinct`	Returns a collection in which every item appears only once
	`Except`	Takes two collections and returns the element in the first collection that isn't part of the second collection
	`Intersect`	Takes two collections and returns the elements that exist in both of them
Sorting	`OrderBy`	Returns an ascending sorted collection by a key
	`OrderByDescending`	Returns a descending sorted collection by a key

3.4.5 *Efficiency by deferred execution*

LINQ is short and readable, but is it fast? The answer (like most things in programming) is that it depends. LINQ isn't always the most optimal solution to query a collection, but most of the time you won't notice the difference. LINQ also works under a deferred execution mode that affects performance and understanding. Consider the next example and try to answer what numbers will print:

```
var numbers = new List<int>{1, 2, 3, 4};
var evenNumbers =
    from number in numbers
    where number%2 == 0
    select number;

numbers.Add(6);        The number 6 is added
                       after the query is created.

foreach (var number in evenNumbers)
{
    Console.WriteLine(number);
}
```

The correct answer is that 2, 4, and 6 will print. How can that be? You created the query before adding the number 6; shouldn't the `evenNumbers` collection hold only the numbers 2 and 4?

Deferred execution in LINQ means that the query is evaluated only on demand. And demand means when there's an explicit traversing on the collection (such as `foreach`) or a call to an operator that does that internally (such as `Last` or `Count`).

To understand how deferred execution works, you need to understand how C# uses `yield` to create iterators.

THE YIELD KEYWORD

The `yield` keyword can be used inside a method that returns `IEnumerable<T>` or `IEnumerator<T>`. When `yield return` is used inside a method, the value it returns is part of the returned collection, as shown in the following example:

```
static IEnumerable<string> GetGreetings()    Returns a collection of strings
{                                            represented by IEnumerable<string>.
    yield return "Hello";
    yield return "Hi";
}
private static void UnderstandingYieldExample()    Each yield return makes the
{                                                  returned item part of the collection
    foreach (var greeting in GetGreetings())       that the method returns.
    {
        Console.WriteLine(greeting);    Each iteration causes the method to
    }                                   execute until it reaches the next yield
}                                       return, yield break, or end of the method.
```

Using `yield return` and `yield break` removes the need to manually create iterators by implementing `IEnumerable<T>` and `IEnumerator<T>` by ourselves; instead you can put all the logic regarding the creation of each item in a collection inside the method that returns the collection. A classic example is the generation of an infinite sequence such as the Fibonacci sequence. What you'll do is hold two variables in the method that holds the two previous items in the sequence. With each iteration, you'll generate a new item by summing the two previous items together and then updating their values:

```
IEnumerable<int> GenerateFibonacci()
{
    int a = 0;
    int b = 1;
    yield return a;          The first two items of the Fibonacci series are
    yield return b;          known and fixed so you can return them.
    while (true)
    {
        b = a + b;
        a = b - a;
        yield return b;      ◁———  Each time an iteration is done on the output collection,
    }                              the next iteration in the while loop happens, which
}                                  causes the calculation of the next item in the sequence.
```

As you can see, `yield` can be used inside loops as well as in regular sequential code. The method that contains the `yield` is controlled from the outside. Each time the `MoveNext` method is called on the `Enumerator` of the output `IEnumerable`, the method that returned the `IEnumerable` is resumed and continues its execution until it reaches the next `yield` statement or until it reaches its end. Behind the scenes, the compiler generated a state machine that keeps track of the method's position and knows how to transition to the next state to continue execution.

The LINQ operators (most of them) are implemented as iterators, so their code is executed lazily on each item in the collection queried. Here's a modified version of the `Where` operator to explain that point. The modified `Where` prints a message for each item it checks:

```
static class EnumerableDefferedExtensions
{
    public static IEnumerable<T> WhereWithLog<T>(this IEnumerable<T> source,
                                                 Func<T, bool> predicate)
    {
        foreach (var item in source)
        {
            Console.WriteLine("Checking item {0}", item);
            if (predicate(item))
            {
                yield return item;
            }
        }
    }
}
```

Now you'll use `WhereWithLog` on a collection and validate that the predicate isn't used on all the items at once but in an iterative way:

```
var numbers = new[] { 1, 2, 3, 4, 5, 6 };
var evenNumbers = numbers.WhereWithLog(x => x%2 == 0);
Console.WriteLine("before foreach");
foreach (var number in evenNumbers)
{
    Console.WriteLine("evenNumber:{0}",number);
}
```

This is the output:

```
before foreach
Checking item 1
Checking item 2
evenNumber:2
Checking item 3
Checking item 4
evenNumber:4
Checking item 5
Checking item 6
evenNumber:6
```

You can see that between each item yielded, a message is printed from the outer `foreach` loop. When you build a method chain of LINQ operators, each item moves through all the operators and is then handled by the code that traverses the query result, and then the next item goes through the chain.

The deferred execution has a good impact on performance. If you need only a limited number of items from a query result, you're not paying for the query execution time on the items you don't care for.

The deferred execution also allows you to build queries dynamically, because the query isn't evaluated until you iterate on it. You can add more and more operators without causing side effects:

```
var numbers = new[] { 1, 2, 3, 4, 5, 6 };
var query = numbers.Where(x => x%2 == 0);
if (/*some condition*/)
{
    query = query.Where(x => x > 5);          ◁─┐
}                                                │ If the condition is true
if (/*another condition*/)                       │ the operator will be
{                                                │ added to the query.
    query = query.Where(x => x > 7);          ◁─┘
}
foreach (var item in query)        ◁─┐ Evaluates
{                                    │ query
    Console.WriteLine(item);
}
```

3.5   *Summary*

C# was introduced in 2002 as an object-oriented language. Since then, C# has collected features and styles from other languages and became a multi-paradigmatic language.

- The functional programming styles aim to create a declarative and concise code that's short and readable.
- Using techniques such as a declarative programming style, first-class functions, and concise coding that were adopted by C# can make you more productive.
- In C# you use delegates to provide the first-class and higher-order functions.
- The reusable `Action` and `Func` types helps you express functions as parameters.
- Anonymous methods and lambda expressions make it easy to consume those methods and send code as arguments.
- In C#, you use a method-chaining technique to build domain-specific languages (DSLs) that express the domain you program.
- Extension methods make it easy to add functionality to types when you don't have access to a type source code or when you don't want to modify their code.
- To accomplish method chaining, use fluent interfaces and extension methods.
- LINQ makes querying over a collection super easy, with an abstraction that allows executing the same query against different underlying repositories.
- You can use LINQ to make simple queries that filter collections and more-complex queries that involve joining two collections together.
- Anonymous types ease your querying because it provides they provide inline creation of types that you use to store the results of your queries that should be visible only inside a scope.
- Deferred execution allows you to create queries that are executed when the results of the query are used instead of when the query is created.

The next chapter discusses the first part of creating an Rx query and the basics of creating the observables that every Rx query is built upon.

Part 2

Core ideas

The eight chapters in this part of *Rx.NET in Action* cover the full capabilities of the Rx library and its application in your programs. You'll start learning with the building blocks of Rx—the observable and the observer—how to create them, connect them, and control their relationship.

Then you'll learn how to build sophisticated Rx pipelines that are composed using the powerful Rx operators. You'll use operators that allow you to create queries on a single observable or a combination of multiple observables. You'll see how to control and parameterize concurrency and time in your queries and how to handle faults and avoid known pitfalls as part of your design.

Creating observable sequences

This chapter covers

- Creating observables of data and events
- Creating observables from enumerables
- Using Rx creational operators
- Getting to know the primitive observables

When people start learning about Rx, they usually ask, "Where do I begin?" The answer is easy: you should start with creating the observable.

In the next two chapters, you'll learn various ways to create observables. This chapter is limited to observables that are synchronous in their creation. Chapter 5 covers observables that involve asynchroncity in their creation and emissions.

Because many types of sources exist from which you want to receive items, it's not surprising that you have more than one way to create an observable. For instance, you can create an observable from traditional .NET events so you can still reuse your existing code, or you can create it from collections of items so it's easier to combine it with other observables. Each way is suited to different scenarios and has different implications, such as simplicity and readability.

4.1   Creating streams of data and events with observables

The `IObservable` interface is the most fundamental building block that Rx is based on, and it includes only a single method: `Subscribe`.

The observable is the source that pushes the items, and on the other end is the observer that receives them. The items can be of many forms: they can be the notification that something happened (events) or a data element you can process like a chat message.

Figure 4.1 shows an observable that represents a stream of chat messages received by a chat application. The chat observer receives each message through the `OnNext` method, and can display it on-screen or save it to a database. At one point, a network disconnection leads to an error notification.

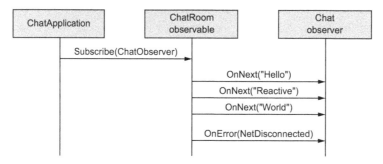

Figure 4.1   An example of a possible observable-observer dialogue. The observer receives notifications after subscribing until the network disconnects, which leads to an error.

We'll discuss a few ways to get to this type of observable. We'll start with the naïve solution.

4.1.1   Implementing the IObservable<T> interface

Before getting into a heavy chat message example, let's look at listing 4.1, which shows the most simple and naïve way to create an observable that pushes a simple series of numbers to observers: manually implementing the `IObservable<T>` interface. Creating observables this way *isn't* the best practice, but I believe it's essential for understanding the mechanics of how observables work.

Listing 4.1   Handcrafted observable that pushes numbers

```
using System;
using System.Reactive.Disposables;

public class NumbersObservable : IObservable<int>
{
    private readonly int _amount;
```

```
                   public NumbersObservable(int amount)
                   {
                       _amount = amount;
                   }

                   public IDisposable Subscribe(IObserver<int> observer)
                   {
                       for (int i = 0; i < _amount; i++)
                       {
                           observer.OnNext(i);
                       }
                       observer.OnCompleted();
                       return Disposable.Empty;
                   }
               }
```

> **Observable is initialized with the amount of numbers it will push to the observers.**

> **Observable notifies of its completeness after all the values have been pushed.**

> **For each observer that subscribes, the observable pushes the series of values.**

> **The Subscribe method returns the disposable that represents the subscription.**

The `NumbersObservable` class implements the `IObservable` interface, which allows any observer of integers to subscribe to it. Note that the `NumbersObservable` pushes the integer values immediately and synchronously as the observer subscribes to it. We'll talk later about observables that make asynchronous execution.

The following listing is an example of an observer that will accompany us throughout the chapter. This observer writes to the console the `OnNext`, `OnComplete`, and `OnError` actions as they happen.

Listing 4.2   `ConsoleObserver` writes the observer actions to the console

```
public class ConsoleObserver<T> : IObserver<T>
{
    private readonly string _name;

    public ConsoleObserver(string name="")
    {
        _name = name;
    }

    public void OnNext(T value)
    {
        Console.WriteLine("{0} - OnNext({1})",_name,value);
    }

    public void OnError(Exception error)
    {
        Console.WriteLine("{0} - OnError:", _name);
        Console.WriteLine("\t {0}", error);
    }

    public void OnCompleted()
    {
        Console.WriteLine("{0} - OnCompleted()", _name);
    }
}
```

> **Subscribing to any observable and printing all the notifications emitted by it**

> **Printing a name (if provided) with every notification, making it useful for debugging**

> **Printing every notification of OnNext**

> **Printing the error notification**

> **Printing the completion of the observable**

The following shows how to subscribe the `ConsoleObserver` to the Numbers-Observable:

```
var numbers = new NumbersObservable(5);
var subscription =
    numbers.Subscribe(new ConsoleObserver<int>("numbers"));
```

If you run the code snippet, this is what you'll see:

```
numbers - OnNext(0)
numbers - OnNext(1)
numbers - OnNext(2)
numbers - OnNext(3)
numbers - OnNext(4)
numbers - OnCompleted()
```

The five numbers that the observables pushed to the observer are displayed in the line with `OnNext`, and after the observable completed, so the last line is the call to `OnCompleted`.

Whenever an observer is subscribed to the observable, the observer receives an object that implements the `IDisposable` interface. This object holds the observer's subscription, so you can unsubscribe at any time by calling the `Dispose` method. In our simple example that emits a series of numbers, the entire communication between the observable and the observer is done in the `Subscribe` method, and when the method ends, so does the connection between the two. In this case, the subscription object doesn't have real power, but to keep the contract correct, you return and empty the disposable by using the Rx static property `Disposable.Empty`.

NOTE   Appendix B covers the Rx Disposables library in more detail.

You can make the subscription of `ConsoleObserver` more user friendly. Instead of creating an instance and subscribing each time you need it, let's create an extension method that does that for you.

Listing 4.3   `SubscribeConsole` extension method

```
public static class Extensions
{
    public static IDisposable SubscribeConsole<T>(
            this IObservable<T> observable,
            string name="")
    {
        return observable.Subscribe(new ConsoleObserver<T>(name));
    }
}
```

`SubscribeConsole` will help you throughout this book, and it may be useful for your Rx testing and investigations, so it's a good tool to have. The previous example now looks like this:

```
var numbers = new NumbersObservable(5);
var subscription =
    numbers.SubscribeConsole();
```
All notifications emitted by the observable will be written to the console.

You've now created an observable and observer by hand, and it was easy. Why, then, can't you always do it this way?

4.1.2 The problem with handcrafted observables

Writing observables by hand is possible, but rarely used, because creating a new type each time you need an observable is cumbersome and error prone. For example, the observable-observer relation states that when OnCompleted or OnError are called, no more notifications will be pushed to the observer. If you change the Numbers-Observable you created and add another call to the observer OnNext method after OnComplete is called, you'll see that it's called:

```
public IDisposable Subscribe(IObserver<int> observer)
{
    for (int i = 0; i < _amount; i++)
    {
        observer.OnNext(i);
    }
    observer.OnCompleted();

    observer.OnNext(_amount);
    return Disposable.Empty;
}
```
Call received by the observer.

This code now causes your ConsoleObserver to output the following:

```
errorTest - OnNext(0)
errorTest - OnNext(1)
errorTest - OnNext(2)
errorTest - OnNext(3)
errorTest - OnNext(4)
errorTest - OnComplete
errorTest - OnNext(5)
```

This is problematic because the unwritten agreement between the observable and the observer is what allows you to create the various operators of Rx. The Repeat operator, for example, resubscribes an observer when the observable completes. If the observable lies about its completion, the code that uses Repeat becomes unpredictable and confusing.

4.1.3 The ObservableBase

You don't often write observables manually, but doing so does make sense in some cases. For example, when you want to name your observable and make it encapsulate complex logic, then a handcrafted observable is good for you. Say you need to create a mapping of what goes into each of the observer methods (as you'll see next when you use a chat service that you talk to), but the service client is represented by a class that provides events for different types of notifications. In this case, you'd like to consume the chat service with an observable that pushes chat messages. When connecting to the chat service, you get a connection object with the following interface:

```
public interface IChatConnection
{
    event Action<string> Received;        Raised when a chat
    event Action Closed;                  message was received.
    event Action<Exception> Error;

    void Disconnect();                    Raised when an unexpected
}                                         error occurred.
```

Raised when the connection was closed. *(marginal note pointing to `event Action Closed;`)*

The connection to the chat service is done using the `Connect` method of the `ChatClient` class:

```
public class ChatClient
{
    ...

    public IChatConnection Connect(string user, string password)
    {
        // Connects to the chat service
    }
}
```

It's much nicer to consume the chat messages with an observable. The mapping, shown in figure 4.2, is clear between the events and what the observer knows to handle:

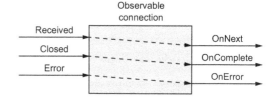

Figure 4.2 Mapping the `ChatConnection` events to the observer methods

- `Received` event can be mapped to the observers' `OnNext`
- `Closed` event can be mapped to the observers' `OnComplete`
- `Error` event can be mapped to the observers' `OnError`

Because logic is involved in wiring the event to the observer method, creating your own observable type makes sense. But you still want to avoid the common pitfalls of creating observables manually, so the Rx team provides a base class: `Observable-Base`. The following listing shows how to use it to create the `Observable-Connection` class.

Listing 4.4 `ObservableConnection`

```
using System;
using System.Reactive;
using System.Reactive.Disposables;

public class ObservableConnection : ObservableBase<string>
{
```

```
                private readonly IChatConnection _chatConnection;

                public ObservableConnection(IChatConnection chatConnection)
                {
                    _chatConnection = chatConnection;
                }

                protected override IDisposable SubscribeCore(IObserver<string> observer)
                {
                    Action<string> received = message =>
                    {
                        observer.OnNext(message);
                    };

                    Action closed = () =>
                    {
                        observer.OnCompleted();
                    };

                    Action<Exception> error = ex =>
                    {
                        observer.OnError(ex);
                    };

                    _chatConnection.Received += received;
                    _chatConnection.Closed += closed;
                    _chatConnection.Error += error;

                    return Disposable.Create(() =>
                    {
                        _chatConnection.Received -= received;
                        _chatConnection.Closed -= closed;
                        _chatConnection.Error -= error;
                        _chatConnection.Disconnect();
                    });
                }
            }
```

Saves the Chat-Connection so you can register and unregister from its events later

ObservableBase class provides the abstract method SubscribeCore where you write the logic of subscribing the observer.

Creates event handlers for the ChatConnection events. You save them in a variable so you can unregister them later.

Disposing of the subscription will unregister the ObservableConnection from all the ChatConnection events and try to disconnect from the service.

TIP The `ObservableConnection` example is based on the way SignalR creates its observable connection. SignalR is a library that helps server-side code push content to the connected clients. It's powerful, so you should check it out.

`ObservableConnection` derives from `ObservableBase<string>` and implements the abstract method `SubscribeCore`, which is called from the `ObservableBase Subscribe` method. `ObservableBase` performs a validity check on the observer for you (in case of null) and enforces the contract between the observer and the observable. It does that by wrapping each observer inside a wrapper called `Auto-DetachObserver`. This wrapper automatically detaches the observer from the client when the observer calls `OnCompleted` or `OnError` or when the observer itself throws an exception while receiving the message. This takes away the burden of implementing this safe execution pipeline yourself in your observables.

After you get the `ObservableConnection`, you can subscribe to it:

```
var chatClient = new ChatClient();
var connection = chatClient.Connect("guest", "guest");
IObservable<string> observableConnection =
    new ObservableConnection(connection);

var subscription=
    observableConnection.SubscribeConsole("receiver");
```

Connecting to the chat service

Creating an ObservableConnection from the ChatConnection. No subscription is made yet.

Subscribing ConsoleObserver shown at the beginning of the chapter

As before, you can make the creation of the `ObservableConnection` more pleasant with an extension method.

Listing 4.5   Creating the `ObservableConnction` with an extension method

```
public static class ChatExtensions
{
    public static IObservable<string> ToObservable(
            this IChatConnection connection)
    {
        return new ObservableConnection(connection);
    }
}
```

Now, you can simply write this:

```
var subscription =
    chatClient.Connect("guest", "guest")
    .ToObservable()
    .SubscribeConsole();
```

Still, it's annoying to create new observable types each time, and most of the time you don't have such complex logic to maintain. That's why it's considered bad practice to create observables by deriving directly from the `ObservableBase` or the `IObservable` interface. Instead, you should use one of the existing factory methods for observable creation that the Rx library provides.

4.1.4   *Creating observables with Observable.Create*

Every observable implements the `IObservable` interface, but you don't have to do it manually. The static type `Observable` that's located under the System.Reactive.Linq namespace provides several static methods to help you create observables. The `Observable.Create` method allows you to create observables by passing the code of the `Subscribe` method. The following listing shows how to use it to create the numbers observable you manually created previously.

Listing 4.6 Creating the numbers observable with `Observable.Create`

```
Observable.Create<int>(observer =>                    ← The lambda expression receives
{                                                       the observer (of type IObserver)
    for (int i = 0; i < 5; i++)     ←                   that subscribes to the observable.
    {                                    The created
        observer.OnNext(i);              observable will push
    }                                    the numbers 0 to 4.
    observer.OnCompleted();
    return Disposable.Empty;
});
```

As with the `ObservableBase` you used previously, the `Create` method does all the boilerplate for you. It creates an observable instance—of type `AnonymousObserv-able`—and attaches the delegate you provided (as a lambda expression, in this case) as the observable `Subscribe` method.

`Observable.Create` takes it even further, and allows you to return not only an `IDisposable` that you create, but also an `Action`. The provided `Action` can hold your cleanup code, and after it returns, the `Create` method will wrap the `Action` inside an `IDisposable` object that it creates by using `Disposable.Create`. If you return `null`, Rx will create an empty disposable for you.

NOTE Appendix B covers the Rx Disposables library in more detail.

Of course, you'd want your observable created with a user-defined amount and a static number of items (five in the previous example). Create the observable inside a method, as shown here:

```
public static IObservable<int> ObserveNumbers(int amount)  ←   Receives the number of
{                                                              items that the
    return Observable.Create<int>(observer =>                  observable will push
    {
        for (int i = 0; i < amount; i++)     ←   Pushes the numbers
        {                                        requested by the
            observer.OnNext(i);                  amount parameter
        }
        observer.OnCompleted();
        return Disposable.Empty;
    });
}
```

`Observable.Create` is heavily used because it's flexible and easy to use, but you may wish to postpone the creation of the observable until it's needed, such as when the observer is subscribed.

4.1.5 Deferring the observable creation

In section 4.1.2, you used the `ChatClient` class to connect to a remote chat server and then converted the returned `ChatConnection` into an observable that pushed the messages into the observers. The two steps of connecting to the server and then converting the connection to the observable always come together, so you want to add the method `ObserveMessages` to the `ChatClient`, encapsulate it, and follow the Don't Repeat Yourself (DRY) principle:

```
public IObservable<string> ObserveMessages(string user, string password)
{
    var connection = Connect(user, password);        Immediately connect
    return connection.ToObservable();                to the chat service.
}
```

Whenever a call to the `ObserveMessages` method is made, a connection to the chat service is created and then it's converted to an observable. This works perfectly fine, but it's possible that after the observable is created, no observer is subscribed to it for a long time or no observer ever subscribes. One reason this could happen is that you may create an observable and pass it to other methods or objects that might use it in their own time (for example, a screen that subscribes only when it's loaded, but loads only when a parent view receives input from a user).

Yet the connection is open and wastes resources on your machine and on the server machine. It would be better to delay the connection to the moment the observer subscribes. This is the purpose of the `Observable.Defer` operator that has the signature shown in figure 4.3.

```
public static IObservable<TResult> Defer<TResult>(Func<IObservable<TResult>> observableFactory)
```

The returned observable is a proxy around the real observable; when the observer subscribes, the observable factory will execute.

The factory method will create the real observable when the observer subscribes.

Figure 4.3 The `Defer` method signature

The `Defer` operator creates an observable that acts as a proxy around the real observable. When the observer subscribes, the `observableFactory` function that was provided as an argument is called and the observer subscribes to the created observable. This sequence is shown in figure 4.4.

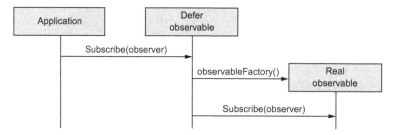

Figure 4.4 Sequence diagram of the subscription of an observer to a deferred observable created with the `Defer` operator.

Defer is good when you want to create observables with any of the observable factory operators you'll learn next, or if you have a factory method of your own (that you might, can't, or don't want to change), but you still want to create that observable when the observer subscribes.

This is how to use Defer to create the ObservableConnection:

```
public IObservable<string> ObserveMessagesDeferred(string user,
                                                   string password)
{
    return Observable.Defer(() =>
    {
        var connection = Connect(user, password);
        return connection.ToObservable();
    });
}
```

I should point out that using Defer *doesn't* mean that the observable that was created with the observableFactory is shared between multiple observers. If two observers subscribe to the observable that was returned from the Defer method, the Connect method will be called twice:

```
var messages = chatClient.ObserveMessagesDeferred("user","password");
var subscription1 = messages.SubscribeConsole();         | **Results in a call to Connect.**
var subscription2 = messages.SubscribeConsole();         |
```

This behavior isn't specific to Defer. The same issue occurred in the observables you created previously. Keep that in mind, and you'll learn when and how to make shareable observables in chapter 6 when we talk about cold and hot observables. Defer also plays another role in the observables "temperature" world because it can be used to turn a hot observable to a cold one, but I'm getting ahead of myself.

Eventually, the observable you created bridged traditional .NET events into the Rx. This is something you often do with Rx, so Rx provides operators that ease that work.

4.2 Creating observables from events

Creating an observable from a traditional .NET event is something you've seen in previous chapters, but we haven't discussed what happens inside. If all you need is to convert a traditional .NET event to an observable, using methods such as Observable.Create will be excessive. Instead, Rx provides two methods to convert from event to observable, namely FromEventPattern and FromEvent. These two methods (or operators) often lead to confusion for people working with Rx, because using the wrong one will cause compilation errors or exceptions.

4.2.1 Creating observables that conform to the EventPattern

The .NET events that you see inside the .NET framework expect the event handler to have the following signature:

```
void EventHandler(object sender, DerivedEventArgs e)
```

The event handler receives an object that's the `sender` that raised the event, and an object of a type that derives from the `EventArgs` class. Because the pattern of passing `sender` and `eventargs` is so commonly used, you can find generic delegates in the .NET Framework that you can use when creating events: `EventHandler` and `Event-Handler<T>`.

Rx recognizes that it's common to create events with delegates of that structure, which is called the event pattern, and therefore provides a method to convert events that follow the event pattern easily. This is the `FromEventPattern` operator. `FromEventPattern` has a few overloads, and the most used one is shown in figure 4.5.

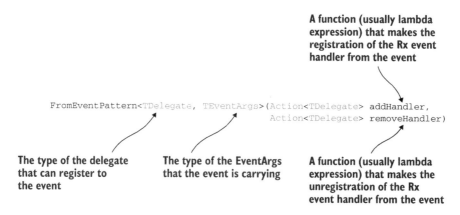

Figure 4.5   One of the `FromEventPattern` method overload's signatures

The `addHandler` and `removeHandler` parameters are interesting. Because they let you specify how to attach and detach the inner event handler that Rx provides, they expect to get an action that performs the registration and deregistration of a delegate (that's provided as the action parameter) from the event. In most cases (if not all), they have the following form:

- addHandler → h => [*src*].[*event*] += h
- removeHandler → h => [*src*].[*event*] -= h

For example, one of the places you see the event pattern is in UI events, such as in WPF. Suppose you want to receive the stream of clicks on a button named `theButton` that's placed in a window. The `Button` class exposes the `Click` event (that's defined in its base class `ButtonBase`):

```
public event RoutedEventHandler Click;
```

The `RoutedEventHandler` is a delegate that's defined in the `System.Windows` namespace:

```
public delegate void RoutedEventHandler(object sender,
                              System.Windows.RoutedEventArgs e)
```

To create an observable from the click event, write the following code:

```
IObservable<EventPattern<RoutedEventArgs>> clicks =
        Observable.FromEventPattern<RoutedEventHandler, RoutedEventArgs>(
                h => theButton.Click += h,
                h => theButton.Click -= h);
clicks.SubscribeConsole();
```

**Writes message to the Visual
Studio Output window**

Here, you convert the `Click` event to an observable, so that every event raised will call
the observers' `OnNext` method. You specify that the generic parameters are `Routed-`
`EventHandler`, because this is the event handler specified in the event definition,
and `RoutedEventArgs`, because this is the `eventargs` type that the event sends to
the event handlers.

The created observable pushes objects of type `EventPattern<RoutedEvent-`
`Args>`. This type encapsulates the values of the `sender` and the `eventargs`.

If the event is defined using the standard `EventHandler<TEventArgs>`, you can
use the `FromEventPattern` overload that expects only the generic parameter of
`TEventArgs`:

```
IObservable<EventPattern<TEventArgs>> FromEventPattern<TEventArgs>(
    Action<EventHandler<TEventArgs>> addHandler,
    Action<EventHandler<TEventArgs>> removeHandler);
```

**Specifies the eventargs
type via TEventArgs.**

**Gets an EventHandler<TEventArgs>
to register/unregister from the event.**

Rx also gives the simplest version for converting events into observables, in which you
need to specify only the name (as a string) of the event and the object that holds it, so
the click event example could've been written as follows:

```
IObservable<EventPattern<object>> clicks =
    Observable.FromEventPattern(theButton, "Click");
```

I'm not fond of this method. Magic strings tend to cause all sorts of bugs and code
confusion.[1] It's easy to make a typo, and you need to remember to change the strings
around your application in case you decide to rename your event. But the simplicity is
attractive, so use it with care.

> **TIP** If you're working with GUI applications and find the conversion between
> UI events to observables appealing, you might find the ReactiveUI framework
> (http://reactiveui.net/) helpful. ReactiveUI isn't covered in this book, but it
> provides many useful Rx utilities. One of them is the built-in conversions of
> many UI events to observables.

---

[1] A possible solution to the magic strings problem is the `nameof` operator that has existed since C# 6.0. See
   https://msdn.microsoft.com/en-us/library/dn986596.aspx.

4.2.2 *Events that aren't following the event pattern*

Not all events follow the event pattern. Suppose you have a class that scans the available Wi-Fi networks in your area. The class exposes an event that's raised when a network become available:

```
public delegate void NetworkFoundEventHandler(string ssid);
class WifiScanner
{
    public event NetworkFoundEventHandler NetworkFound = delegate { };
    // rest of the code
}
```

The event doesn't follow the standard event pattern because the event handler needs to receive a string (for the network SSID). If you try to convert the event to an observable by using the FromEventPattern method, you'll get an argument exception, because the NetworkFoundEventHandler delegate isn't convertible to the standard EventHandler<TEventArgs> type.

To overcome this, Rx provides the FromEvent method that looks similar to the FromEventPattern method:

```
IObservable<TEventArgs> FromEvent<TDelegate, TEventArgs>
    (Action<TDelegate> addHandler, Action<TDelegate> removeHandler);
```

This overload of the FromEvent method gets two generic parameters: one for the delegate that can attach to the event, and another for the type of the eventargs that's passed to the delegate by the event. The important part here is that you have no constraint on the type of the delegate or on the eventargs; they can be whatever you like. This is how to write the WifiScanner class:

```
var wifiScanner = new WifiScanner();
IObservable<string> networks =
    Observable.FromEvent<NetworkFoundEventHandler, string>(
            h => wifiScanner.NetworkFound += h,
            h => wifiScanner.NetworkFound -= h);
```

In the code, you create an observable from the event that the WifiScanner exposes. The event expects an eventHandler that conforms to the NetworkFoundEvent-Handler delegate, and the value that the event handlers receives is string, so the resulting observable is of type IObservable<string>.

4.2.3 *Events with multiple parameters*

The more complex overload of the FromEvent method is used when the event you want to convert to an observable has more than one parameter in the eventHandler signature. Take, for example, the case that the WifiScanner is sending not only the network name, but also its strength:

```
public delegate void ExtendedNetworkFoundEventHandler(string ssid,
                                                       int strength);
```

**The event handler needs to receive
the SSID and the signal strength.**

```
class WifiScanner
{
    public event ExtendedNetworkFoundEventHandler ExtendedNetworkFound =
      delegate { };
}
```

Trying to write the same code you wrote for the one parameter version won't work. Observables can pass only one value when they call the OnNext method of their observers. You need to somehow wrap the two parameters in a single object. The FromEvent overload that you'll use takes a conversion function that converts the Rx event handler to an event handler that can be used with the event. First, let's look at the method signature and then I'll explain what exactly you're seeing.

Creates a reference to a method that can attach to the event. This method needs to call the provided Action<TEventArgs>. This is the Rx handler that will call the observer OnNext.

```
IObservable<TEventArgs> FromEvent<TDelegate, TEventArgs>
    (Func<Action<TEventArgs>, TDelegate> conversion,
    Action<TDelegate> addHandler,
    Action<TDelegate> removeHandler);
```

The conversion handler is then passed to the addHandler and removeHandler.

This method signature takes time to digest, so I'll explain it with an example to help you understand. The following example converts the ExtendedNetworkFound event into an observable of Tuple<string, int>:

```
IObservable<Tuple<string, int>> networks =
Observable.FromEvent<ExtendedNetworkFoundEventHandler, Tuple<string, int>>(
    rxHandler =>
        (ssid, strength) =>  rxHandler(Tuple.Create(ssid, strength)),
    h => wifiScanner.ExtendedNetworkFound += h ,
    h => wifiScanner.ExtendedNetworkFound -= h);
```

The returned handler is provided to the add\removeHandler.

Creates a handler that calls the rxHandler with the values the event is sending, wrapped in a tuple.

First let's talk about addHandler and removeHandler. As before, this pair of actions receives a reference to a method that can be registered to the event in question. The addHandler registers it, and the removeHandler unregisters it. But how does Rx know what handler to create? This is the job of the *conversion function*. In the previous example, the conversion function is the lambda expression. Its purpose is to create a handler of its own that has the signature of the delegate defining the event. The lambda expression receives the parameter rxHandler, which holds the method that eventually calls the OnNext method in the observers. The lambda expression builds the event handler that can be registered to the ExtendedNetworkFound event; this event handler calls rxHandle, and so it acts as a mediator between what the event expects and what Rx expects.

4.2.4   *Dealing with events that have no arguments*

Not every event sends arguments to its event handlers. Certain events state that something happens; for example, the next event is raised by your `WiFiScanner` when the network connects:

```
event Action Connected = delegate { };
```

When trying to convert the event to an observable, you face a problem. Every observable must implement `IObservable<T>`, and `T` is the type of the data that will be pushed to the observers. What will type `T` be for the observable created from the `Connected` event? You need a neutral type that could represent a void. In mathematics, a neutral element with respect to an operation (such as multiplication or addition) is called the `Unit` (it's really called the `Identity` element, but under a broader context it's referred to as the `Unit`). You're already familiar with the `Unit` element in your day-to-day life: it's the number 1 under multiplication, and 0 under addition. That's why Rx includes the struct `System.Reactive.Unit`. This struct has no real members, and you can think of it as an empty entity that represents a singular value. It's often used to denote the successful completion of a void-returning method, as in the case of our event. This how to convert your event to an observable:

```
IObservable<Unit> connected = Observable.FromEvent(
    h => wifiScanner.Connected += h,
    h => wifiScanner.Connected -= h);

connected.SubscribeConsole("connected");
```

Because `Unit` has only a default value (that represents void), its `ToString` methods return the string of empty parentheses "()", so the following output is what you'll get from the previous example:

```
connected - OnNext(())
connected - OnNext(())
```

> **NOTE** We didn't cover a few of the overloads to `FromEventPattern` and `FromEvent`. Those overloads allow you to simplify hooking events for simple cases (when the event handler is just `Action<T>`, for example) or to convert from an event that doesn't conform to the event pattern into `IObservable` of `EventPattern`. You should take a look.

Converting events into observables can be helpful, because after you have the observable, there's no limit to the event processing you can do with Rx operators. But events aren't the only constructs you'd like to convert to an observable; sometimes you'll want to take something that's the complete opposite of an observable and turn it into an observable. I'm talking about enumerables.

4.3   *From enumerables to observables and back*

Enumerables provide the mechanism to work in a pull model, whereas observables enable you to work in a push model. Sometimes you'll want to move from a pull model to a push model to create a standard handling of both worlds, such as creating the same logic for adding chat messages that are received on the fly and for messages that were stored and read later from a repository. Sometimes it might even make sense to move from a push model to a pull model. This section explores those transitions and their effects on your code.

4.3.1 Enumerable to observable

Enumerables and observables are dual; you can go from one to the other by following several simple steps. Rx provides a method that helps you convert an enumerable into an observable: `ToObservable`. In this example, you create an array of strings and convert it to an observable:

```
IEnumerable<string> names = new []{"Shira", "Yonatan", "Gabi", "Tamir"};
IObservable<string> observable = names.ToObservable();

observable.SubscribeConsole("names");
```

If you run this code, the following is printed:

```
names - OnNext(Shira)
names - OnNext(Yonatan)
names - OnNext(Gabi)
names - OnNext(Tamir)
names - OnCompleted()
```

Under the hood, the `ToObservable` method creates an observable that, once subscribed into, iterates on the collection and passes each item to the observer. When the iteration is done, the `OnComplete` method is called on the observer.

If an exception occurs while iterating, it will be passed to the `OnError` method.

Listing 4.7 Creating an observable that throws

```
class Program
{
    static void Main(string[] args)
    {
        NumbersAndThrow()
            .ToObservable()                          The enumerable returned from
            .SubscribeConsole("names");              the method will give the values 1–3
                                                     and then throws an exception.
        Console.ReadLine();
    }

    static IEnumerable<int> NumbersAndThrow()
    {
        yield return 1;
        yield return 2;
        yield return 3;
        throw new ApplicationException("Something Bad Happened");
        yield return 4;
    }
}
```

The output of this example is as follows:

```
enumerable with exception - OnNext(1)
enumerable with exception - OnNext(2)
enumerable with exception - OnNext(3)
enumerable with exception - OnError:
        System.ApplicationException: Something Bad Happened
. . .
```

If all you need is to eventually subscribe to the enumerable, you can use the `Subscribe` extension method on the enumerable. This converts the enumerable to an observable and subscribes to it:

```
IEnumerable<string> names = new[] { "Shira", "Yonatan", "Gabi", "Tamir" };
names.Subscribe(new ConsoleObserver<string>("subscribe"));
```

WHERE TO USE IT

At the beginning of this chapter, you created an `ObservableConnection` that helped you consume chat messages through an observable. The nature of the `ObservableConnection` is that only new messages will be received by the client, but as users, you'd like to enter the chat room and see the messages that were there before you connected.

For the simplicity of our scenario, let's assume that while you were offline, no messages were sent. This leaves the problem of loading the messages saved from all the previous sessions. Usually, this is where a database is needed. Your application is saving every message it receives into a database, and when you connect, those messages are loaded and added to the messages screen.

With the `ObservableConnection`, you already have code that knows how to add messages to the screen. This is code you'd also like to use for the messages loaded from the database. It would've been great to represent the messages in the database as an observable, merge it with the observable of the new messages, and use the same observer to receive the messages from both worlds. Here's a small example that does that: two messages are saved to the database, and two messages are received while connected:

```
ChatClient client = new ChatClient();
IObservable<string> liveMessages    =                          ◁── An observable for the
    client.ObserveMessages("user","pass");                          messages that are received
IEnumerable<string> loadedMessages = LoadMessagesFromDB(); ◁──      while connected

loadedMessages.ToObservable()                                      A collection with all the
    .Concat(liveMessages)             ◁──                          messages that were
    .SubscribeConsole("merged");                                   stored in the database
```

Messages from the liveMessages observable will be sent to the observers only after loadedMessages has finished.

This example uses the operator `Concat`. This operator will concatenate the `liveMessages` observable to the `loadedMessages` observable, such that, only after all the loaded messages are sent to the observers, the live messages will be sent. The following is the output:

```
merged - OnNext(loaded1)
merged - OnNext(loaded2)
merged - OnNext(live message1)
merged - OnNext(live message2)
```

You could write the same example without converting the enumerable by yourself:

```
liveMessages
    .StartWith(loadedMessages)
    .SubscribeConsole("loaded first");
```

The `StartWith` operator first sends to the observers all the values in the enumerable and then starts to send all messages received on the `liveMessages` observable.

In the previous chapters, where we talked about the enumerable/observable duality, you saw that it allows going in both directions, from enumerable to observable, as you saw here, and from observable to enumerable, as you'll see next.

4.3.2   *Observable to enumerable*

In the same way that you converted an enumerable to an observable, you can do the opposite, using the `ToEnumerable` methods. This creates an enumerable that, once traversed, will block the thread until an item is available or until the observable completes. Using `ToEnumerable` *isn't* something that you *want* to do, but sometimes can't do otherwise, as in the cases when you have a library code that accepts only enumerables and you need to use it on a known subset of items from the observable, for example, sorting a fraction of items that you can define by time or amount. Using `ToEnumerable` is simple, as you'll see here.

> **Listing 4.8   Using the `ToEnumerable` operator**

```
var observable =
    Observable.Create<string>(o =>
    {
        o.OnNext("Observable");
        o.OnNext("To");
        o.OnNext("Enumerable");
        o.OnCompleted();
        return Disposable.Empty;
    });
```

⟵ If you comment this line, the thread will enter a waiting state after all the values in OnNext have been consumed.

```
var enumerable = observable.ToEnumerable();
foreach (var item in enumerable)
{
    Console.WriteLine(item);
}
```

The loop will print every value that you send with OnNext. When the observable completes, the loop will end.

Because of the blocking behavior of the enumerable returned from `ToEnumerable`, using it isn't recommended. You should stay with the push model as much as possible.

NOTE The Next operator also returns an enumerable, but it acts differently than the one ToEnumerable is returning. Chapter 6 covers this topic.

Rx includes methods that can convert the observable to a list and an array in a non-blocking way (keeping it an observable), namely ToList and ToArray, respectively. Unlike ToEnumerable, these methods return an observable that provides a single value (or no value if an error occurs), which is the list or the array. The list (or array) is sent to the observers only when the observable completes.

> **Listing 4.9 Using the `ToList` operator**

```
var observable =
    Observable.Create<string>(o =>
    {
        o.OnNext("Observable");
        o.OnNext("To");
        o.OnNext("List");
        o.OnCompleted();
        return Disposable.Empty;
    });

IObservable<IList<string>> listObservable =
    observable.ToList();

listObservable
    .Select(lst => string.Join(",", lst))
    .SubscribeConsole("list ready");
```

Only if the observable completes will the list be sent to the observers. (points to `o.OnCompleted();`)

Converts the list to a string, where each item is separated with a comma. (points to `.Select(lst => string.Join(",", lst))`)

Running this sample results in this output:

```
list ready - OnNext(Observable,To,List)
list ready - OnCompleted()
```

In the spirit of converting an observable to an enumerable, I should also mention the ToDictionary and ToLookup methods. Though they sound similar, they have different use cases.

CONVERTING AN OBSERVABLE TO A DICTIONARY

In .NET, types that implement the interface System.Collections.Generic .IDictionary<TKey, TValue> are said to be types that contain key-value pairs. For each key, there can be only one corresponding value or no value at all. In this case, we say the key isn't part of the dictionary.

Rx provides a way to turn an observable into a dictionary, by using the method ToDictionary that has a few overloads. The following example is the simplest one:

```
IObservable<IDictionary<TKey, TSource>> ToDictionary<TSource, TKey>(
    this IObservable<TSource> source,
    Func<TSource, TKey> keySelector)
```

keySelector returns the value of the key for each observable value. (points to `Func<TSource, TKey> keySelector)`)

This method runs `keySelector` for each value that's pushed by the `source` observable and adds it to the dictionary. When the `source` observable completes, the dictionary is sent to the observers. Here's a small example that demonstrates how to create a dictionary from city names, where the key is the name length.

Listing 4.10 Using the `ToDictionary` operator

```
IEnumerable<string> cities = new[] { "London", "Tel-Aviv", "Tokyo", "Rome" };

var dictionaryObservable =
    cities
    .ToObservable()
    .ToDictionary(c => c.Length);

dictionaryObservable
    .Select(d => string.Join(",", d))
    .SubscribeConsole("dictionary");
```

> The key can be whatever you wish, but if two items share the same key, you'll get an exception.

> Joins all the key-value pairs together, separated by a comma

Running the example displays the following:

```
dictionary - OnNext([6, London],[8, Tel-Aviv],[5, Tokyo],[4, Rome])
dictionary - OnCompleted()
```

If the two values in the observable share the same key, when trying to add them to the dictionary you'll receive an exception that says the key already exists. Dictionaries maintain a 1:1 relationship between the key and the value; if you want multiple values per key, you need a lookup.

CONVERTING AN OBSERVABLE TO A LOOKUP

If you need to convert your observable into a dictionary-like structure that holds multiple values per key, `ToLookup` is what you need. The `ToLookup` signature looks similar to the signature of `ToDictionary`:

```
IObservable<ILookup<TKey, TSource>> ToLookup<TSource, TKey>(
    this IObservable<TSource> source, Func<TSource, TKey> keySelector)
```

As with `ToDictionary`, you need to specify the key for each observable value (other overloads allow you to also specify the value itself). You can look at the lookup as a dictionary in which each value is a collection.

The next example creates a lookup from an observable of city names, where the key is the length of the name. This time, the observable will have multiple cities with the same name length.

Listing 4.11 Using the `ToLookup` operator

```
IEnumerable<string> cities =
    new[] { "London", "Tel-Aviv", "Tokyo", "Rome", "Madrid" };

var lookupObservable =
    cities
```

> London and Madrid have the same length.

```
    .ToObservable()
    .ToLookup(c => c.Length);
```

In the lambda expression, you specify the key for each value.

```
lookupObservable
    .Select(lookup =>
    {
        var groups = new StringBuilder();
        foreach (var grp in lookup)
            groups.AppendFormat("[Key:{0} => {1}]",grp.Key,grp.Count());
        return groups.ToString();
    })
    .SubscribeConsole("lookup");
```

When you receive the lookup, you iterate on each of its inner groups and join them to a string that shows the key and the number of items.

This is the output after running the example:

```
lookup - OnNext([Key:6 => 2][Key:8 => 1][Key:5 => 1][Key:4 => 1])
lookup - OnCompleted()
```

You can see that because *London* and *Madrid* have the same length (of 6), the output shows that the key 6 has two values.

The duality between observables and enumerables allows you to operate in both worlds and makes it easy for you to transform one to the other according to your needs. But remember that it comes with a warning. You have more ways to create observables than "implementing" their logic or converting from other types. Common patterns are nicely abstracted with creational operators and can be used as factories.

4.4   Using Rx creational operators

Up to this point, you've seen how to create observables by hand or convert from known types such as enumerables and events. Over time, it's become clear that certain patterns in the observable creation are being repeated, such as emitting items inside a loop or emitting a series of numbers. Instead of writing it ourselves, Rx provides operators that help do it in a standard and concise way. The observables created by the creational operators are often used as building blocks in much more complex observables.

4.4.1   Generating an observable loop

Suppose you have an iterative-like process that you need to run to produce the observable sequence elements a few lines at a time, as in the case of reading a file in batches. For this type of scenario, you can use the `Observable.Generate` operator. Here's its simplest overload:

```
IObservable<TResult> Generate<TState, TResult>(
    TState initialState,
    Func<TState, bool> condition,
    Func<TState, TState> iterate,
    Func<TState, TResult> resultSelector)
```

An initial state for loop

Determines whether you should run the next iteration based on the current state.

Returns the next state value.

Selects the value in the observable based on the current state. The result can be a different type than the state.

For example, if you want to generate an observable that pushes the first 10 even numbers (starting from 0), this is how you do it:

```
IObservable<int> observable =
    Observable.Generate(
        0,                  //Initial state
        i => i < 10,        //Condition (false means terminate)
        i => i + 1,         //Next iteration step
        i => i*2);          //The value in each iteration

observable.SubscribeConsole();
```

Running this example prints the numbers 0, 2, 4, 6, 8, 10, 12, 14, 16, 18.

To make this even simpler, if what you're trying to create is an observable that creates a range of elements, you can use another operator that does only that: the `Observable.Range` operator:

```
IObservable<int> Range(int start, int count)
```

This creates an observable that pushes the integral numbers within a specified range.

If you add the `Select` operator, you can create the same observable you created by using `Generate`:

```
IObservable<int> observable =
    Observable
        .Range(0, 10)          ◁——  Creates an observable
        .Select(i => i*2);           that pushes 10 numbers
                                     starting from 0
```

`Generate` or `Range` can be used to create more than numbers generators. Here's an example that uses `Generate` to create an observable that emits the lines of a file.

4.4.2 Reading a file

Basically, reading a file is an iterative process. You need to open the file and read line by line until you reach the end. In the observable world, you'd like to push the content to your observers. The following code shows how to do that with `Observable.Generate`:

```
IObservable<string> lines =              Open the stream to the file.
    Observable.Generate(                 Note: There's a flaw here that
        File.OpenText("TextFile.txt"),  ◁——  we'll discuss shortly.
        s => !s.EndOfStream,                              The state is the stream
        s => s,                                        ◁—  itself (it contains its
        s => s.ReadLine());  ◁——                          position in the file).
                                    Returns the line
lines.SubscribeConsole("lines");    from the file
```

Continue until
you reach the
end of the file.

This is what I got when running the example on a file with four lines:

```
lines - OnNext(The 1st line)
lines - OnNext(The 2nd line)
lines - OnNext(The 3rd line)
lines - OnNext(The 4th line)
lines - OnCompleted()
```

FREEING THE FILE RESOURCE

The previous example has a flaw you may not see immediately. The call to `File.OpenText` creates a stream that holds the file open. Even after the observable completes—either when it reaches the end or when it is disposed of from the outside—the stream is still active and the file remains open. To overcome this and so that your application will handle resources correctly, you need to let Rx know that a disposable resource is involved. This is where the `Observable.Using` operator fits in. The `Using` operator receives a factory method that creates the resource (and the factory method that creates the observable with that resource). The returned observable will make sure that when the inner observable completes, the resource will be disposed of.

> **NOTE** The `Using` operator, together with other resource management considerations, is covered in chapter 10.

This listing shows how to correct our example.

Listing 4.12 Freeing resources with the `Using` operator

```
IObservable<string> lines =
    Observable.Using(
        () => File.OpenText("TextFile.txt"),        ◁——  Opens the file and returns the
        stream =>                                         stream you work with
            Observable.Generate(
                stream,                              ◁——  The initial state is the stream itself
                s => !s.EndOfStream,                       (pointing to the start of the file).
                s => s,.                             ◁——  The state is the stream.
                s => s.ReadLine())                   ◁——  Returns the line
    );                                                     from the file

lines.SubscribeConsole("lines");
```

Continue until you reach the end of the file. (annotation pointing to `s => !s.EndOfStream,`)

Now you know for sure that when your observable is used, no resource you create will remain undisposed, which makes your code more efficient.

4.4.3 *The primitive observables*

A few creational operators can come in handy during certain times, to combine with other observables to create edge cases. This can be useful when testing or for demonstrations and learning purposes, but also when building operators of your own that need to deal with certain inputs that require special handling.

CREATING A SINGLE-ITEM OBSERVABLE

The `Observable.Return` operator is used to create an observable that pushes a single item to the observer and then completes:

```
Observable.Return("Hello World")
    .SubscribeConsole("Return");
```

Running this example results in this output:

```
Return - OnNext(Hello World)
Return - OnCompleted()
```

CREATING A NEVER-ENDING OBSERVABLE

`Observable.Never` is used to create an observable that pushes no items to observers and never completes (not even with an error):

```
Observable.Never<string>()
    .SubscribeConsole("Never");
```

The generic parameter is used to determine the observable type. You can also pass a fake value of the type you want to do the same. Running this example prints nothing on the screen.

CREATING AN OBSERVABLE THAT THROWS

If you need to simulate a case that an observable notifies its observers about an error, `Observable.Throw` will help you do this:

```
Observable.Throw<ApplicationException>(
    new ApplicationException("something bad happened"))
    .SubscribeConsole("Throw");
```

This is what prints after running the example:

```
Throw - OnError:
        System.ApplicationException: something bad happened
```

CREATING AN EMPTY OBSERVABLE

If you need an observable that doesn't push any items to its observers and completes immediately, you can use the `Observable.Empty` operator:

```
Observable.Empty<string>()
    .SubscribeConsole("Empty");
```

This prints the following:

```
Empty - OnCompleted()
```

4.5   *Summary*

Wow, you learned a lot in this chapter. You should feel proud of yourself. The material covered in this chapter will be carried with you in almost every observable pipeline you'll create:

- All observables implement the `IObservable<T>` interface.
- Creating observables by manually implementing the `IObservables` interface is discouraged. Instead, use one of the built-in creation operators.
- The `Create` operator allows you to create observables by passing the `Subscribe` method that will run for each observer that subscribes.

- The `Defer` operator allows you to defer or delay the creation of the observable until the time when an observer subscribes to the sequence.
- To create an observable from events that conform to the event pattern (where the delegate used receives a sender and `EventArgs`), use the `FromEvent-Pattern` operator.
- To convert events that don't conform to the event pattern, use the `FromEvent` operator.
- The `FromEventPattern` and `FromEvent` operators receive a function that adds an event handler to the event, and a function that removes an event handler from the event.
- You can use an overload of the `FromEventPattern` operator that allows you to pass an object and to specify the name of the event to create the observable from. This should be used mostly for standard framework events.
- Enumerables can be converted to observables as well using the operator `ToObservable`.
- Observables can be converted to enumerables by using the operators `ToEnumerable`, `ToList`, `ToDictionary`, and `ToLookup`. But they'll cause the consuming code to block until an item is available or until the entire observable is completed, depending on the operator.
- To create an observable from an iterative process, use the `Generate` operator.
- The `Range` operator creates an observable that emits the sequence of numbers in the specified range.
- To create an observable that emits one notification, use the `Observable.Return` operator.
- To create an observable that never emits notifications, use the `Observable.Never` operator.
- To create an observable that notifies failure, use the `Observable.Throws` operator.
- To create an empty observable, use the `Observable.Empty` operator.

Still, throughout the chapter, we ignored important types that wrap asynchronous execution. The next chapter will extend your knowledge about creating observables. You'll learn about the asynchronous patterns in .NET and how to bridge them into Rx.

Creating observables from .NET asynchronous types

This chapter covers

- Understanding the importance of asynchronous code
- Writing asynchronous code in C#
- Bridging .NET asynchronous code to Rx
- Creating observables of periodic behaviors

If there's one thing I really dislike, it's standing in line, especially a long line. I always feel I'm wasting time that I could invest in other things (such as writing a book). I always love the restaurants that allow you to come in and leave your name for a seat, which then frees you to walk around, admire the view, shop, and so forth. When your seat is available, or when your time slot arrives, you're notified by a phone call or buzzer. For me, this is customer service at its best.

Like you and me, our code sometimes needs to stand in line and wait for something; this is what we call the *synchronous way*. Like you and me, our code can be notified when a task is complete and can harvest the result; this is the *asynchronous way*. Writing asynchronous code is crucial for modern apps to be responsive (and react in a timely manner) and it's a key trait for being reactive. In this chapter, you'll look at patterns for executing code asynchronously in .NET and see how they relate to your observables. You'll look at ways to create observables from asynchronous types and learn about obstacles you might face when doing so.

> **NOTE** This chapter and the rest of the book use the Task-Based Asynchronous Pattern (TAP) and `async-await` as the pattern for writing asynchronous code. Appendix A covers the common .NET patterns for writing asynchronous code as well as references to other sources on the subject.

5.1   Bridging .NET asynchronous types with Rx

Rx observables are wonderful when working with asynchronous sources. The observable and observer interfaces allow the separation between a producer that can run anywhere, synchronously or asynchronously, and the consumer (the observer) that can receive the notifications and handle them. This has benefits including testability and flexibility, because it's easy to create a *fake*[1] observable to emulate your test scenarios, and easy to make changes in the producer side without affecting the consumer. This producer-consumer separation is shown in figure 5.1.

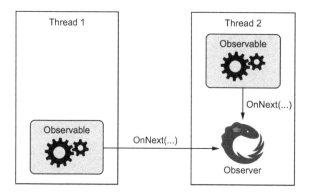

Figure 5.1 From the observer standpoint, the observable can run on any thread and emit the notifications by computing them asynchronously or synchronously.

Here you can see that the observer that subscribes to an observable doesn't know where the notifications are emitted from and whether the observable computes them in an asynchronous way. But in chapter 10 you'll learn that sometimes it's necessary for the observer to handle those notifications on a specific thread. For example, in WPF and WinForms applications, it's possible to make changes to UI controls only from the UI thread, and so it's necessary for observers that are modifying elements in the application screens to observe the notifications on the special UI thread.

Rx provides operators to support that and control the execution of the observable pipeline. You'll learn about them in chapter 10. In the next few pages, you'll look at an example of converting from synchronous code to asynchronous code that you consume through the observable.

---

[1] A fake is also known as a mock or stub; see http://mng.bz/b2b8.

5.1.1 Changing the synchronous method to asynchronous

Suppose you have a magical prime numbers generator. This class can generate as many prime numbers as you want, but the processing time to produce a number is long. Your first attempt to create a synchronous version, the `MagicalPrimeNumbers Generator`, looks like this:

```
class MagicalPrimeGenerator
{
    public IEnumerable<int> Generate(int amount){. . .}
}
```

The `Generate` method receives an integer for the number of primes you want to generate and returns an enumerable with those numbers.

Now you can write a small program that prints the numbers:

```
var generator = new MagicalPrimeGenerator();
foreach (var prime in generator.Generate(5))          ← Blocks the main thread
{                                                       for a few seconds
    Console.Write("{0}, ", prime);
}
```

Because it takes your magical primes generator time to generate each number (for example, 2 seconds), your main thread will block here for 5 * 2 = 10 seconds. Even if you change the primes generator to generate each item on demand with `yield`, it'll still block the calling thread for 2 seconds between two numbers.

Another attempt could generate the full collection of the requested primes in an asynchronous way, which means you can change the `Generate` signature to this:

```
Task<IReadOnlyCollection<int>> GenerateAsync(int amount);
```

The method now returns `Task<IReadOnlyCollection<int>>`. I've used `IReadOnlyCollection<T>` to make it clear that the method generates the full collection before returning.

This change doesn't block the calling thread, but from the client perspective, it performs worse because the client will have to wait (asynchronously) a long time before processing any items in the collection. For instance, the previous program that prints the five prime numbers will now have to wait 10 seconds before printing anything. In a way, you've returned to the original version of the program.

The iterative model doesn't fit here, so let's convert it into a push model.

5.1.2 Creating the primes observable

If the pull model doesn't work, even when making it asynchronous, you should move to the push model. This way, you won't have to wait for the entire computation to finish to see some progress. Instead of creating an enumerable of the prime numbers, you need to create an observable that will emit every prime number when it's ready.

This is how the method signature looks now:

```
public IObservable<int> GeneratePrimes(int amount)
```

The method still receives as a parameter the number of prime numbers to generate, but now it returns an observable of type IObservable<int>.

Now you can implement the method; here's the first try:

```
public IObservable<int> GeneratePrimes(int amount)
{
    return Observable.Create<int>(o =>
    {
        foreach (var prime in Generate(amount))
        {
            o.OnNext(prime);
        }
        o.OnCompleted();
        return Disposable.Empty;
    });
}
```

> **Produces an enumerable using yield; you won't wait for the entire collection.**

> **Pushes each prime number to the observer immediately**

> **You'll reach this point after all the primes are generated, so disposing of the subscription has no effect.**

To create the observable, you're using the Create method you learned about in chapter four. The code provided to the Create method is still synchronous, so the observer will receive all the generated primes upon subscription, and the call to Subscribe won't return until the generation is finished. You can see this in the following code. You use the operator Timestamp to also display a timestamp for every item emitted:

```
var generator = new MagicalPrimeGenerator();

var subscription = generator
    .GeneratePrimes(5)
    .Timestamp()
    .SubscribeConsole("primes observable");

Console.WriteLine("Generation is done");
Console.ReadLine();
```

When you run it you'll see

```
primes observable - OnNext(2@01/08/2015 12:50:02 +00:00)
primes observable - OnNext(3@01/08/2015 12:50:04 +00:00)
primes observable - OnNext(5@01/08/2015 12:50:06 +00:00)
primes observable - OnNext(7@01/08/2015 12:50:08 +00:00)
primes observable - OnNext(11@01/08/2015 12:50:10 +00:00)
primes observable - OnCompleted()
Generation is done
```

The Timestamp operator wraps the observable items in an object of type System.Reactive.Timestamped<TSource> that contains two properties: Value for the inner item and Timestamp for the time in which the item was produced. It also overrides ToString to return a string in the format Value@Timestamp.

You can see that the Generation is done message is printed after all the prime numbers are generated. You can see that the numbers are received with a 2-second gap between them. Let's fix our observable so the subscription won't block. For this, you can run the inner generation code inside a new task.

TIP   Creating a new task for running the observable code is considered a bad practice. I'm doing it in the next example to keep things simple at this stage. In chapter 10, you'll learn about the Rx concurrency model and how you should change the code written here.

Now that the observable code is going to run concurrently, the observer's ability to unsubscribe becomes much more important. Until now, the emissions from all the observables you saw happened immediately when the observer subscribed (synchronously), so the observer didn't have the opportunity to unsubscribe. Now the observer can unsubscribe at any time. To allow this, you attach the returned disposable to a `CancellationToken` that you'll check in every iteration, so the new version looks like this:

```
public IObservable<int> GeneratePrimes(int amount)        Creates the CancellationTokenSource
{                                                          from which you produce
    var cts = new CancellationTokenSource();        ←──   cancellation tokens
    return Observable.Create<int>(o =>
    {                                                Runs the code inside a new
        Task.Run(() =>                         ←──   task to make it asynchronous
        {
            foreach (var prime in Generate(amount))
            {
                cts.Token.ThrowIfCancellationRequested();
                o.OnNext(prime);
            }                                        Ensures that the task won't
            o.OnCompleted();                         run in case the subscription was
        }, cts.Token);                         ←──   disposed of before starting

        return new CancellationDisposable(cts);  ←──┐ Cancels the CancellationTokenSource
    });                                              │ when disposed of
}
```

Checks whether cancellation was requested and stopping

In this version of `GeneratePrimes`, you start a new task at the point where, as before, you're iterating on the enumerable returned from the `Generate` method that yields the next prime number in every iteration. Now that your code is running in the background, you can enable the cancellation of the subscription. To do this, you create a `CancellationTokenSource` instance that you later attach to the returned disposable by using the `CancellationDisposable` class. When the user disposes of it, the `CancellationTokenSource` will be canceled as well. Inside each iteration, you check to see whether cancellation was requested and stops the loop.

TIP   When you run code examples that introduce concurrency inside a console application (for example, with `Task.Run`), the main thread will exit even if the concurrent code is still running. Adding a call to `Console.ReadLine` (or any other `Console` read method) is an easy way to keep the application from exiting before the example is done.

The pattern of running code inside a task and enabling cancellation with a `CancellationToken` object that's connected to the returned disposable is common,

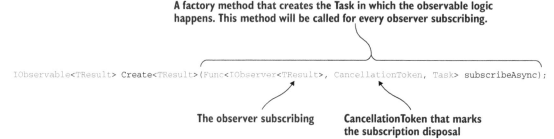

A factory method that creates the Task in which the observable logic happens. This method will be called for every observer subscribing.

```
IObservable<TResult> Create<TResult>(Func<IObserver<TResult>, CancellationToken, Task> subscribeAsync);
```

The observer subscribing

CancellationToken that marks the subscription disposal

Figure 5.2   The asynchronous version of the `Create` **operator**

so the Rx team provides an overload of the `Observable.Create` method (shown in figure 5.2) that does the plumbing for you.

The asynchronous version of the `Create` operator receives a `Func` that's invoked for each observer that subscribes to the returned observable—therefore, it's called `subscribeAsync`. The `subscribeAsync` function receives two parameters: the observer that's subscribing and a `CancellationToken` that's tied to the subscription disposable. `subscribeAsync` returns a task, thus allowing the asynchronous code to be written inside.

Here's how to use this method to simplify your `GeneratePrimes` method:

```
public IObservable<int> GeneratePrimes (int amount)
{
    return Observable.Create<int>((o, ct) =>        ◁─┐ Your lambda expression
    {                                                  │ receives the observer (o) and
        return Task.Run(() =>                          │ a CancellationToken (ct).
        {
            foreach (var prime in Generate(amount))
            {
                ct.ThrowIfCancellationRequested();
                o.OnNext(prime);
            }
            o.OnCompleted();
        });

    });
}
```

The previous code is almost similar to what you did before, only this time you don't need to create `CancellationToken` and its connection to the subscription disposal.

Let's recap what you've learned so far:

1   The `Create` operator receives an asynchronous function named `subscribeAsync`.
2   The `subscribeAsync` function is executed each time an observer is subscribed to the observable. The function must return a `Task` to represent its asynchronous operation.

3 When invoked, the `subscribeAsync` function receives `CancellationToken`, which acts as a communication channel of the observer's subscription disposal.

4 Inside `subscribeAsync` is where you'll write the code that emits the notifications to the subscribed observer.

TIP If you need more control over the way the subscription disposal affects your observable logic, you should know that the `Create` operator also includes overloads that return a disposable from the `subscribeAsync` method.

TIP In the previous chapter, you learned about using `Defer` to defer the creation of an observable to when the first observer subscribes. Rx also provides a version of the `Defer` operator that supports an asynchronous observable factory, as well as a cancellable version called `DeferAsync`.

Next I'll show you how the combination of observables with `async-await` shows the real strength of Rx.

5.1.3 *Using async-await in observable creation*

The async version of `Create` also allows you to use `async-await` inside the `subscribeAsync` code. By combining observables and `async-await`, you can see the real value Rx brings. Instead of waiting for two (or more) separate asynchronous operations to complete, and only then merge their results so they can be consumed as a whole, you can start to emit elements the moment you have something meaningful.

Figure 5.3 illustrates an observable that emits search results from two search engines whose call is `async`.

Figure 5.3 With observables, observers can start to receive notifications even if not all the sequence sources (like search engines) have completed.

The code for this example is:

```
IObservable<string> Search(string term)
{
    return Observable.Create<string>(async o =>
    {
        var searchEngineA = ...
        var searchEngineB = ...
```

Marks the code with async because you're going to use await inside; your lambda expression now returns the task.

```
var resultsA = await searchEngineA.SearchAsync(term);
foreach (var result in resultsA)
{
    o.OnNext(result);
}
var resultsB = await searchEngineB.SearchAsync(term);
foreach (var result in resultsB)
{
    o.OnNext(result);
}
o.OnCompleted();
});
}
```

Calls the asynchronous search method and awaits it → (points to first block)

Emits each of the search results (points to first foreach)

Another asynchronous call you await → (points to second block)

Emits the results from the second search engine (points to second foreach)

The previous code in the `Search` method creates an observable by using the asynchronous version of `Observable.Create`. The `subscribeAsync` I provided as a lambda expression uses `async-await` and therefore returns a task. The code is simple, calling to two search engines, one after the other, each time emitting the results.

What you're missing in this code is the possibility to cancel the process if the subscription is disposed of. As an exercise, add this feature yourself and check what happens when you dispose of the subscription at different stages. You can see my solution at the book's source code.

5.1.4   *Converting tasks to observables*

The preceding example that demonstrates using the `Observable.Create` method with the asynchronous subscribe method can be improved. You might have noticed the repetition in the code. For every search engine, you called the search method and then iterated the results.

To improve the code, you can take advantage of the fact that a natural conversion occurs between the task and the observable; a task can be looked at as an observable of potentially one item (zero if it never returns). To convert a task to an observable, all you need to use is the extension method `ToObservable` on the task.

> **TIP** Rx recognizes the deep connection between tasks and observables, and therefore allows, with certain operators, you to provide tasks in the same way you provide observables, without the need to convert to observables before.

The search method of each search engine returns `Task<IEnumerable <string>>`, in our case, so converting it to an observable will give `IObservable<IEnumerable <string>>`, still different from the observables you want—`IObservable <string>`. You need one more step that I'll explain shortly.

Here's how to change the previous code to convert the two searches from tasks to observables and then concatenate them together:

```
IObservable<string> Search (string term)
{
    var searchEngineA = new SearchEngineA();
    var searchEngineB = new SearchEngineB();
```

```
IObservable<IEnumerable<string>> resultsA =
    searchEngineA.SearchAsync(term).ToObservable();
IObservable<IEnumerable<string>> resultsB =
    searchEngineB.SearchAsync(term).ToObservable();

return resultsA
    .Concat(resultsB)
    .SelectMany(results => results);
}
```

Converting each task's results from the search engine to an observable

Concatenating the observables together so that the results from the second search engine will be emitted only after the results from the first completed

Changing the observable from an observable of collections to an observable of the items in the collections (also called flattening).

This method needs a little explanation. The first part of the method calls the search methods and converts the tasks to observables; it's easy.

With two observables in your hands, you can do numerous things. Because you want to keep the semantics of the methods you saw until now, in which the results from the second search engine are provided only after you finish emitting the results from the first search, you need to `Concat` the observables:

```
IObservable<TSource> Concat<TSource>(
    this IObservable<TSource> first,
    IObservable<TSource> second)
```

This overload accepts only two observables.

`Concat` receives two or more observables (depending on the overload) and returns an observable that's a concatenation of the input observables, which emit their values without interleaving. All the items from the first observables are emitted, and only then all the items from the second, and so forth. Figure 5.4 provides a marble diagram so you can visualize it.

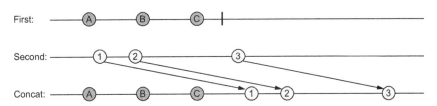

Figure 5.4 The `Concat` operator marble diagram. All items from the first observable are emitted. Only after the first observable completes will the items from the second observable be emitted.

Still, after you concatenate the observables, you get `IObservable<IEnumerable<string>>`. You need to flatten each enumerable so that the items will be pushed one by one, and so your observable will become `IObservable<string>`. This is where the `SelectMany` operator comes in. I'll show the overload I used, and then I'll explain it:

```
IObservable<TResult> SelectMany<TSource, TResult>(
    this IObservable<TSource> source,
    Func<TSource, IEnumerable<TResult>> selector)
```

The selector function projects the item to an enumerable whose items will be emitted in the resulted observably

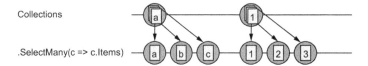

Figure 5.5 The `SelectMany` **operator marble diagram. Each item produces an enumerable by the selector, and the items from each enumerable are emitted to the resulting observable.**

`SelectMany` projects each element of an observable sequence to an enumerable sequence and concatenates the enumerables into one observable sequence. `Select-Many` gets a selector of type `Func<TSource, IEnumerable<TResult>>`; this selector is called on every item in the observable and returns a collection from that item. The elements of the collection will afterward be emitted on the resulting observable. The marble diagram in figure 5.5 makes this clearer.

Going back to our example, you concatenated the observables created from the search engines, and each observable carries one item that's the collection of the search results. When you wrote `SelectMany(results => results)`, you made it so that the returned observables will carry each search result separately.

> **NOTE** It's also possible to convert from an observable to a task that you can later await to get the last value (or exception) produced by the observable. This is done with the `ToTask` operator. You also can await the observable itself because it provides its own `Awaiter` class.

Besides the use of `SelectMany` to project observables that emit collections into observables that emit the items from the collections, `SelectMany` has an important use when running asynchronous code as part of your observable pipeline, as you'll see next.

5.1.5   *Running asynchronous code as part of the pipeline*

Running asynchronous code is beneficial not only for creating observables; it's also extremely useful for running inside the operators that compose the observable pipeline, as shown in figure 5.6. This way, you don't have to block your pipeline while processing an emitted element and can let your observable emit the next one while the processing happens in the background.

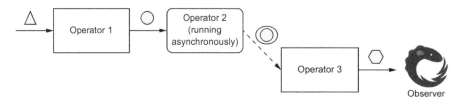

Figure 5.6   Asynchronicity can also be necessary in one of the pipeline operators. Operator 2 performs an async operation that, once completed, is passed to operator 3.

As you can see, an item begins its journey in the pipeline in operator 1, and then operator 2 performs an asynchronous operation. You'd like operator 3 to handle the result after the asynchronous operation completes.

Consider the next example in which you want to use the `Where` operator to check each item in the observable against an asynchronous service that determines whether the number is a prime:

```
var svc = new PrimeCheckService();
var subscription = Observable.Range(1, 10)
    .Where(async x => await svc.IsPrimeAsync(x))         This won't
    .SubscribeConsole("AsyncWhere");                     compile.
```

The `Where` operator expects from the given predicate to return a Boolean that will determine whether the item will be allowed to proceed on the observable. But the `IsPrimeAsync` method returns a `Task<bool>` so you naïvely try to await it, which causes your lambda expression return type to again be `Task<bool>`. Unfortunately, `Where` (and most other operators) doesn't support tasks, and that's why your code doesn't compile. But don't lose hope; together we can make it work!

> **NOTE** In the observer's `OnNext` method, nothing prevents you from running code with `async-await` (as long as the method is marked with `async`). But remember that because the method returns void, it will return to the caller the moment the first `await` is reached, so that the next `OnNext` might be called while still processing the previous one. Many times, this process turns out to be confusing and hard to track.

As you remember, `Task<T>` can be converted to `IObservable<T>`, so `Task<bool>` can become an `IObservable<bool>` on which the `Where` operator can work without a problem.

Here's how the magic happens:

1 Run the `IsPrimeAsync` method for each number.
2 Convert the return task into an observable.
3 Merge all the observables that were created, while still keeping the source (the number being checked) of each one.
4 Allow only the observables that will emit the value `true`—meaning the number is prime—to proceed to the resulted observable.

Sounds complex, but it's simple thanks to the `SelectMany` operator. In the previous example, the `SelectMany` operator was used to flatten a collection by passing a `selector` function that determined the enumerable to flatten. Here's another overload of `SelectMany` (illustrated in figure 5.7 and the following bit of code) that will help here but is a little frightening at first look. Don't worry about it; after the next code example, it will become clear, and you can return here and read the description again.

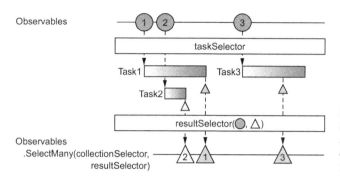

Figure 5.7   The SelectMany operator allows you to generate an asynchronous task from each element and then emit the task results on the resulted observable.

The overload of SelectMany does the same as before, but instead of *selecting* a collection from the item of the observable, it projects it to a task, invokes the result selector with the source element and the task result, and merges the results into one observable sequence:

```
IObservable<TResult> SelectMany<TSource, TTaskResult, TResult>(
    this IObservable<TSource> source,
    Func<TSource, Task<TTaskResult>> taskSelector,
    Func<TSource, TTaskResult, TResult> resultSelector)
```

The observable you work on ←

Receives the item from the observable and selects the task

Creates the end result to be emitted from the item and the result of the task that the taskSelector created for that item

Using this overload, the previous example can be written like so:

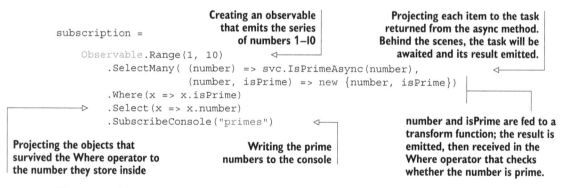

```
subscription =
    Observable.Range(1, 10)
        .SelectMany( (number) => svc.IsPrimeAsync(number),
                     (number, isPrime) => new {number, isPrime})
        .Where(x => x.isPrime)
        .Select(x => x.number)
        .SubscribeConsole("primes")
```

Creating an observable that emits the series of numbers 1–10

Projecting each item to the task returned from the async method. Behind the scenes, the task will be awaited and its result emitted.

Projecting the objects that survived the Where operator to the number they store inside

Writing the prime numbers to the console

number and isPrime are fed to a transform function; the result is emitted, then received in the Where operator that checks whether the number is prime.

These are the printed results when I run it on my machine:

```
primes - OnNext(1)
primes - OnNext(2)
primes - OnNext(3)
primes - OnNext(5)
primes - OnNext(7)
primes - OnCompleted()
```

It takes time to digest, but what you see has a natural beauty and elegance. Let's review it step by step.

In the example, you create a simple observable that emits the sequence 1 to 10. Each item is then received by the `SelectMany` operator that calls the asynchronous method `IsPrimeAsync`. This method returns a task, which isn't interesting to the rest of your query; but what you want is the future result the task will give you, and so `SelectMany` awaits this result for you behind the scenes. When the result is ready, the transformed function you provided to the `SelectMany` operator is called. The transform method receives the number on which you ran `IsPrimeAsync` together with the result of the task, and in this case, you combine them into an object. This combined object is what's emitted on the resulted observable and then received in the `Where` and `Select` operators.

This entire process is depicted in figure 5.8. (I've shortened variable names to reduce noise.)

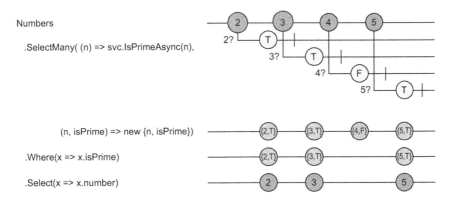

Figure 5.8   A marble diagram that shows the use of the `SelectMany` operator with asynchronous code. Each number is checked (asynchronously) to see whether it's prime. When the result is ready, the observable pipeline continues.

One thing that's important in figure 5.8 is that I describe each task returned from the `IsPrimeAsync` method as an observable, which in the case of tasks have only one item, and then it emits no more.

I should be honest with you: not everybody agrees that this chain of methods is as beautiful as I think it is (shocking, isn't it?). Luckily, the same query can be written in the query expression, which makes it more readable; judge for yourself:

```
IObservable<int> primes =
    from number in Observable.Range(1, 10)
    from isPrime in svc.IsPrimeAsync(number)
    where isPrime
    select number;

primes.SubscribeConsole("primes");
```

This query is the same as the one you used before, and translates to the same method chains. It's important to understand the internal mechanics of things so you can control them better, so I started with the more complex approach. Also, not everything can be converted to the query syntax, so knowing how to use the `SelectMany` operator will be a powerful tool in your belt.

Now that we have that covered, see if you can predict what will be printed if the time that it takes for the `IsPrimeAsync` method to complete is different for different numbers. For example, if the time it takes for 3 is longer than it takes for 4. Can you predict the order?

5.1.6   *Controlling the results order*

`SelectMany` projects the items to tasks in the same order that they're emitted. But the order of the items in the resulting observable (the results of the tasks) that `SelectMany` creates depends on the order that the tasks complete—which can be different from the original order.

For example, run the previous prime check example when the time to check the number 4 is a few seconds more than all the other numbers:

```
var svc = new VariableTimePrimeCheckService(numberToDelay: 3);
IObservable<int> primes =
    from number in Observable.Range(1, 10)
    from isPrime in svc.IsPrimeAsync(number)
    where isPrime
    select number;
```

Configuring the service to delay the response of the check on the number 3

Same query: produces only the prime numbers in sequence 1–10

```
primes.SubscribeConsole("primes - unordered");
```

This yields the following output:

```
primes - unordered - OnNext(1)
primes - unordered - OnNext(2)
primes - unordered - OnNext(7)
primes - unordered - OnNext(5)
primes - unordered - OnNext(3)
primes - unordered - OnCompleted()
```

Notice that the number 3 is emitted last in our resulting observable.

You don't always need or want the order of the resulted observable to be the same as the source observable, but when you do, `SelectMany` won't help. Instead, you can take advantage of the `Concat` operator you used earlier in a different context.

The `Concat` operator provides an overload that works on an observable sequence of tasks, and emits the result of each task in the order the task was positioned in the sequence. The result of the first task is emitted first, and then of the second task, and so forth, even if the result of the first task is completed long after the second task. This is exactly what you need! Here's the overload's signature you'll be using:

```
static IObservable<TSource> Concat<TSource>(
        this IObservable<Task<TSource>> sources)
```

NOTE   The same behavior exists for collections of tasks, or observable of observables (where the values from the first observable are emitted before the values from the second observable). The `Concat` operator provides overloads for each case.

What's left is to create the observable of tasks that you could feed onto the `source` parameter of the `Concat` operator. Doing so is easy with the help of the `Select` operator that enables you to project an item into a different form, and you can use it to return the task that the `IsPrimeAsync(number)` returns:

```
IObservable<Task<bool>> observable =
    Observable.Range(1, 10)
        .Select(number => svc.IsPrimeAsync(number));
```

But there's a problem. Note that the observable type is `IObservable<Task<bool>>`, which means you lost the original item from which the task was created.

To include the original item, you wrap the task and the original item together in a new task that yields them both. The final solution looks like this:

```
IObservable<int> primes =
    Observable.Range(1, 10)
        .Select(async (number) => new { number, IsPrime = await
        ➥ svc.IsPrimeAsync(number) })
        .Concat()
        .Where(x => x.IsPrime)
        .Select(x => x.number);
```

Keeps the order of the emitted aligned with the order of the source items

Using async-await in your lambda expression causes the compiler to implicitly deduce the return type of the selector function to be a task of the anonymous type defined inside.

Running the example gives this output, which keeps the numbers ordered:

```
primes - OnNext(1)
primes - OnNext(2)
primes - OnNext(3)
primes - OnNext(5)
primes - OnNext(7)
primes - OnCompleted()
```

The lambda expression you provided as the selector function is using the `async-await` pattern. Inside it, you're creating an anonymous type that has two properties: the original number and the result (due to the `await`) of the `IsPrime` asynchronous check. And so the return type of your lambda expression is a task of the anonymous type created inside.

The `Concat` operator is now working on an observable that pushes tasks of this new anonymous type—named `'a` in Visual Studio IntelliSense, as you can see in figure 5.9.

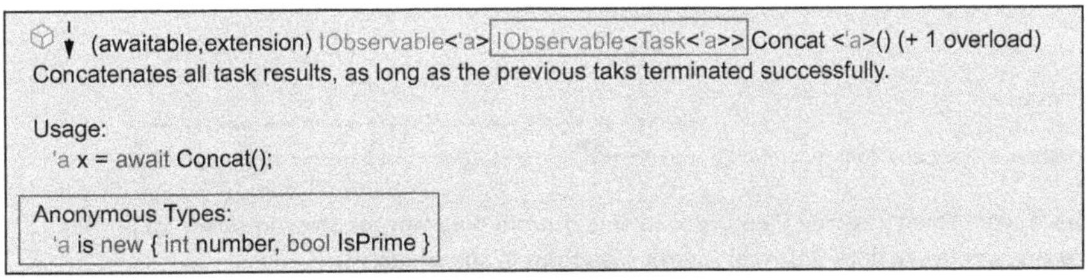

Figure 5.9   Visual Studio IntelliSense names the anonymous type in the selector function `'a`.

You can see that the `Concat` operator is working on `IObservable<Task<'a>>` but produces an observable of type `IObservable<'a>`. It seems you've solved the problem, but what if a task never completes? What will happen to your system?

Internally, the `Concat` operator must keep in memory the results of all the tasks that have completed, but their time hasn't arrived yet. For example, if the source observable emits five tasks, and the last four complete successfully, but the first task takes an hour to complete, the four results will be kept in memory until the first task completes.

If one of the tasks never completes (if it's stuck in a loop or a deadlock), `Concat` might cause memory pressure. As a general approach, it's better to not rely on order when it comes to asynchronous execution.

You now have the power to add asynchronous code execution as part of your observable pipeline. When order isn't mandatory, use `SelectMany`. When the order is a must, use `Concat`. `SelectMany` and `Concat` are explored further in chapter 8.

5.2 Creating observables of periodic behavior

One common request I see from developers who start to use Rx is to create observables that process in a periodic way (for example, every 2 seconds) and emit their results. In the imperative programing style, this is done with a timer. An example of such behavior might be checking for updates against a web service and emitting the updated items.

Rx provides two operators that enable creating observables of periodic behavior or scheduled emission that we'll cover in this part of the chapter.

5.2.1 Emitting values in time intervals

The `Interval` operator creates an observable that produces a value periodically every time interval:

> Determines the time interval to produce the first and subsequent elements.

```
static IObservable<long> Interval(TimeSpan period)
```

The `Interval` operator creates an observable of type `IObservable<long>` that periodically emits the next long value (starting with 0). The time between two subsequent notifications is determined by the `period` parameter. Figure 5.10 is a marble diagram that shows the operator effects with a period of 1 second.

With a period of 1 second, the first notification is emitted after 1 second, and the second notification occurs 1 second later, and so on.

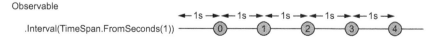

Figure 5.10   The `Interval` operator in this marble diagram creates an observable that emits a value every time interval (every 1 second in the diagram).

Here's an example that shows how to use the `Interval` operator to create a WPF window that polls a web service for updates every minute, and displays them in a list box:

```
public partial class MessagesWindow : Window
{
    private IDisposable _subscription;

    public MessagesWindow()
    {
        InitializeComponent();

        var updatesWebService = new UpdatesWebService();
        _subscription = Observable
            .Interval(TimeSpan.FromMinutes(1))
            .SelectMany(_ => updatesWebService.GetUpdatesAsync())
            .SelectMany(updates => updates)
            .ObserveOnDispatcher()
            .Subscribe(/*an observer the update the ListBox*/);
    }
}
```

Annotations:
- **Emitting a notification every minute** → `.Interval(TimeSpan.FromMinutes(1))`
- **Marshalling the rest of the processing to the UI thread** → `.ObserveOnDispatcher()`
- **Calling the web service for updates, the call returns a task<IEnumerable<string>> that the SelectMany awaits on your behalf** → `.SelectMany(_ => updatesWebService.GetUpdatesAsync())`
- **Flattening the updates that were received, so you'll process each update separately** → `.SelectMany(updates => updates)`

Keeping the periodic call to the web service in the observable pipeline allows you to create elegant solutions, as you can see in the previous example. I owe you an explanation on the `ObserveOnDispatcher` operator. Until now, I deliberately ignored the elephant in the room: where are the `Interval`s coming from, on which threads? In chapter 10, you'll learn the concurrency model that Rx uses and see the connection to the `Interval` operator as well as other time-based operators. For now, you should know that by default, the `Interval` operator runs on a different thread of the observer subscription. In WPF and other GUI frameworks, code that mutates the UI controls can run in only the UI thread. The `ObserveOnDispatcher` operator guarantees that the observer code will run on the UI thread (by using the WPF Dispatcher).

> **NOTE** In the example, it's possible that a call to the web service will happen even if the previous one hasn't yet returned. The `Interval` operator has no knowledge about the asynchronous action you perform at each cycle.

It's important to note that the `Interval` operator supports the same period between all emissions, including the first one. The `Timer` operator that you'll see next gives more flexibility.

5.2.2 Creating an observable timer

At times you may want to create an observable that periodically emits a value, but to differentiate the time that the first emission is made, perhaps you'd want it to be immediate or delayed to a future schedule. Using the `Timer` operator, you can achieve such flexibility. Here's one of the overloads that's commonly used:

```
static IObservable<long> Timer(TimeSpan dueTime, TimeSpan period)
```

Observable

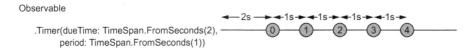

.Timer(dueTime: TimeSpan.FromSeconds(2),
       period: TimeSpan.FromSeconds(1))

Figure 5.11 The `Timer` **operator marble diagram creates an observable sequence that periodically produces a value (1 second in the diagram) after the specified initial relative due time has elapsed (2 seconds in the diagram).**

Calling this overload creates an observable that periodically produces a value after the specified initial relative due time has elapsed from the moment an observer subscribes. Figure 5.11 shows an example of creating an observable that produces a value every second, but starting 2 seconds after subscription. You can say that the `Interval` operator that you saw earlier is a special case of the `Timer` operator, in which the `dueTime` and `period` are the same.

The timer also includes overloads to schedule the beginning of the periodicity in both *relative* and *absolute* times. You'll explore those definitions when you look at another special case, scheduling the emission of a single value.

5.2.3   *Scheduling an emission with a timer*

The `Timer` operator can also be used to schedule the production of a value (0 of type `long`) to a future time:

```
static IObservable<long> Timer(TimeSpan dueTime)
static IObservable<long> Timer(DateTimeOffset dueTime)
```

> **Returns an observable that produces a single value at the specified dueTime**

> **Returns an observable that produces a single value after the relative dueTime has passed**

As you can see, `Timer` has two overloads that receive the due time to emit the single value. The difference between the two overloads is in the way you represent the time to emit the value:

- *Relative time*—Defined as `TimeSpan`, which reflects a time interval from the moment of the observer subscription. For example, in 5 seconds

  ```
  Observable.Timer(TimeSpan.FromSeconds(5))
  ```

- *Absolute time*—Defined as `DateTimeOffset`, which reflects a particular date and time, regardless of the time of the observer subscription. For example, July 4 or today at midnight

  ```
  Observable.Timer(DateTimeOffset.Parse("00:00:00"))
  ```

Creating an observable that emits a value in a preconfigured time can be useful when combining with other observables. Here's an example that uses the `Switch` combinator (combining operator) to change from one observable to the other after 5 seconds:

```
IObservable<string> firstObservable =
    Observable
        .Interval(TimeSpan.FromSeconds(1))
        .Select(x => "value" + x);
IObservable<string> secondObservable =
    Observable
        .Interval(TimeSpan.FromSeconds(2))
        .Select(x => "second" + x)
        .Take(5);

IObservable<IObservable<string>> immediateObservable =
    Observable.Return(firstObservable);

//Scheduling the second observable emission
IObservable<IObservable<string>> scheduledObservable =
    Observable
        .Timer(TimeSpan.FromSeconds(5))
        .Select(x => secondObservable);

immediateObservable
    .Merge(scheduledObservable)
    .Switch()
    .Timestamp()
    .SubscribeConsole("timer switch");
```

Creates an observable that emits every second

Creates an observable that emits every 2 seconds, but only 5 notifications

Creates an observable that emits the first observable

Creates an observable that emits the second observable after 5 seconds

Merges the two observables that emit observables

Switches from the first emitted observable to the second

Running this example yields this output on my machine:

```
timer switch - OnNext(first0@10/08/2015 20:30:52 +00:00)
timer switch - OnNext(first1@10/08/2015 20:30:53 +00:00)
timer switch - OnNext(first2@10/08/2015 20:30:54 +00:00)
timer switch - OnNext(first3@10/08/2015 20:30:55 +00:00)
timer switch - OnNext(first4@10/08/2015 20:30:56 +00:00)
timer switch - OnNext(second0@10/08/2015 20:30:58 +00:00)
timer switch - OnNext(second1@10/08/2015 20:31:00 +00:00)
timer switch - OnNext(second2@10/08/2015 20:31:02 +00:00)
timer switch - OnNext(second3@10/08/2015 20:31:04 +00:00)
timer switch - OnNext(second4@10/08/2015 20:31:06 +00:00)
timer switch - OnCompleted()
```

You can see that after 5 seconds, the second observable begins emitting its values (every 2 seconds), and so the control switches from the first observable to the second. Switch is an interesting combinator that's covered further in chapter 8.

You have more to learn about asynchronous code execution and handling inside your Rx code: How can you transition to another thread in the middle of the pipeline and go back to the original context later (as in the case of a UI), and how can those transitions affect the building of the pipeline and the results you may see? These topics are discussed in upcoming chapters, but for now you have solid ground to start creating your observables and using asynchronicity in your application. Let's summarize what you've learned.

5.3   *Summary*

You've completed this two-part series of the ways to create observables, which makes you observables qualified. This chapter covered ways to create observables through asynchronous code execution.

Here's a summary of what you learned:

- Rx observables provide an abstraction over the source that emits the notification in a way that makes it thread transparent so that the observers don't need to know or care about the origin of the notification.
- Rx observables can be created from code via asynchronous operations by using the overloads of the `Observable.Create` or `Observable.Defer` operators. Those overloads accept an asynchronous subscribe function that can even be written using `async-await`.
- Rx can take care of connecting tasks cancellation and subscription disposal by providing you with a `CancellationToken` that Rx attaches to the disposable subscription object that's returned after an observer subscribes.
- You can easily convert asynchronous types such as tasks into observables by using the extension method `ToObservable`.
- To run asynchronous code as part of the operators in your pipeline, you can use the `SelectMany` operator that can await the asynchronous code (which can be represented as `Task` or another `IObservable`) and then continue the pipeline upon completion or emission.
- Use the `Concat` operator if you want the order of processing the results of the asynchronous code that was started from different emissions to be the same as the order of the emissions.
- Creating observables that emit notification in a periodic way is also possible in Rx by using the `Interval` operator, or the `Timer` operator if you need further control of the due time of the emission.

Because there's no real use for observables without the observers that subscribe to them, the next chapter concentrates on the observer's side and the various ways to create them and control their lifetimes.

Controlling the observer-observable relationship

6

This chapter covers

- Creating observers without a fuss
- Controlling the length of the observer/observable relationship
- Adding and controlling side effects in the pipeline

Imagine you're a singer with the most beautiful voice, the greatest lyrics, and the best performance moves. It doesn't pay to be such a singer if you have no listeners. The same goes for observables; they sit there, doing nothing and wasting resources, if there's no observer to subscribe to and receive their notifications. It's also interesting to think about when the relationship between the singer and the listener begins and ends, especially if the music is coming from an album, and the listener can skip tracks or stop playing.

This chapter covers the methods you can use to create observers, and the importance of each action that observers need to implement. The subscription of the observer to the observable is also something you'll need to maintain, but you can control when it begins and how long it lasts by the number of notifications or a timespan, a combination of the two, or with advanced logic that you define. All of these options are provided by a set of operators that you'll learn about throughout this chapter. At the end of the chapter, you'll combine them to create a fully reactive drawing application.

6.1 Creating observers

The *observer* is the consumer of the observable notifications. There can be many observers to a single observable, and there can be many observables that an observer observes, as shown in figure 6.1.

Figure 6.1   An observable can have multiple observers, and an observer can observe multiple observables.

Our goal with Rx is to simplify your event-processing code, so in this part I'll show you how to create observers so you can pick the one that's most suitable for your needs. This is a good place to review the role the observer plays in the communication protocol between the observable and observer.

6.1.1 The observable-observer communication

The protocol between the observable and the observer is shown in figure 6.2.

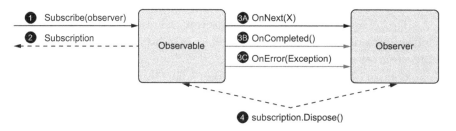

Figure 6.2   The communication protocol between the observable and the observer

This is how the communication protocol you see in figure 6.2 works:

1 The communication between the observable and the observer begins by sub-scribing the observer to the observable.

2 The observable returns a subscription object that implements the `IDisposable` interface.

3 Once the observer is subscribed, the observable can emit notifications of different kinds to it. For example:

– The observable can emit any number of notifications by calling the observer's `OnNext` method and passing the payload as an argument.

– When the observable reaches completion, meaning no more notifications will be emitted, it signals that to the observer by calling the `OnCompleted` method.

– If an error occurs in the observable, which also means that no more notifications will be emitted, the observer is notified with a call to the `OnError` method that takes the exception object as an argument.

– The `OnCompleted` and `OnError` methods are mutually exclusive, so the Rx protocol mandates that only one of them (or none) can be called on the observer.

4 Anytime after the observer is subscribed, the subscription can be disposed of. The observable must ensure that after the subscription is disposed of, no more notifications of any kind will be emitted to the observer.

The next section covers ways to control the observer lifetime and the length of the subscription.

6.1.2 *Creating observers without leaving the pipeline*

By far, the most desirable way to create an observer is doing it without leaving your pipeline so that everything is centralized and, thus, easier to read and maintain. Luckily, it's also the easiest and most straightforward way of creating an observer, as shown in figure 6.3. All it takes is using one of the overloads of the `Subscribe` extension method that resides under the static `ObservableExtensions` class, which is under the `System` namespace.

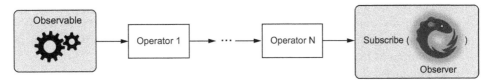

Figure 6.3 Creating the observer and subscribing it as part of the pipeline with the `Subscribe` operator

Here's an example that creates and subscribes an observer that prints to the screen (much like the `ConsoleObserver` created in chapter 4). In this case, you pass all the observer's functions as arguments to the `Subscribe` operator:

```
Observable.Range(1, 5)        Creates an observable that
    .Subscribe(               emits the numbers 1 to 5      Provides the implementation
                                                            for the OnNext method of the
        x => Console.WriteLine("OnNext({0})", x),           observer that will be created
        ex => Console.WriteLine("OnError: {0}", ex.Message),
        () => Console.WriteLine("OnCompleted")
    );                        Provides the implementation for      Provides the
                              the OnCompleted method of the        implementation for the
                              observer that will be created        OnError method of the
                                                                   observer that will be created
```

In the example, I provide lambda expressions as arguments to the `Subscribe` method. This results in an observer that prints to the screen every notification it receives.

The output for this example is

```
OnNext(1)
OnNext(2)
OnNext(3)
OnNext(4)
OnNext(5)
OnCompleted
```

The overloads of the `Subscribe` method let you specify different functions as arguments and create an observer that uses those functions as its implementation. Here's a list of most of the overloads:

```
IDisposable Subscribe<T>(this IObservable<T> source,
    Action<T> onNext)
IDisposable Subscribe<T>(this IObservable<T> source,
    Action<T> onNext,
    Action<Exception> onError)
IDisposable Subscribe<T>(this IObservable<T> source,
    Action<T> onNext,
    Action onCompleted)
IDisposable Subscribe<T>(this IObservable<T> source,
    Action<T> onNext,
    Action<Exception> onError,
    Action onCompleted)
```

As you can see from the overloads shown, you can specify the implementation of each observer method (`OnNext`, `OnCompleted`, and `OnError`), and you can do it only for those methods you care about (for example, creating an observer by specifying only what happens in its `OnNext` method).

The nicest thing about creating an observer with the `Subscribe` method is that it allows you to keep everything together—the observable pipeline and the observer that subscribes to it.

Using the `Subscribe` overloads is easy and powerful. Although it's tempting to use the simplest form of the `Subscribe` method (the one that requires only an `onNext` argument), it's also a place that hides many bugs.

Consider the next example, where I create a pipeline to add a small math calculation on each number and deliberately create a condition to throw an exception after the two first notifications:

```
Observable.Range(1, 5)                                    Creates an observable that
    .Select(x=> x/(x-3) )                                 emits the numbers 1 to 5
    .Subscribe(x => Console.WriteLine("{0}",x));          When number 3 is reached, a
                                                          DivideByZeroException is thrown.
```

In this case when the exception is thrown, just as with regular exceptions, our application will crash. An application that crashes is undesirable. Worse than that are those instances where you don't know how and why (let alone where) the application crashed. To avoid the worst-case scenario, you should add an implementation to the created observer `OnError` method. For example:

```
Observable.Range(1, 5)
    .Select(x => x/(x - 3))                               Regular notifications
    .Subscribe(x => Console.WriteLine("{0}", x),          will be treated here.
        ex =>{/* do something with the exception */});    Error notifications will be
                                                          processed here or swallowed.
```

Now, the raised exception won't crash the application; instead, the error-handling code will run, and the observer will be detached from the observable.

Leaving the error-handling code empty is possible, of course, just like creating an empty `catch` block, which is known as *exception swallowing* or *error hiding*,[1] but this is considered bad practice because doing so will hinder your ability to investigate any bugs in your application, especially when asynchroncity is involved.

6.1.3 *Not passing OnError and asynchronous observables*

In the previous chapter, you saw ways to create observables that perform asynchronous behaviors. Let's explore what happens if you add asynchronicity to our example. What do you think will happen if you write this:

```
                                                          Perform the calculation
                                                          asynchronously by creating
                                                          another task. When x = 3, an
Observable.Range(1, 5)                                    exception will be thrown.
    .Select(x => Task.Run(() => x / (x - 3)))
    .Concat()
    .Subscribe(x => Console.WriteLine("{0}", x));         Concatenate the task (as
                                                          observables) to observe the
Console.WriteLine("Press any key to continue...");        results in the same order as
Console.ReadKey();                                        that of task creation.
```

---

[1] For more about exception swallowing or error hiding, see https://en.wikipedia.org/wiki/Error_hiding.

Running the example provides this output:

```
0
-2
Press any key to continue . . .
```

You know there's an exception somewhere, but you don't see it, and you're not even aware that it happened. More puzzling is that in production, you'll suddenly stop seeing the output (or other types of results) from your observable pipeline, and this isn't a good thing.

When you create tasks that fail (unintentionally, of course) and don't handle the exceptions within the task continuation or inside a catch block that wraps the `await`, your application continues to work although the task was kicked out of your system.

> **TIP** To capture and handle all the unhandled exceptions thrown from tasks, you can use the `TaskScheduler.UnobservedTaskException` event that will be triggered when a task is disposed of because its exception wasn't observed. You can also change the default behavior so that the process will terminate by setting a configuration in your app.config\web.config file.[2]

I recommend that you always include some implementation of the `OnError` method; at the very least, log it so you can investigate it later. Chapter 11 provides more details about error handling and recovery.

6.1.4 *Replacing the subscription disposal with cancellation*

Another interesting variation of the `Subscribe` method is one that accepts a `CancellationToken` as a parameter and lets you replace the disposable subscription with a cancellation mechanism. For example:

```
void Subscribe<T>(
    this IObservable<T> source,
    /* onNext,OnCompleted,OnError permutations */,
    CancellationToken token)
```

As with the Subscribe overload, you can pass an implementation of the OnNext, OnCompleted, and OnError methods.

These variations of `Subscribe` return `void` instead of `IDisposable`, so the ability to unsubscribe the observer needs to be provided in some other way. This is the job of `CancellationToken`. As figure 6.4 shows, Rx monitors `CancellationToken` for cancellation and, when this happens, it disposes of the inner subscription and disconnects the observer from the observable.

Figure 6.4   Rx monitors the `CancellationToken` for cancellation. When this happens, it will dispose of the inner subscription.

---

[2] More details on unhandled exceptions can be found on MSDN: http://mng.bz/57Fv.

The next example uses the cancellation token to unsubscribe the observer 5 seconds after it subscribes to the observable:

Registers an operation to invoke when there's a cancellation

```
var cts = new CancellationTokenSource();
cts.Token.Register(() => Console.WriteLine("Subscription canceled"));
```

```
Observable.Interval(TimeSpan.FromSeconds(1))
    .Subscribe(x => Console.WriteLine(x), cts.Token);
```

Passes the cancellation token while subscribing

Creates an observable that emits a value every 1 second

```
cts.CancelAfter(TimeSpan.FromSeconds(5));
```

Waits 5 seconds before canceling, which results in unsubscribing the observer

Passing a cancellation token to the Subscribe method can be useful when you need to synchronize the cancellation of other parts of your system (such as other tasks).

6.1.5 Creating an observer instance

In the previous sections, the methods used in the overloads of the Subscribe method create the observer instance behind the scenes, so you have no real interaction with it.

Sometimes, you may want to access the observer instance. Let's say you need to pass it to a method as an argument, or you need to create an observer inside a method and return it. In Microsoft StreamInsight (a high throughput, event-processing tool), you can create observables and deploy them to a remote server, and then you can create observers and pass them to a method that will attach them to the remote observables.

To create an implementation of the IObserver interface, you could, of course, create a new class and implement each of its methods, but that's an error-prone and daunting task (much like creating an observable from scratch, as discussed in chapter 4).

Instead of creating new classes to implement new observers, I recommend an easier way using the Observer.Create method that resides in the System.Reactive namespace. This will save you time and errors:

```
IObserver<T> Create<T>(
    Action<T> onNext,
    Action<Exception> onError,
    Action onCompleted)
```

Like the Observable.Subscribe overloads, you can pass an implementation of the OnNext, OnError, and OnCompleted methods (or any subset of those) to Observer.Create, and it returns an object that implements the IObserver<T> interface, which calls the functions you provided.

Here's a small example that creates an observer that prints only the notifications received in its OnNext method and then subscribes it to two observables:

```
var observer = Observer.Create<string>(x => Console.WriteLine(x));

Observable.Interval(TimeSpan.FromSeconds(1))
    .Select(x=>"X"+x)
    .Subscribe(observer);
```

```
Observable.Interval(TimeSpan.FromSeconds(2))
    .Select(x => "YY" + x)
    .Subscribe(observer);
```

Running this example for 5 seconds shows this output:

```
X0
YY0
X1
X2
YY1
X3
```

In the example, you create two observables—one that emits a value every 1 second (prefixed with X) and another that emits a value every 2 seconds (prefixed with YY). You then use the same observer to subscribe to both observables. Figure 6.5 shows the marble diagram of this program.

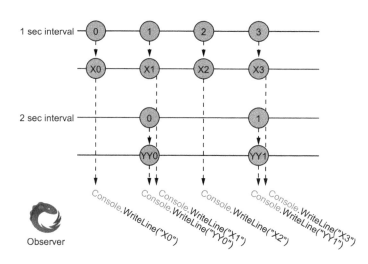

Figure 6.5 Subscribing the same observer to multiple observables lets you share and reuse the subscriber's functionality.

In most cases, manually creating an instance of the observer is unnecessary, but when it's needed, use `Observer.Create`. This will ensure that the observer behaves correctly with regard to the observable-observer protocol.

After an observer is created and subscribed, you might want to end the relationship at some point. In addition, you might want to gain better control of when the relationship starts. Rx gives you tools to control the lifetime of your observer.

6.2   *Controlling the observable-observer relationship lifetime*

Subscribing an observer to an observable is easy; it's as simple as calling the `Subscribe` method. Unsubscribing is also easy. You need only to dispose of the subscription. You

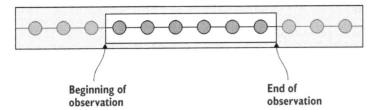

Beginning of
observation

End of
observation

Figure 6.6 Given an observable, the beginning of the emissions observed
by the observers as well as the end of the emissions are configurable and
create an observation box.

can, however, tweak the observable pipeline so that, even though the observer
subscribes, notifications are observed at only a specific time (or condition) and stop
being observed after a specific time (or condition), as shown in figure 6.6.

Just like the singer and its audience, each listener in the audience is an observer
(or subscriber) that can arrive at the show at any time, but is allowed to enter the hall
only when the organizers decide. Moreover, the listener can leave the show whenever
they decide to do so (disposing of the subscription). The singer, on the other hand,
will start the show when they decide to do so and will stop the show as determined by
some predefined condition, such as the number of songs, a specific duration, or when
another singer is ready to perform onstage (another observable).

The same applies to observables. In some scenarios, you might want to configure
the notifications to be observed after a certain time or to complete based on a particular condition. Instead of writing the code to handle those repeatable patterns yourself,
Rx provides operators to make your job super easy.

6.2.1 Delaying subscription

Calling the `Subscribe` method will immediately make the observable aware of the
observer and, from that point, emit notifications to it. For some scenarios, it may be
necessary to delay the time the subscription is made. For example, if you're planning
a trip, you would want to observe notifications about the weather at your destination
closer to the time of your flight and not necessarily when you booked the tickets.

The `DelaySubscription` operator receives a `TimeSpan` or `DateTimeOffset`
that marks the point to make the subscription. This is how to delay the subscription 5
seconds:

```
Console.WriteLine("Creating subscription at {0}", DateTime.Now);
Observable.Range(1, 5)                                          ⟵ Creates an observable
    .Timestamp()                                                  that emits 5 values
    .DelaySubscription(TimeSpan.FromSeconds(5))    ⟵
    .SubscribeConsole();                           ⟵
                                                          Delays the subscription
                                                          by 5 seconds
```

Adds a
timestamp to
every value

Subscribes an observer that writes
every notification to the console

Here's the output:

```
Creating subscription at 06/09/2015 00:00:00
 - OnNext(1@05/09/2015 00:00:05 +00:00)
 - OnNext(2@05/09/2015 00:00:05 +00:00)
 - OnNext(3@05/09/2015 00:00:05 +00:00)
 - OnNext(4@05/09/2015 00:00:05 +00:00)
 - OnNext(5@05/09/2015 00:00:05 +00:00)
 - OnCompleted()
```

You can see that although you created the subscription at 00:00:00, the notification started at 00:00:05, meaning the subscription happened only at that time. Because the observable is cold (cold observables are described in the next chapter), a sequence of notifications will be generated the moment the observer subscribes. The observer will receive five notifications, but only from the moment it subscribes. Our observer won't miss any emission.

These are the overloads for the `DelaySubscription` operator—one for relative time and one for absolute time:

```
IObservable<TSource> DelaySubscription<TSource>(
    this IObservable<TSource> source,          Delay by a
    TimeSpan dueTime)                          relative TimeSpan
IObservable<TSource> DelaySubscription<TSource>(
    this IObservable<TSource> source,          Delay to an absolute
    DateTimeOffset dueTime)                    DateTimeOffset
```

It's important to note that the relative `TimeSpan` is started only from the point the subscription is requested and not from the moment `DelaySubscription` is added to the pipeline as the next example shows:

```
Console.WriteLine("Creating the observable pipeline at {0}", DateTime.Now);
var observable =
    Observable.Range(1, 5)              Creates an observable that emits
        .Timestamp()                    five notifications with a timestamp
        .DelaySubscription(TimeSpan.FromSeconds(5));    Delays each subscription
Thread.Sleep(TimeSpan.FromSeconds(2));                  to this observable by
                                                        5 seconds
Console.WriteLine("Creating subscription at {0}", DateTime.Now);
observable.SubscribeConsole();                   Subscribes an
                                                 observer that writes
                                                 to the console
```

**Creates a short pause between creating the observable
pipeline and the point of subscribing the observer**

Now, when you run this example, you get these results:

```
Creating the observable pipeline at 06/09/2015 00:00:10
Creating subscription at 06/09/2015 00:00:12
 - OnNext(1@05/09/2015 00:00:17 +00:00)
 - OnNext(2@05/09/2015 00:00:17 +00:00)
 - OnNext(3@05/09/2015 00:00:17 +00:00)
 - OnNext(4@05/09/2015 00:00:17 +00:00)
```

```
 - OnNext(5@05/09/2015 00:00:17 +00:00)
 - OnCompleted()
Done
```

You can see from the results that the 5-second delay took place after the call to the `Subscribe` method and not when the `DelaySubscription` operator was added. Another important aspect of the observer lifetime is that you can control when it stops receiving the notifications, as you'll see next.

6.2.2 Stop emitting notifications at a scheduled time

If you need the observable to complete and to stop emitting notifications at an absolute time (for example, at midnight January 1, 2020), there's no reason to subscribe to its updates. Rather than creating a `Timer` and disposing of the subscription, there's an easier way. You can use the `TakeUntil` operator.

The `TakeUntil` operator receives a `DateTimeOffset`, which is an absolute date and time in a specific time zone. When that time arrives, the observable will notify its observers that it has completed. There's no relative time overload for `TakeUntil`, but here's a simple example that uses the absolute time version to schedule the unsubscribe in a relative time of 5 seconds:

```
Observable.Timer(DateTimeOffset.Now,TimeSpan.FromSeconds(1))
    .Select(t => DateTimeOffset.Now)
    .TakeUntil(DateTimeOffset.Now.AddSeconds(5))
    .SubscribeConsole("TakeUntil(time)");
```

Takes the current time in every iteration →

Produces a value every second, but starts immediately

Schedules the unsubscribe to 5 seconds from now

This generates the following output:

```
TakeUntil(time) - OnNext(07/09/2015 10:00:10 +03:00)
TakeUntil(time) - OnNext(07/09/2015 10:00:11 +03:00)
TakeUntil(time) - OnNext(07/09/2015 10:00:12 +03:00)
TakeUntil(time) - OnNext(07/09/2015 10:00:13 +03:00)
TakeUntil(time) - OnNext(07/09/2015 10:00:14 +03:00)
TakeUntil(time) - OnCompleted()
```

You can see from the output that the first notification was emitted at *10:00:10* and because you scheduled the observable to stop receiving notification after 5 seconds, you see that the last notification was received at *10:00:14* (5 seconds later). This is the complete signature for `TakeUntil`:

```
IObservable<TSource> TakeUntil<TSource>(
    this IObservable<TSource> source,
    DateTimeOffset endTime)
```

The time the observer will stop taking notifications from the observable

6.2.3 Discarding items when another observable emits

Rx makes it easy to combine observables to build powerful pipelines. Among those operators that allow combining observables is another variation of `TakeUntil`. This

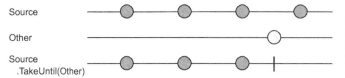

Figure 6.7 The `TakeUntil` operator allows notifications from the observable source to proceed until the other observable emits a notification.

lets you make the observable stop emitting notifications based on external conditions that are represented by another observable emission, as shown in figure 6.7.

If you want your observable to stop emitting notifications after a certain period (instead of an absolute time), you can write code like this:

```
Observable.Timer(DateTimeOffset.Now,TimeSpan.FromSeconds(1))
    .Select(t => DateTimeOffset.Now)
    .TakeUntil(
            Observable.Timer(TimeSpan.FromSeconds(5)))
    .SubscribeConsole("TakeUntil(observable)");
```

Creates an observable that produces a single value after 5 seconds and passes it to the TakeUntil operator. The observer stops receiving notifications after that time.

Running this code produces

```
TakeUntil(observable) - OnNext(07/09/2015 18:39:18 +03:00)
TakeUntil(observable) - OnNext(07/09/2015 18:39:19 +03:00)
TakeUntil(observable) - OnNext(07/09/2015 18:39:20 +03:00)
TakeUntil(observable) - OnNext(07/09/2015 18:39:21 +03:00)
TakeUntil(observable) - OnNext(07/09/2015 18:39:22 +03:00)
TakeUntil(observable) - OnCompleted()
```

In this example, you can see that 5 seconds after the first notification (which is produced immediately when the observer subscribes), the `OnCompleted` message is received.

The method signature for the `TakeUntil` operator is shown next. Because the other observable can be of any type, you can use whatever observable you want to control the observations of the emissions.

```
IObservable<TSource> TakeUntil<TSource, TOther>(
    this IObservable<TSource> source,
    IObservable<TOther> other)
```

Terminates propagation of elements of the source sequence

USING OBSERVABLES AS EXTERNAL TRIGGERS FOR TAKEUNTIL

Of course, more-complex scenarios could determine when to stop receiving notifications. For example, you can specify that a chat message observer will stop "listening" to chat messages when a certain control message arrives:

```
IObservable<string> messages = ...
IObservable<string> controlChannel = ...

messages
    .TakeUntil(controlChannel.Where(m => m == "STOP"))
    .Subscribe(
```

Allows the notification to be observed only until the message STOP is received. No more messages will be observed after that.

```
msg => {/* add to message screen */ },
ex => { /* error handling */},
() => { /* completion handling */});
```

Using observables as the parameter for an operator is seen frequently in Rx and is a flexible mechanism of control.[3]

6.2.4 Skipping notifications

At times you might want to subscribe an observer to an observable, but receive notifications only when a particular condition is met. For instance, in a chat message, you could specify to receive messages only after a specific control message is sent. Or, you may want to skip a specified number of search results if you know in advance that the first results are irrelevant. The `Where` operator used in previous chapters (and explained in-depth in chapter 8) can filter notifications, but after you add a condition, you can't disable it when it evaluates to `true` for the first time. Notifications will keep being pushed, even if not all of them survive the filtering.

SKIPPING UNTIL . . .
The `SkipUntil` operator, depicted in figure 6.8, lets you specify when to start receiving notifications from the observable source, giving you finer control over your application's operations.

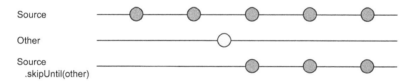

Figure 6.8 The `SkipUntil` operator lets you skip notifications from the observable source until the other observable emits a notification.

Suppose a chat application needs to start showing messages from a certain user only when a specific control message is sent, like the traffic cop who allows traffic to proceed only after receiving an order from the commander. This is how it could be done:

```
IObservable<string> messages = ...
IObservable<string> controlChannel = ...

messages
    .SkipUntil(controlChannel.Where(m => m == "START"))   <—┐
    .Subscribe(
        msg => {/* add to message screen */ },
        ex => { /* error handling */},
        () => { /* completion handling */});
```

> The moment the message START is received, notifications will be observed.

---

[3] This powerful mechanism is a result of the `IObservable<T>` being a monad. Good explanations of monads with .NET types can be found at http://mng.bz/E381 and http://ericlippert.com/2013/02/21/monads-part-one/.

The `SkipUntil` operator has two overloads: one that accepts a `DateTimeOffset` for absolute time scheduling (which is relatively straightforward at this point) and one that accepts an observable that acts as an external trigger. For example:

```
IObservable<TSource> SkipUntil<TSource>(this IObservable<TSource> source,
    DateTimeOffset startTime)                                    ◁─────┐
IObservable<TSource> SkipUntil<TSource, TOther>(            | **Skipping notifications**
    this IObservable<TSource> source,                      | **until an absolute time**
    IObservable<TOther> other)   ◁───┐
                                     | **Skipping notifications until another**
                                     | **observable emits a notification**
```

TIP   You can also skip items based on relative time by using the `Skip` operator.

If you need to specify the number of items to skip, the `Skip` operator is what you're looking for.

SKIPPING A NUMBER OF NOTIFICATIONS

Sometimes you want to skip notifications by a predefined number of items (for example, you want to combine an observable with a shifted version of itself, so you can process two adjacent notifications). Just as in LINQ, you can use the `Skip` operator to do that:

```
IObservable<TSource> Skip<TSource>(this IObservable<TSource> source,
    int count)
```

The following shows an example for bypassing the first two notifications:

```
Observable.Range(1, 5)
    .Skip(2)
    .SubscribeConsole("Skip(2)");
```

This example produces this output:

```
Skip(2) - OnNext(3)
Skip(2) - OnNext(4)
Skip(2) - OnNext(5)
Skip(2) - OnCompleted()
```

TIP   If you want to stop receiving notifications after a predefined number of notifications, just as in LINQ, use the `Take` operator that receives the number of elements you want as an integer.

6.2.5   *Taking or stopping when a condition is met*

If none of the methods for starting or stopping notifications is suitable for your needs, you can use the configurable `TakeWhile` or `SkipWhile` overloads, which receive a predicate that indicates when to start or stop:

```
IObservable<TSource> TakeWhile<TSource>(this IObservable<TSource> source,
    Func<TSource, bool> predicate)                              ◁─────┐
IObservable<TSource> TakeWhile<TSource>                    | **Accepts the notifications as long**
    (this IObservable<TSource> source,                     | **as the predicate on the**
                                                           | **notification data evaluates to true.**
```

```
Func<TSource, int, bool> predicate)
IObservable<TSource> SkipWhile<TSource>(this IObservable<TSource> source,
Func<TSource, bool> predicate)
IObservable<TSource> SkipWhile<TSource>(this IObservable<TSource> source,
Func<TSource, int, bool> predicate)
```

Bypasses notifications as long as the predicate on the notification data evaluates to true.

Bypasses notifications as long as the predicate on the notification data and its index evaluate to true.

Accepts the notifications as long as the predicate on the notification data and its index evaluate to true.

Figures 6.9 and 6.10 show that when the predicate evaluates to `true`, something happens—either you start or you stop accepting notifications.

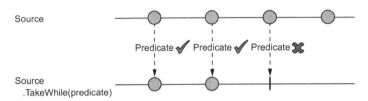

Figure 6.9 The `TakeWhile` operator accepts notifications while a predicate function evaluates to `true` and discards all items after the predicate evaluates to `false`.

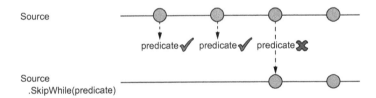

Figure 6.10 The `SkipWhile` operator discards the notifications as long as a predicate evaluates to `true` and accepts all notifications after the predicate evaluates to `false`.

You can use the two operators together to observe only a subrange of values:

```
Observable.Range(1, 10)
    .SkipWhile(x => x < 2)
    .TakeWhile(x => x < 7)
    .SubscribeConsole();
```

This example allows only a range of numbers between 2 (inclusive) and 7 (exclusive) to be observed:

- `OnNext(2)`
- `OnNext(3)`
- `OnNext(4)`
- `OnNext(5)`
- `OnNext(6)`
- `OnCompleted()`

With operators that take or skip notifications, you can easily adjust the *source* observable you subscribe to and control the input your code responds to. How wonderful is that? After the observable you subscribe to completes, no matter whether it's due to the completion of the source or because you discard further notifications, you can choose to start all over again, just as when you hear your favorite album and want to hear it one more time.

6.2.6   *Resubscribing*

After an observable completes, no more notifications are received by the observer. Sometimes, however, you may want to restart and subscribe to the observable. This is usually done when you have a *cold observable* (covered in chapter 7) that starts emitting notifications when the observer subscribes. Resubscribing will make the observable emit the notifications again. This can also occur with *hot observables*. For example, you can subscribe to a mouse movement observable until a click is made and then resubscribe to capture the movements until the next click happens, and so on.

To automatically resubscribe in Rx, you use the `Repeat` operator. For example, you can create an observable that emits the range 1 to 3 twice:

```
Observable.Range(1, 3)
    .Repeat(2)
    .SubscribeConsole("Repeat(2)");
```

This example generates this output

```
Repeat(2)  -  OnNext(1)
Repeat(2)  -  OnNext(2)
Repeat(2)  -  OnNext(3)
Repeat(2)  -  OnNext(1)
Repeat(2)  -  OnNext(2)
Repeat(2)  -  OnNext(3)
Repeat(2)  -  OnCompleted()
```

The `Repeat` operator has two overloads, as shown next. With both overloads, when the source observable completes successfully, an observer will be subscribed to it again:

```
IObservable<TSource> Repeat<TSource>(this IObservable<TSource> source)
IObservable<TSource> Repeat<TSource>(this IObservable<TSource> source,
    int repeatCount)
```

Repeats the sequence a specified number of times   **Repeats the sequence indefinitely**

> **TIP** Another operator that allows "repeating" an observable is `DoWhile`, which repeats the observable if a predicate is `true`.

You need to remember that `Repeat` calls the `Subscribe` method according to the number of times you specified. So if there's a side effect taking place in the observable `Subscribe` method (such as connecting to an external source), it'll repeat.

Side effects are another interesting topic. When thinking about observable pipelines, how can you add an invocation to an operation (such as logging) in the middle of the pipeline? We'll discuss that next.

6.2.7   *Adding side effects in the observable pipeline*

In chapter 3, you learned that a side effect is a change in the environment that influences the way your application behaves. You also discovered that functional programming languages try to avoid creating side effects, but at times they're necessary. And, frankly, many of your applications would be limited if they couldn't change state or call operations to change the environment.

The important part about side effects is that you want them to be visible and discoverable. Until now, the only place that you could change state or call operations was inside the Rx observer methods, which means only at the end of the notification journey when something reacted to it. This is limiting. What if you wanted to do something simple like writing a log between operators?

To allow this kind of operation as part of your observable pipeline, Rx provides the Do operator (illustrated in figure 6.11).

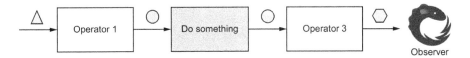

Figure 6.11   Adding a side effect between operators

Here's how to use the Do operator to add logs that'll make it easy to debug your observable pipeline:

```
Observable.Range(1, 5)
    .Do(x=> { Console.WriteLine("{0} was emitted",x); })
    .Where(x=>x%2==0)
    .Do(x => { Console.WriteLine("{0} survived the Where()", x); })
    .Select(x=>x*3)
    .SubscribeConsole("final");
```

This little application creates an observable that emits a range of values (1 to 5), filters the odd numbers, and multiplies the even numbers by 3. Between each operator, you added code to print to the console with the Do operator. This is the output:

```
1 was emitted
2 was emitted
2 survived the Where()
final - OnNext(6)
3 was emitted
```

```
4 was emitted
4 survived the Where()
final - OnNext(12)
5 was emitted
final - OnCompleted()
```

Like the `Subscribe` operator, the `Do` operator has several overloads that let you add functionality to the various source observable emissions:

```
IObservable<TSource> Do<TSource>(this IObservable<TSource> source,
    Action<TSource> onNext)
IObservable<TSource> Do<TSource>(this IObservable<TSource> source,
    Action<TSource> onNext,
    Action onCompleted)
IObservable<TSource> Do<TSource>(this IObservable<TSource> source,
    Action<TSource> onNext,
    Action<Exception> onError)
IObservable<TSource> Do<TSource>(this IObservable<TSource> source,
    Action<TSource> onNext,
    Action<Exception> onError,
    Action onCompleted)

IObservable<TSource> Do<TSource>(this IObservable<TSource> source,
    IObserver<TSource> observer)
```

> **Invokes the appropriate actions for each notification in the observable sequence; you can choose which actions you want to provide.**

> **Passes an observer, instead of each individual action**

You can take the logging example one step further and create a reusable `Log` operator that prints all the source observable notifications for you. The `Log` operator will use `Do` to print various emissions coming from the observable source.

Listing 6.1   The `Log` operator

```
public static IObservable<T> Log<T>(this IObservable<T> observable,
                                    string msg="")
{
    return observable.Do(
        x => Console.WriteLine("{0} - OnNext({1})", msg, x),
        ex =>
        {
            Console.WriteLine("{0} - OnError:", msg);
            Console.WriteLine("\t {0}", ex);
        },
        () => Console.WriteLine("{0} - OnCompleted()", msg));
}
```

This `Log` operator is nice to play with when investigating your observable's pipeline, and you might find it useful in your applications. Here's how I use it in the example:

```
Observable.Range(1, 5)
    .Log("range")
    .Where(x => x%2 == 0)
    .Log("where")
    .Select(x => x*3)
    .SubscribeConsole("final");
```

This produces

```
range  -  OnNext(1)
range  -  OnNext(2)
where  -  OnNext(2)
final  -  OnNext(6)
range  -  OnNext(3)
range  -  OnNext(4)
where  -  OnNext(4)
final  -  OnNext(12)
range  -  OnNext(5)
range  -  OnCompleted()
where  -  OnCompleted()
final  -  OnCompleted()
```

As mentioned previously, adding side effects to the observable pipeline could introduce some confusion, but when used correctly, they can improve the code you write, in both readability and correctness. Next, I'll show you how combining the operators you've learned about in this chapter can turn a large complex application into a small yet comprehensible one.

6.3   *Putting it all together*

All the operators you've learned about let you process complex events easily, especially when combining them. Did you ever think that your mouse could be treated as an observable? It's an observable that's capable of producing notifications about the state of the mouse buttons and, of course, the current cursor position.

You can take advantage of this to create a reactive drawing application. The application draws lines by adding points based on the mouse position in a window, starting when the mouse button is pressed down, and stopping when the mouse button is released. An example of a simple drawing is shown in figure 6.12.

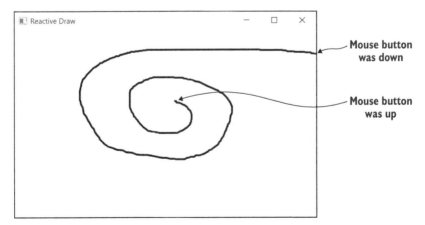

Figure 6.12   The Reactive Draw application. A line is created by adding points based on the position of the mouse, starting from the point the mouse button is down and stopping when it's up.

This is how the application looks when writing it in a WPF window.

First, you need to create observables from the traditional MouseDown, MouseUp, and MouseMove events:

Subscribes to the events raised by the window, passing the this (the window object) as an argument and the name of the event to the FromEventPattern method.

```
var mouseDowns =
Observable.FromEventPattern<MouseButtonEventArgs>(this, "MouseDown");
var mouseUp =
Observable.FromEventPattern<MouseButtonEventArgs>(this, "MouseUp");
var movements =
Observable.FromEventPattern<MouseEventArgs>(this, "MouseMove");
```

Now, for each movement, you select the mouse position and add a point to a polyline drawn in the window's inner panel:

Observes the mouse movements (of type MouseEventArgs)

```
movements
    .Select(m => m.EventArgs.GetPosition(this))
    .Subscribe(pos => line.Points.Add(pos));
```

Takes the mouse position relative to the window's coordinate system

Adds a point to the polyline

This code creates an application that draws a continuous line, without stopping. So now you need to add a condition that will stop taking the movements when the mouse button is up. This is exactly the job for TakeUntil:

```
movements
    .Select(m => m.EventArgs.GetPosition(this))
    .TakeUntil(mouseUp)
    .Subscribe(pos => line.Points.Add(pos));
```

Observes the mouse position only until the mouse button is up.

Here the mouseUp observable is passed to the TakeUntil operator. When a notification that that mouse button is up is emitted, the observer will be detached from the observable.

You still need to add the trigger to start drawing the line when the mouse button is down. This is achieved by using the SkipUntil operator. For example:

```
movements
    .SkipUntil(mouseDowns)
    .Select(m => m.EventArgs.GetPosition(this))
    .TakeUntil(mouseUp)
    .Subscribe(pos => line.Points.Add(pos));
```

Movements aren't observed by the observer until a mouse-button-down notification is emitted.

After a mouse-button-down notification is emitted, the mouse movements are observed by the observer that adds the points to the line. And when the mouse button is up, the observer stops.

This creates a situation in which only one transaction is allowed (only one cycle of a mouse-down and mouse-up event). For this application, you want to repeat this cycle again and again, which is (of course) the job of Repeat. For example:

```
movements
    .SkipUntil(mouseDowns)
    .Select(m => m.EventArgs.GetPosition(this))
    .TakeUntil(mouseUp)
    .Repeat()                              ◁──┐  Resubscribe to the mouse movements,
    .Subscribe(pos => line.Points.Add(pos));      only after the mouse button is down
```

Great, you now have an application that draws a line, but it always adds points to the same line. A drawing application that draws only one line, reactive as it may be, isn't useful.

What you want is to add a new line when the mouse button is down and have the points received from the mouse move added to that line, which becomes the current line. This is a side effect you need to take care of. Luckily, you have the `Do` operator. The following listing shows the complete application code that handles the drawing. As always, you can find the entire application's source code in the book's Git repo (http://mng.bz/IZ4B).

Listing 6.2 Reactive Draw application—full code

```
Polyline line = null;                    ◁──┐  The current line will be
                                              held by this variable.
movements
    .SkipUntil(
        mouseDowns.Do(_ =>        ◁──┐  Adding a side effect to
        {                              each mouse-down
            line = new Polyline() {Stroke = Brushes.Black, StrokeThickness = 3};    notification that
            canvas.Children.Add(line);      creates a new line and
        }))                            adds it to the window
    .TakeUntil(mouseUp)
    .Select(m => m.EventArgs.GetPosition(this))
    .Repeat()
    .Subscribe(pos => line.Points.Add(pos));
```

This example shows the beauty of the operator composability you have in Rx. Each operator logically follows another to create a clear chain of execution, in which one observable created by an operator becomes the source observable of the next operator. You created a complete drawing application with just a few lines of code, and modifying our pipeline as you built it was simple.

6.4 Summary

Another chapter comes to its end, and this one was fundamental for understanding how to work correctly with the observer and observables. The concepts in this chapter aren't easy to understand, so you should commend yourself for making it such a long way.

Here's what you learned in this chapter:

- You can easily create and subscribe an observer by using the `Subscribe` extension method, which accepts the `OnNext`, `OnError`, and `OnCompleted` methods.

- If you want to use the observer more than once, you can create an observer instance with the `Observer.Create` method and subscribe it yourself.
- You can replace the disposable subscription object with a `CancellationToken` and then pass it to the `Subscribe` method.
- To delay the subscription of an observer to an observable, you use the `Delay-Subscription` method and pass it the relative `TimeSpan` or the absolute `DateTimeOffset`.
- The `TakeUntil` operator lets you specify the time the observer will stop receiving notifications or lets you pass another observable that marks the stop by emitting a notification.
- The `SkipUntil` operator lets you specify the time the observer will start receiving notifications or lets you pass another observable that marks the start by emitting a notification.
- You can skip any number of notifications by using the `Skip` operator, and stop receiving notifications after a specified number by using the `Take` operator.
- You can set a condition to start receiving notifications and to stop receiving notifications by using the `SkipWhile` and `TakeWhile` operators, respectively.
- An observer can automatically be subscribed to an observable with the `Repeat` operator, which lets you specify a certain number of times or an indefinite number of times.
- To show a side effect explicitly as part of your observable pipeline, use the `Do` operator, where you can specify the actions to do in the `OnNext`, `OnError`, and `OnCompleted` notifications.
- The Reactive Drawing application you created in this chapter used many of these operators to make a powerful application with just a few lines of code.
- In the next chapter, you'll explore the concept of an observable's temperature and learn what cold and hot observables mean.

7
Controlling the observable temperature

This chapter covers

- Creating publishers with subjects
- Working with hot and cold observables
- Moving from hot to cold and vice versa
- Controlling the hot observable lifetime

The abstraction provided by observables hides from the observers the knowledge of how the underlying source makes the emissions. Depending on the way the observable is implemented, the same emissions (the object instance) might be shared between the various observers, or alternatively, each observer might get different instances. The observable might be implemented so that each observer receives the entire sequence, or instead receives part of the sequence, depending on when it subscribed.

Say an observable emits sound waves. As an observer, you don't know whether the sound is coming from a live concert, or played from an album that was started the moment the observer subscribed. During a concert, all the listeners (the observers) share the same tunes. But when played from an album, the tunes are played to each listener independently, and the full sequence of songs can be consumed no matter when the observer subscribed.

The term *observable temperature* refers to the state of the observable at the moment of its subscription. This state describes the time an observable begins and stops its emissions and whether the emissions are shared between observers. A *hot observable* is in an active state, like a singer performing live or an observable that emits the mouse's current position. In contrast, a *cold observable* is in a passive state, like an album waiting to be played or an observable that pushes the elements in a loop when an observer subscribes.

To control and change the observable temperature—for example, when you want to make sure all observers observe the same items, or when you want to "record" notifications to replay them later—you need to use one of the Rx building blocks—the `Subject`, a type that's both an observable and an observer. `Subject` acts as a hub that allows multicasting notifications. You can also use `Subject` to create a PubSub inside your application. At the end of the chapter, you'll know how to identify and control the shareability of your observable so that the results of your queries will always be predictable.

7.1   *Multicasting with subjects*

A type that implements the `IObservable<T>` interface and `IObserver<M>` interface is called a *subject*. This type acts as both an observer and an observable, as shown in figure 7.1. It allows you to create an object that becomes a hub, which is able to intercept notifications it receives as an observer and push them to its observers. This, for example, can be used inside a shopping-cart class to notify various observers (such as the relevant UI component) about items added or removed from the cart. The cart exposes `Subject` as an observable, and the cart `Add` and `Remove` methods call the subject's `OnNext` method to notify about the change.

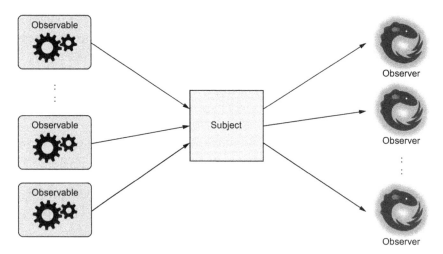

Figure 7.1   A subject is a type that's both an observable and an observer. It allows multicasting the notifications emitted by the sources to the observers.

The following listing provides the definition of the `ISubject` interface that resides in the `System.Reactive.Subjects` namespace.

Listing 7.1 The `ISubject` interface

```
interface ISubject<in TSource, out TResult> : IObserver<TSource>,
                                              IObservable<TResult>
{
}
```

The `Subject` type represents a PubSub (publisher-subscriber) pattern: the subject consumes notifications on one side (or is triggered by a notification) and emits notifications on the other side. This lets you create types that add special logic (transformations, caching, buffering, and so on) within the notifications received before they're published, or allows multicasting from one source to multiple destinations.

When `TSource` and `TResult` generic parameters are of the same type, you can use the simpler version of the `ISubject` interface.

Listing 7.2 `ISubject` interface with `Source` and `Result` types that are the same

```
interface ISubject<T> : ISubject<T, T>
{
}
```

Rx provides these subject implementations:

- `Subject<T>`—Broadcasts every observed notification to all observers.
- `AsyncSubject<T>`—Represents an asynchronous operation that emits its value upon completion.
- `ReplaySubject<T>`—Broadcasts notifications for current and future observers.
- `BehaviorSubject<T>`—Broadcasts notifications and saves the latest value for future observers. When created, it's initialized with a value that emits until changed.

In all the standard implementations of subjects inside the Rx library, the observers receive the notifications sequentially, in the order that they subscribed.

Why is it called a subject?

In chapter 1, I mentioned that Rx drew its inspiration from the original GoF observer design pattern. In this pattern, the *subject* is observed by the observers and can be externally triggered to raise the notifications. The Rx `Subject` plays the same role as the *subject* in the observer pattern, therefore its name.

7.1.1   *Simple broadcasting with Subject<T>*

The simplest subject implementation is `Subject<T>`, which serves as a simple broad-caster, as shown in figure 7.2. This type adds no behavior around the received notifica-tion. Each observed notification is broadcast to the observers without any additional processing. This is why it makes `Subject<T>` a good fit for a backing field to an observ-able that's exposed by your class. All you need to do is tell it to push notifications from various methods in the class (such as the shopping cart that needs to notify parts of the application that it has changed).

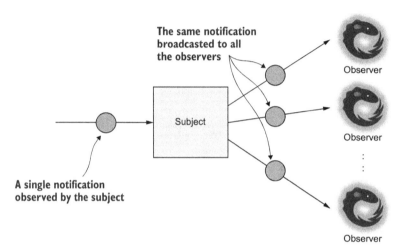

Figure 7.2 `Subject<T>` **is a broadcaster. Each notification it observes is broadcast to its observers.**

Because `Subject<T>` is an observer, it exposes the `OnNext`, `OnCompleted`, and `OnError` methods, so when they're called, the same methods are called on all the observers. You can manually signal a subject to emit notifications by calling its exposed methods.

This example uses a subject to publish two notifications to two observers and then completes:

```
using System.Reactive.Subjects;

Subject<int> sbj = new Subject<int>();       ⟵──┐ Creates a subject
                                                 │ of integers

sbj.SubscribeConsole("First");               ⎫ Subscribes two observers
sbj.SubscribeConsole("Second");              ⎭

sbj.OnNext(1);        ⎫ Emits two notifications
sbj.OnNext(2);        ⎭
sbj.OnCompleted();    ⟵──┐ Notifies subscribed observers about
                         │ the end of the observable sequence
```

Running this example displays the following output:

```
First - OnNext(1)
Second - OnNext(1)
First - OnNext(2)
Second - OnNext(2)
First - OnCompleted()
Second - OnCompleted()
```

Each time you call the OnNext or OnCompleted methods on the subject, the observers receive the notification in the order in which they subscribe.

MULTIPLE SOURCE, BUT ONE COMPLETION

One misunderstanding I see when working with Subject<T> is that although there can be many source observables, only one completion will occur and be passed to the observers. Subjects conform to the observable-observer protocol mandate that after completion, no more notifications are emitted.

Consider this example: a subject subscribes to two observables representing two chat rooms, each emitting messages as they're received from participants. Each observable emits five notifications but at different rates—every 1 second and every 2 seconds. The desired behavior is that the observer subscribing to the subject will receive the messages from both chat rooms and, if one chat room completes (all the participants leave), the messages from the other chat room will continue to be observed. But, confusingly, the real behavior is that the observer will receive the values emitted only until either observable completes; the rest of the notifications from the other observable won't pass through, as shown in figure 7.3.

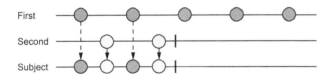

Figure 7.3 The subject can subscribe to multiple sources, but when any of the sources completes (the second in this figure), so does the subject.

Listing 7.3 Subscribing the subject to multiple observables

```
Subject<string> sbj = new Subject<string>();

Observable.Interval(TimeSpan.FromSeconds(1))
    .Select(x => "First: " + x)
    .Take(5)
    .Subscribe(sbj);
Observable.Interval(TimeSpan.FromSeconds(2))
    .Select(x => "Second: " + x)
    .Take(5)
    .Subscribe(sbj);

sbj.SubscribeConsole();
```

Creates a subject of type string

Creates an observable that simulates the first chat room the subject is subscribed to. Chat room emits five notifications before completion, one every 1 second.

Simulates a second chat room which emits five notifications before completion, one every 2 seconds.

Subscribes an observer to the subject

After running this example, you'll get this output:

```
- OnNext(First: 0)
- OnNext(Second: 0)
- OnNext(First: 1)
- OnNext(First: 2)
- OnNext(Second: 1)
- OnNext(First: 3)
- OnNext(First: 4)
- OnCompleted()
```

The output shows that after the five values are emitted by the first observable, a completion notification from the first observable is observed by the subject and then published to its observer. Afterward, no more notifications are received.

CLASSIC MISUSE OF A SUBJECT

Typically, developers naively try to merge observables together by using a subject, but the built-in `Merge` operator should be used instead. The following listing shows a classic example of a subject misuse: the subject subscribes to multiple sources to merge them. And the surprisingly confusing result is that the resulting sequence isn't merged at all. The scenario here merges an enumerable that was fetched from a database and transformed to an observable (everything is a stream, remember?[1]) together with an observable of real-time notifications. The observable created from the enumerable completes first and, therefore, the rest of the notification won't be observed, making the result confusing.

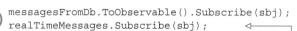

Listing 7.4   The wrong way to merge observables

```
Subject<string> sbj = new Subject<string>();        Creates a subject and
sbj.SubscribeConsole();                             subscribes an observer

    //at some point later...
                                                     Fetches a collection of
IEnumerable<string> messagesFromDb = ...        ◁── messages from the database
IObservable<string> realTimeMessages = ...      ◁─┐
                                                   Creates an observable of messages
                                                   that emits messages in real time
```

Don't do it.
Use Merge
instead.
```
messagesFromDb.ToObservable().Subscribe(sbj);                              ◁
realTimeMessages.Subscribe(sbj);      ◁──────────┐
                                                  Converts the collection to an observable
        Subscribes the subject (because the previous    that synchronously emits all the
        observable already completed, none of this      messages to the subject subscribed
        observable's notifications will be observed)     to it and publishes its completeness
```

In the example, you create a subject at the beginning of the application and subscribe an observer to it. (In a real application, the observer can be the screen that shows the messages.) Later, somewhere in the code (for example, after the initialization process), you subscribe the subject to two observables: the first is an enumerable of the

---

[1]   Chapter 1 introduced the concept that everything is a stream.

items that the database loads (and transforms to the observable), and the second is the observable of the messages received in real time. This creates a simple implementation of a merge; however, the correct way to implement the merge is by using the `Merge` operator.

The first observable is created from a finite collection of messages because a finite number of messages are stored in the database. The moment the subject subscribes to it, all the messages are synchronously emitted, and then the `OnCompleted` method is called on `Subject`.

Calling the `OnCompleted` method at this point means the subject discards any message emitted afterward. This makes the subscription to the second observable useless, as it has no effect.

> **TIP** As a general rule, use subjects (of any kind) with caution, and make sure you're not reinventing the wheel; instead, use the built-in Rx operators.

One problem with `Subject<T>` you may encounter is that if the source observable emits a value before an observer subscribes, this value will be lost. This is specifically problematic if the source always emits only a single notification. Luckily, `AsyncSubject` provides a remedy for those cases.

7.1.2 *Representing asynchronous computation with AsyncSubject*

You can add inner behavior to the way subjects handle source notifications. `AsyncSubject<T>` adds logic to your code that fits nicely with asynchronous emissions. This is useful when the source observable might complete before the observer has a chance to subscribe to it, as shown in figure 7.4. This behavior is often seen when dealing with concurrent applications, where order of execution can't be predicted.

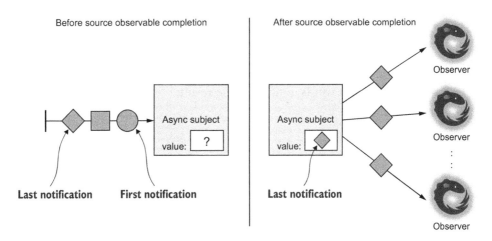

Figure 7.4 `AsyncSubject` **emits only the last value to current and future observers.**

Internally, `AsyncSubject` stores the most recent value so that when the source observable completes, it emits this value to current and future observers. For example, you can use `AsyncSubject` inside Rx to convert `Task` and `Task<T>` into observables. Listing 7.5 shows the conceptual implementation of this conversion. The Rx implementation for the `ToObservable` operator is different and includes performance optimizations and edge-case handling.

The code shows how to create an `AsyncSubject` and redirect each possible completion status for the task to the observable notifications. Even though the task is completed, the subject emits the notification to the observer.

Listing 7.5   Converting `Task<T>` to an observable by using `AsyncSubject`

```
var tcs = new TaskCompletionSource<bool>();
var task = tcs.Task;

AsyncSubject<bool> sbj = new AsyncSubject<bool>();
task.ContinueWith(t =>
{
    switch (t.Status)
    {
        case TaskStatus.RanToCompletion:
            sbj.OnNext(t.Result);
            sbj.OnCompleted();
            break;
        case TaskStatus.Faulted:
            sbj.OnError(t.Exception.InnerException);
            break;
        case TaskStatus.Canceled:
            sbj.OnError(new TaskCanceledException(t));
            break;
    }
} ,TaskContinuationOptions.ExecuteSynchronously);
tcs.SetResult(true);
sbj.SubscribeConsole();
```

Creates a Task from a TaskCompletionSource that you can control in the code

If the Task completes successfully, emits its result and then completes

Takes the exception that was thrown and notifies the observers

If the Task is canceled, notifies the observers with a TaskCanceledException

Sets the continuation to work on the same thread as the completed Task

Sets the Task to completion before the observer subscribes

The program output shows that even though the `Task` completed before the observer subscribed, the observer is notified of the result:

```
- OnNext(True)
- OnCompleted()
```

Keep in mind that `AsyncSubject` emits only one value, and only after the source observable completes. Sometimes, however, you'll want to emit notifications as they come and preserve the ability to cache the latest value for future observers, as `AsyncSubject` does. For that, you need to use `BehaviorSubject`.

7.1.3   *Preserving the latest state with BehaviorSubject*

The type `BehaviorSubject<T>` is useful when you need to represent a value that changes over time, such as an object state. Say you need to store an object's possible states (`PreLoad`, `Loaded`, `Rendering`, and so forth).

Every observer that subscribes to `BehaviorSubject` receives the last value and all subsequent notifications, as shown in figure 7.5. Therefore, when creating an instance of `BehaviorSubject`, you pass an initial value (a default). You can also read the last (or initial) value through the `Value` property that `BehaviorSubject` exposes, making it ideal as a backing field for a state property that allows change notifications.

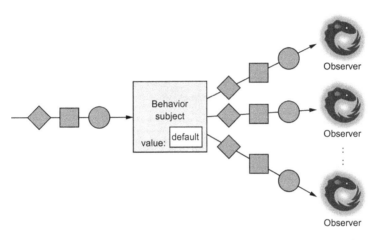

Figure 7.5 `BehaviorSubject` **represents a value that changes over time. Observers receive the last (or initial) value and all subsequent notifications.**

This example uses `BehaviorSubject` to maintain the state of the network connectivity while still making changes in the connectivity observable:

Creates a BehaviorSubject that represents the connectivity state and initializes as Disconnected

If an observer subscribes before a connection is made, the subscriber receives the Disconnected value.

```
BehaviorSubject<NetworkConnectivity> connection =
  new BehaviorSubject<NetworkConnectivity>(
    NetworkConnectivity.Disconnected);
    connection.SubscribeConsole("first");
//After connection
connection.OnNext(NetworkConnectivity.Connected);
connection.SubscribeConsole("second");
Console.WriteLine("Connection is {0}", connection.Value);
```

If another observer subscribes after a connection is made, the subscriber receives the cached Connected value.

Emits a notification with the Connected value which is cached inside BehaviorSubject.

Shows the last emitted or initialized BehaviorSubject value through the Value

Running this example shows this output:

```
first - OnNext(Disconnected)
first - OnNext(Connected)
second - OnNext(Connected)
Connection is Connected
```

BehaviorSubject keeps a cache of one value only (the last one). For more than one value, use ReplaySubject.

7.1.4   *Caching the sequence with ReplaySubject*

ReplaySubject<T> is a subject that holds a cache of the notifications it observes inside an inner buffer, as shown in figure 7.6.

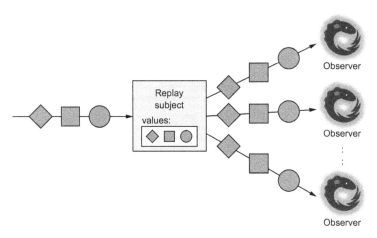

Figure 7.6 ReplaySubject **broadcasts each notification to all subscribed and future observers, subject to buffer trimming policies.**

ReplaySubject lets you, for example, store notifications and replay them for various observable pipelines that you're testing, and compare the results to see which is the best. To prevent unwanted memory leaks, you can control the caching policy that limits the buffer size, time, or both.

Listing 7.6 shows how to limit ReplaySubject by time and size. This example uses Rx with a health sensor. Like Microsoft Band,[2] the client application connects to the sensor when started, but the user can add a heart-rate parameter to the UI later. To display a nice graph, you want to keep the last 20 readings from the last 2 minutes.

---

[2] A repository that adds Rx support to Microsoft Band can be found at GitHub (https://github.com/Reactive-Extensions/RxToBand).

Listing 7.6 Limiting the `ReplaySubject` **cache by time and size**

Gets an observable of the heart
rate from Microsoft Band

```
IObservable<int> heartRate = ...
ReplaySubject<int> sbj = new ReplaySubject<int>(bufferSize: 20,
 window: TimeSpan.FromMinutes(2));
```

Subscribes the subject
when the application starts

```
heartRate.Subscribe(sbj);

// After the user selected to show the heart rate on the screen)
sbj.SubscribeConsole("HeartRate Graph");
```

If the user displays the heart rate onscreen,
subscribes an observer to receive the cached
readings and all the ones that follow

Creates ReplaySubject
with a buffer size of 20
and notifications
cached at 2 minutes

For the heart rate, I simulated five readings (70–74) and, instead of displaying a graph, I printed them onscreen:

```
HeartRate Graph - OnNext(70)
HeartRate Graph - OnNext(71)
HeartRate Graph - OnNext(72)
HeartRate Graph - OnNext(73)
HeartRate Graph - OnNext(74)
HeartRate Graph - OnCompleted()
```

Like everything that involves caching in software, you should be aware of the memory footprint it leaves and the cache invalidation you use. There's no way to manually clean the cache that `ReplaySubject` contains (nor access it and read it), so pay special attention when you use the unbounded version of `ReplaySubject`. You can free the cache's memory only by disposing of `ReplaySubject`.

Next, we'll talk about guidelines and best practices for subjects.

7.1.5   *Hiding your subjects*

You should be aware of a risk when working with subjects: it's easy to lose control of them. Suppose you have a class that holds an inner subject and then exposes it when a property returns an observable, as this example shows:

```
class BankAccount
{
    Subject<int> _inner = new Subject<int>();

    public IObservable<int> MoneyTransactions { get { return _inner; } }
}
```

Returns the
subject instance

Although you expose the `IObservable` type only, the encapsulation can still be broken. That's because it's possible for a hostile or inexperienced developer to cast the observable back to a subject, as in this example:

Makes a regular subscription
as the class author intended

```
var acct = new BankAccount();
acct.MoneyTransactions.SubscribeConsole("Transferring");
```

```
var hackedSubject = acct.MoneyTransactions as Subject<int>;   ◄──┐ A hostile casting
                                                                  │ of the observable
hackedSubject.OnNext(-9999);        ◄──┐ Your encapsulation is broken, and
                                       │ all the account money is taken.
```

After casting back to `Subject` (or `ISubject`), the code can now emit notifications from the outside. This will cause confusion and unwanted bugs.

HOW TO PROTECT FROM OUTSIDE EMISSIONS

Your subject was compromised because you returned an inner object that has accessible methods. To fix that, you need to return a different object—one that won't reveal the ability to reach your observers even by accident.

For that purpose, Rx provides the `AsObservable` operator. `AsObservable` creates a proxy that wraps your subject and exposes only the `IObservable` interface, so the observer can still subscribe, but no code can cast the observer to a subject, and no code can access the observers. This is demonstrated in figure 7.7.

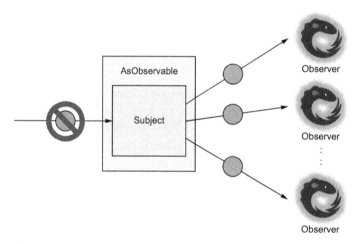

Figure 7.7   Instead of exposing your subject, use the `AsObservable` operator to create a proxy that hides the inner subject.

The following example proves that the observable returned by the `AsObservable` operator (the proxy) can't be cast to a subject:

```
Subject<int> sbj = new Subject<int>();
var proxy = sbj.AsObservable();
var subject = proxy as Subject<int>;
var observer = proxy as IObserver<int>;
Console.WriteLine("proxy as subject is {0}",subject == null
                                              ? "null"
                                              : "notnull");
Console.WriteLine("proxy as observer is {0}",observer == null
                                              ? "null"
                                              : "not null");
```

This, of course, prints the following:

```
proxy as subject is null
proxy as observer is null
```

`Subject` plays a big role in Rx operators and is a powerful tool if used correctly. Unfortunately, `Subject` can be used incorrectly. The next section provides a few guidelines that can help you decide whether `Subject` is the right object for you to use.

7.1.6   *Following best practices and guidelines*

One of the areas that causes a lot of debate in the Rx world is whether subjects are good or bad, and if using them is right or wrong. As Erik Meijer once said, "Once you start seeing yourself using `Subject`, something is wrong. Because subjects are stateful things."[3]

But let's set the record straight: subjects aren't bad and, when used correctly, can be useful indeed. They're used extensively inside the Rx code itself. It's true, however, that some developers use subjects when they don't need them. So when should you use a subject and when should you avoid them? The following list contains the points you should consider:

- Use the built-in factory methods such as `Observable.Create` whenever possible, instead of using a subject. Use a subject only if no suitable built-in factory method exists.
- Use a subject only if the source of the notifications is local (your code raises the notifications and not an external source); for example, to create a notifying property with `BehaviorSubject`.
- Use a subject for controlling an observable's temperature (as you'll learn next).
- Use a subject when creating an operator of your own that needs a notification's hub.
- Don't expose subjects; use `AsObservable` to prevent that from happening.

The important thing to remember is that before you create an operator, you should always check whether an operator that does what you intended to write by yourself already exists in Rx.

Dave Sexton wrote a wonderful blog post about the correct use of subjects that drills down into these guidelines (http://mng.bz/Pv9). I recommend reading it after you read the next section, where I'll show one area that depends on subjects for its existence—controlling the observable temperature.

7.2   *Introducing temperature: cold and hot observables*

It may sound funny, but observables have a notion of temperature. Observables can be cold or hot, and each has different effects on your applications. A *cold observable* is *passive* and emits only when the observer subscribes; for each observer, a complete

---

[3] "RX: Reactive Extensions for .NET," PDC 2009, http://mng.bz/3qu4, and Erik Meijer on Twitter, http://mng.bz/Weiq.

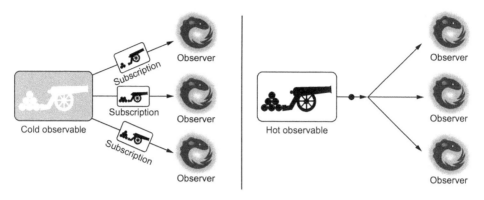

Figure 7.8   A cold observable is passive and starts emitting only when an observer subscribes. A hot observable is active, and its emissions are shared among all the observers.

sequence is generated. A *hot observable* is *active* and emits regardless of the observers. All the observers of the hot observable will observe the same emissions, so we say that the items are shared. Observables can also move from one temperature to the other with the techniques you'll learn in this section that will help make your observable queries predictable. Figure 7.8 summarizes the differences between hot and cold observables.

7.2.1   *Explaining cold and hot observables*

To understand the difference between hot and cold observables, I created the following simple program. It creates an observable that emits two string values with a short delay between them. Look at the following example and try to predict the output:

```
var coldObservable =
    Observable.Create<string>(async o =>
    {
        o.OnNext("Hello");                              Emit the words Hello
        await Task.Delay(TimeSpan.FromSeconds(1));      and Rx with a 1-second
        o.OnNext("Rx");                                 delay between the words
    });

coldObservable.SubscribeConsole("o1");              Subscribes two observers
await Task.Delay(TimeSpan.FromSeconds(0.5));        with a half-second delay
coldObservable.SubscribeConsole("o2");              between the subscriptions
```

Many developers new to Rx find it surprising that the output of this small program shows the message of both observers intertwined:

```
o1 - OnNext(Hello)
o2 - OnNext(Hello)
o1 - OnNext(Rx)
o1 - OnCompleted()
o2 - OnNext(Rx)
o2 - OnCompleted()
```

You can see that the second observer receives the message *Hello* even though it sub-scribes after the first observer receives it.

For each observer that subscribes, the observable begins its work from the start and generates the entire sequence of notifications for that observer. You can also say that the observable isn't running until an observer subscribes to it. Those characteristics are typical for cold observables.

7.2.2 Cold observable

Here's my more formal definition of a *cold observable*:

> *A cold observable is an observable that starts emitting notifications only when an observer subscribes, and each observer receives the full sequence of notifications without sharing them with other observers.*[4]

Most of the observables you've created thus far in this book are cold observables. When you use the operators `Create`, `Defer`, `Range`, `Interval`, and so on, you get an observable that's cold. From the observer's standpoint, if the observable it subscribes to is cold, then the observer can be certain that it hasn't missed any notifications.

7.2.3 Hot observables

Here's my formal definition of a *hot observable*:

> *A hot observable is an observable that emits notifications regardless of its observers (even if there are none). The notifications emitted by hot observables are shared among their observers.*

The classic example of a hot observable is the one you create from an event, such as a mouse-move event. The mouse movement's observable sequence is "live," so even if there's no subscribed observer, the mouse movements still happen. And when there are multiple observers, they all get notified of the same mouse movement.

From the observer standpoint, if the observable it subscribes to is hot, then the observer might have already missed some notifications.

When learning about observable temperatures, it's typical to wonder whether the temperature is fixed or can somehow change. The next section answers just that.

7.3 Heating and cooling an observable

Now that you know what *cold* and *hot* mean in terms of observables, the next step is to figure out the ways to switch from cold to hot, or from hot to cold. In this section, you'll learn how and why you would want to perform the transformation from one temperature to the other.

7.3.1 Turning cold into hot

Suppose you want to create a few queries over an observable; for example, you want to filter certain elements with a few filter functions, and observe the ones that survived

---

[4] This doesn't mean the data carried inside the notification can't reference the same object (thus making them shared); rather, the notifications that carry the data are independent from one another.

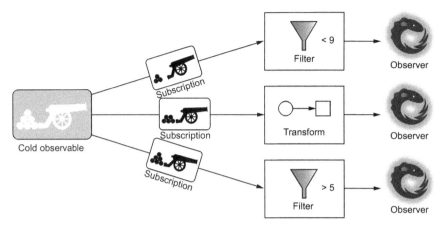

Figure 7.9 Even though each observer subscribes to the same observable, each observer receives a different sequence and the operator processes different elements.

from each filter in a specific way. As a good practice, you'd probably encapsulate each observation (per each filter) in its own query, possibly in its own method. As mentioned previously, cold observables don't share their emissions between their subscribers, so multiple subscriptions, as in the case of the multiple queries, to a cold observable will result in different streams of elements for each one—shown as cannons in figure 7.9. The elements aren't shared and might be different in their values. This is exactly like calling a method twice, which could result in two different return values.

To overcome the possibility that multiple subscriptions will end up with different elements observed by each observer, you need to turn the cold observable into a hot observable, so that the observers will subscribe to the hot one instead, and you can then guarantee they'll observe the same notifications. You have to make sure that turning an observable from cold to hot won't cause you to lose any notifications. You'll have to take that into account inside your process, as you'll see next.

Conceptually, all it takes to make a cold observable hot is putting a proxy between the cold observable and the observers, and letting it broadcast all the notifications to the observers. Luckily, not so long ago, you learned about excellent types that can be programmed as those proxies: subjects. The process of turning an observable from cold to hot is shown in figure 7.10.

To turn a cold observable into a hot observable:

1 Create the subject that will be placed in front of the cold observable. The subject can now accept subscriptions from observers interested in the notifications of the cold observable.

2 Subscribe the observers that are interested in the notifications of the cold observable to the subject.

3 Subscribe the subject, as an observer, to the cold observable. This causes the cold observable to start emitting its sequence of notifications, which are broadcast by

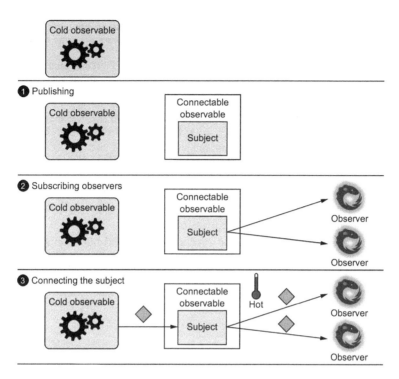

Figure 7.10   The steps for turning a cold observable into a hot observable. The order of the steps is important! After connecting the subject to the cold observable, data starts flowing and it is sent only once.

the subject to all of the observers. This is also the way to guarantee that you don't lose any notifications from the source observable.

Whenever you create an observable and know there will be more than one observable pipeline (and observers), you may want to make the observable hot. This may occur, for example, when you want to model periodic data retrieval from a web service as an observable and don't want each observer to initiate different calls to the web service. Instead, you want to make one call and share the retrieved data with all observers.

Don't be scared of this lengthy process. The code you need to write to turn the cold observable into a hot one is simple. The steps in figure 7.10 correspond to the Rx operators `Publish`, `Subscribe`, and `Connect`. First, I'll show the code that uses those operators and then I'll explain each operator.

Listing 7.7   Turning a cold observable hot

```
var coldObservable=Observable.Interval(TimeSpan.FromSeconds(1)).Take(5);  ◁
var connectableObservable = coldObservable.Publish();
```

Publishes the observable to let multiple observers share the notifications

Creates a cold observable that emits five notifications, one per second

```
connectableObservable.SubscribeConsole("First");
connectableObservable.SubscribeConsole("Second");

connectableObservable.Connect();

Thread.Sleep(2000);
connectableObservable.SubscribeConsole("Third");
```

Subscribes two observers; both will share the same notifications.

Connects the inner subject to the source observable

Subscribes a third observer that will share ensuing notifications with the previous observers

This small application creates a cold observable that emits five notifications, one every second. The application then makes the observable hot by converting it to a `ConnectableObservable` (more on that in a moment) and connects it to the source observable (by calling the `Connect` operator) after two observers subscribe. Then, after another 2 seconds, it subscribes another observer.

The output shows that all notifications are indeed shared between all observers:

```
First - OnNext(0)
Second - OnNext(0)
First - OnNext(1)
Second - OnNext(1)
Third - OnNext(1)
First - OnNext(2)
Second - OnNext(2)
Third - OnNext(2)
First - OnNext(3)
Second - OnNext(3)
Third - OnNext(3)
First - OnNext(4)
Second - OnNext(4)
Third - OnNext(4)
First - OnCompleted()
Second - OnCompleted()
Third - OnCompleted()
```

You can see that the same notification values are shared between the observers. A few new concepts have arisen here, so let's explore the first one: `ConnectableObservable`.

7.3.2   *Using ConnectableObservable*

To turn the cold observable to hot, you need a proxy around it. But you don't want the proxy to create a subscription to the cold observable before you finish setting all the observers you need (otherwise, you might miss some notifications). To help with that, Rx introduces the connectable observable. `ConnectableObservable` implements the `IConnectableObservable` interface and subscribes to the source observable only when explicitly told to do so by calling the `Connect` method.

> **Listing 7.8   The `IConnectableObservable` interface**

```
interface IConnectableObservable<T> : IObservable<T>
{
    IDisposable Connect();
}
```

Subscribes the observable wrapper to its source and returns a disposable object representing the subscription

IConnectableObservable is an observable by itself and can (and will) have observers. As long as the connection is established, all the observers will receive the notifications from the source observable.

To get an instance that implements the IConnectableObservable interface, you need to call the Publish operator on your source observable. The Publish operator has a few overloads; each overload creates a ConnectableObservable with some tweaks, as you'll see next.

7.3.3 *Publishing and multicasting*

The Publish operator creates a ConnectableObservable wrapper around the source observable. This is a required step for allowing multicasting of the observable notifications. The Publish operator has a few overloads, so let's examine those one by one.

SIMPLE PUBLISH

This is the simplest overload:

```
IConnectableObservable<TSource> Publish<TSource>(
    this IObservable<TSource> source)
```

It creates a ConnectableObservable that holds a Subject<T> internally. So, from the moment you Connect it, all the observers share the same notifications. These are the code steps to follow:

```
var coldObservable= ...
var connectableObservable = coldObservable.Publish();

connectableObservable.Subscribe(...);
:
connectableObservable.Subscribe(...);

connectableObservable.Connect();
```

Publishes a cold observable by creating a ConnectableObservable that wraps it and holds a single subscription to it

Subscribes all observers interested in the shared notifications from the source observable

Subscribes the ConnectableObservable to the source observable

In most cases, you'd like to subscribe all observers before calling Connect, so no observer will miss a notification; but that's not always the case. In case new observers subscribe later, it's important for you to note that they'll receive only the next notification that follows their subscription.

But you can tweak this behavior so that an observer will immediately receive the latest notification when it subscribes. This is done using the following overloads of Publish, which accept an initial value and create the ConnectableObservable with an inner BehaviorSubject<T>:

```
IConnectableObservable<TSource> Publish<TSource>(
    this IObservable<TSource> source,
    TSource initialValue)
```

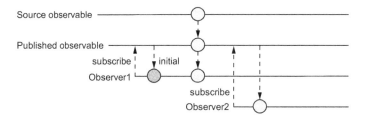

Figure 7.11 Publishing an observable with an initial value. Observers receive either the last value that was emitted from the source observable or the initial value, if no notification was yet emitted.

The inner `BehaviorSubject<T>` this overload creates for the `Connectable-Observable` is initialized with an initial value, so every observer that subscribes before `Connect` was called will receive this value. Every observer that subscribes after `Connect` was called will receive the last value that was emitted from the source observable or the initial value, if no notification was yet emitted. This behavior is shown in figure 7.11

REUSING THE PUBLISHED OBSERVABLE TO CREATE A NEW OBSERVABLE

Things get a little interesting (and complex) when you need to combine the cold observable multiple times to create new observables. The following `Publish` overload is useful in these cases:

```
IObservable<TResult> Publish<TSource, TResult>(
    this IObservable<TSource> source,
    Func<IObservable<TSource>, IObservable<TResult>> selector)
```

The cold source observable

Selector function that can use the multicasted source sequence as many times as needed. Subscriptions made inside are deferred until the real subscription takes place.

Notice that this overload returns an observable and not a `ConnectableObservable`. With this overload, you can easily create observables that reuse the source observable. Consider the next example in which you want to use the `Zip` operator on an observable with itself. The `Zip` operator takes two (or more) observables and merges them by calling a function on the corresponding notifications. The normal expectation that developers have when they use the `Zip` operator on an observable with itself is that the two function arguments will be identical. This example shows why this expectation is false:

```
int I = 0;
var numbers = Observable.Range(1, 5).Select(_ => i++);

var zipped = numbers
    .Zip(numbers, (a, b) => a + b)
    .SubscribeConsole("zipped");
```

Emits a sequence of numbers but causes a side effect on a shared variable.

Because the "numbers" observable is cold, this results in the sequence of values in the form I + (i + 1) and not i + i.

In the example, you use an observable twice in order to create a new observable by using the `Zip` operator. Because the `numbers` observable is cold, the sequence is generated twice, and the side effect caused by incrementing the variable `i` happens twice per notification. Ultimately, what I did in this example is the same as if I had created two different observables that happen to use the same variable `i` and advance it independently (causing the side effect to be reflected in the other observable); thus the function arguments in iteration k will be with the values $a = k$ and $b = k + 1$. You can see this effect in the output:

```
zipped  -  OnNext(1)          ⟵  = 0 + 1
zipped  -  OnNext(5)          ⟵  = 2 + 3
zipped  -  OnNext(9)          ⟵  = 4 + 5
zipped  -  OnNext(13)
zipped  -  OnNext(17)
zipped  -  OnCompleted()
```

You can publish the source observable by yourself, but then it can be hard to decide when exactly to call `Connect`, especially if you want to share the zipped observable. To solve that, you want to defer `Connect` until the subscription happens. As the next example shows, the `Publish` operator can do this:

Calls the Connect method on the published numbers observable

```
var publishedZip = numbers.Publish(published =>
    published.Zip(published, (a, b) => a + b));
publishedZip.SubscribeConsole("publishedZipped");
```

Now, the `numbers` observable is published, so the notifications are shared among all its observers. The same notification will be received both as `a` and `b`. The output is

```
publishedZipped  -  OnNext(0)
publishedZipped  -  OnNext(2)
publishedZipped  -  OnNext(4)
publishedZipped  -  OnNext(6)
publishedZipped  -  OnNext(8)
publishedZipped  -  OnCompleted()
```

PUBLISHLAST

`ConnectableObservables`, created by the `Publish` operator, publishes the notifications from the source observable until it completes. At that point, `Connectable-Observable` completes as well.

Any observer that was late to subscribe won't see any values. This is especially bad when you have an observable that produces a single value, and that's the value you need. This source observable might even be a hot observable.

To help with that, Rx provides the `PublishLast` operator, which publishes only the last value of the source observable:

```
IConnectableObservable<TSource> PublishLast<TSource>(
    IObservable<TSource> source)
```

The PublishLast operator works similarly to the Publish operator, but instead of sharing all notifications from the source observable, the ConnectableObservable it creates will share only the last notification emitted before the source observable completes, both for existing observers and future ones. This is similar to working with an asynchronous type, as you saw earlier in this chapter, and PublishLast will create an AsyncSubject<T> that's used internally by the ConnectableObservable. Here's an example that shows it in action:

```
                                                    Simulates an asynchronous operation
                                                    that takes a long time to complete
var coldObservable = Observable.Timer(TimeSpan.FromSeconds(5))
                        .Select(_ => "Rx");

var connectableObservable = coldObservable.PublishLast();    Shares the last value
connectableObservable.SubscribeConsole("First");             between all current
connectableObservable.SubscribeConsole("Second");            and future observers
connectableObservable.Connect();

Thread.Sleep(6000);                                    Subscribes an observer after
connectableObservable.SubscribeConsole("Third");       the source observable completes
```

Running this example shows that the last notification emitted by the source observable was shared among all observers:

```
First - OnNext(Rx)
First - OnCompleted()
Second - OnNext(Rx)
Second - OnCompleted()
Third - OnNext(Rx)
Third - OnCompleted()
```

7.3.4   *Using Multicast*

Both Publish and PublishLast are good for all of the common scenarios in which you need to heat a cold observable. But if you need more control or need to enforce policies on an internal subject used inside ConnectableObservable (for example, setting its buffer size and other configurations), then you need to use the Multicast operator. Multicast lets you pass the pending subject inside the Connectable-Observable

```
IConnectableObservable<TResult> Multicast<TSource, TResult>(
    this IObservable<TSource> source,
    ISubject<TSource, TResult> subject)
```

Multicast is a powerful low-level operator that's used to create other operators. All the Publish versions use Multicast in their implementations. For example, this implementation from the Rx source code for the Publish overload creates a BehaviorSubject for ConnectableObservable:

```
virtual IConnectableObservable<TSource> Publish<TSource>(
    IObservable<TSource> source,
    TSource initialValue)
```

```
{
    return source.Multicast(new BehaviorSubject<TSource>(initialValue));
}
```

As explained earlier, this `Publish` overload creates a `ConnectableObservable`. Every observer that subscribes to it, after its `Connect` method is called, will receive the last value emitted from the source observable or the initial value, if no notification was yet emitted. The implementation shows that in order to provide this behavior, `Behavior-Subject` is used as the underlying subject passed to the `Multicast` operator.

7.3.5 *Managing the ConnectableObservable connection*

After you connect `ConnectableObservable` to the source observable by calling the `Connect` method, you get back the subscription object that enables you to disconnect it whenever you want. What happens if you reconnect again? What if there are still observers? What if the observers are no longer there? To find the answers, keep on reading.

RECONNECTING

You can reconnect `ConnectableObservable` at any time. Doing so will cause the subscribed observers to see the notifications again. Reconnecting might be useful when you want to keep the observers but need to change the original source of the observable pipeline. For example, if the source observable is a chat server, and you know that server needs to be replaced, you can reconnect, which will cause the new server to be picked up again.

Listing 7.9   Reconnecting `ConnectableObservable`

Subscribes two observers to the connectable observable

Creates and publishes an observable that connects to the current server and emits the messages coming from it

```
var connectableObservable =
    Observable.Defer(() => ChatServer.Current.ObserveMessages())
        .Publish();

connectableObservable.SubscribeConsole("Messages Screen");
connectableObservable.SubscribeConsole("Messages Statistics");
var subscription = connectableObservable.Connect();

//After the application was notified on server outage
Console.WriteLine("--Disposing the current connection and reconnecting--");
subscription.Dispose();
subscription = connectableObservable.Connect();
```

Connects the connectable observable to the source observable to connect to the server

Disposes of the connection to the servers without losing the current observers and reconnects to a new server

---

In this example, the source observable is created using the `Defer` operator, which makes it a cold observable and, therefore, every observer shares the connection logic.

Because you publish it, the connection happens only once, and the notifications are shared among the observers.

The observer begins to receive notifications when you call `Connect` and stops receiving them when you dispose of the subscription object. When you call `Connect` a second time, an underlying connection to the new server is made (because `Chat-Server.Current` points to the new server), and the observers receive the messages coming from it. This is shown in the program output:

```
Messages Screen - OnNext(Server0 - Message1)
Messages Statistics - OnNext(Server0 - Message1)
Messages Screen - OnNext(Server0 - Message2)
Messages Statistics - OnNext(Server0 - Message2)
Messages Screen - OnNext(Server0 - Message3)
Messages Statistics - OnNext(Server0 - Message3)
--Disposing the current connection and reconnecting--
Messages Screen - OnNext(Server1 - Message1)
Messages Statistics - OnNext(Server1 - Message1)
Messages Screen - OnNext(Server1 - Message2)
Messages Statistics - OnNext(Server1 - Message2)
Messages Screen - OnNext(Server1 - Message3)
Messages Statistics - OnNext(Server1 - Message3)
```

PERFORMING AUTOMATIC DISCONNECTION

If you dispose of the subscription object while there are still observers, you might see different results than expected. Moreover, when disposing of the subscription object, the subscribed observers won't see any notifications, and you have no way of telling that the `ConnectableObservable` is no longer connected.

If you keep the subscription when there are no observers, you're wasting expansive resources, and the source observable will keep pushing notifications for no reason. The best option is to make an automatic disconnect when there are no more observers. In addition, you should dispose of the subscription to the source observable.

To achieve this kind of automatic disconnect, you need to use the `RefCount` operator, which manages an inner counter for the number of subscribed observers and then disposes of the subscription when the count is zero.

The next example shows how to subscribe two observers to the observable and, when you unsubscribe them, no more notifications are emitted.

Listing 7.10   Automatic disconnection with `RefCount`

Prints a message to the console every
time the observable emits a value

Creates an observable that
emits a value every second

```
var publishedObservable = Observable.Interval(TimeSpan.FromSeconds(1))
    .Do(x => Console.WriteLine("Generating {0}",x))
    .Publish()
    .RefCount();
var subscription1 = publishedObservable.SubscribeConsole("First");
var subscription2 = publishedObservable.SubscribeConsole("Second");
```

Subscribes the
two observers

Publishes with a reference count so that when the last
observer unsubscribes, there will be no more notifications

```
Thread.Sleep(3000);
subscription1.Dispose();
Thread.Sleep(3000);
subscription2.Dispose();
```

Waits 3 seconds before unsubscribing the first observer

Waits 3 seconds before unsubscribing the second observer

As you can see from the following program output, after the second observer unsubscribes, no more notifications are emitted:

```
Generating 0
First - OnNext(0)
Second - OnNext(0)
Generating 1
First - OnNext(1)
Second - OnNext(1)
Generating 2
Second - OnNext(2)
Generating 3
Second - OnNext(3)
Generating 4
Second - OnNext(4)

Press any key to continue . . .
```

Using `RefCount` when publishing is a good practice that helps ensure that you're not keeping unneeded resources in use. Next you'll look at the other side of the temperature scale and see how to "cool" a hot observable to replay its emissions.

7.3.6 *Cooling a hot observable to allow replaying*

We defined a cold observable as an observable that generates the complete sequence of notifications for each observer that subscribes to it. Just as when you have a live broadcast that you want to watch later, it makes sense that if you could somehow record an observable and replay it later, each observer could subscribe when needed and be guaranteed to receive the entire recorded sequence. Therefore, you can conclude that a recorded observable is a cold observable.

It's important to note that if you have a hot observable, you can make it cold only from the moment you run the conversion. If by the time you make the conversion a notification is already emitted, you can't reproduce them.

To make an observable cold, you need to use the same tools that made a cold observable hot. The only difference is that, in addition to multicasting notifications as they happen, you need to store the notifications and replay them when an observer subscribes. This is what the `Replay` operator does (shown in figure 7.12), and it has many overloads to support doing just that. All of the overloads create a `Replay-Subject<T>` that you can use inside `ConnectableObservable`.

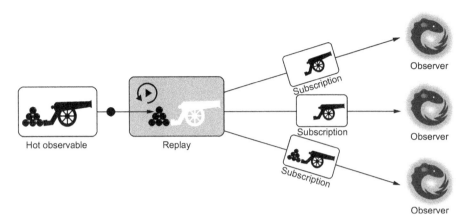

Figure 7.12   Turning a hot observable to a cold observable is necessary when you want to capture emissions and replay them.

The Replay operator has many overloads that let you constrain both the time and the number of items to remember and replay. Here's an example that lets you replay the last two items for any observer that subscribes:

```
                                                          Creates a connectable observable that
                                                                replays the last two items

var publishedObservable = Observable.Interval(TimeSpan.FromSeconds(1))
        .Take(5)
        .Replay(2);                                       ←
publishedObservable.Connect();
var subscription1 = publishedObservable.SubscribeConsole("First");
Thread.Sleep(3000);                                       ←
Var subscription2 = publishedObservable.SubscribeConsole("Second");
```

Connects to the source observable → publishedObservable.Connect();

Receives the last two values and all the subsequent ones

Waits 3 seconds before subscribing the second observable (meaning you missed three values)

Running this application shows this output:

```
First - OnNext(0)
First - OnNext(1)
First - OnNext(2)
Second - OnNext(1)   ← subscribing the second observable
Second - OnNext(2)
First - OnNext(3)
Second - OnNext(3)
First - OnNext(4)
Second - OnNext(4)
First - OnCompleted()
Second - OnCompleted()
```

The preceding results show how the `Replay` operator caches and then re-emits notifications from the source observable. Figure 7.13 shows the marble diagram.

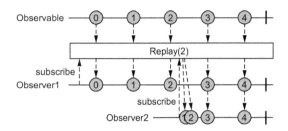

Figure 7.13 Marble diagram showing the result of the `Replay` operator with a buffer size of two items

It's important to understand the implications of the operators you use and how they might make an observable hot or cold. By using the operators you've seen in this chapter, such as `Publish` and `Replay`, you can control the temperature so that there will be no doubt about the results of the queries you write, therefore making your code more readable and predictable.

7.4 Summary

In this chapter, you've learned the definition of the observable temperature and the difference between cold and hot observables. You've also seen how to control the temperature by using special groups of Rx types called subjects.

Here are the important points of this chapter:

- A type that's both an observable and an observer is called a subject.
- Subjects implement the interface `ISubject<TSource, TResult>`, or `ISubject<T>` if the source and result are of the same type.
- Rx provides four built-in subjects: `Subject<T>`, `AsyncSubject<T>`, `ReplaySubject<T>`, and `BehaviorSubject<T>`.
- A subject broadcasts the notifications it receives to all its observers.
- Observables have a notion of temperature; they can be cold or hot.
- A cold observable emits the full sequence of notifications when the observer subscribes.
- A hot observable emits notifications regardless of its observers and may share the notifications among the observers.
- To make a cold observable hot, you use the `Publish` and `Multicast` operators to create a `ConnectableObservable` with an inner subject.
- Calling the `Connect` method on the `ConnectableObservable` subscribes it to the source observable, and the notifications are shared with all observers.
- To automatically unsubscribe the `ConnectableObservable` when there are no more observers, use the `RefCount` operator.
- The `Replay` operator renders a hot observable cold by replaying the notifications to the observers. You can limit the amount of memory used for replaying by specifying the number of items and/or time to keep the items in memory.

In the next chapter, you'll deepen your knowledge of the querying operators Rx has to offer.

Working with basic
query operators

This chapter covers

- Mapping and transforming the notification datum
- Filtering and choosing which notifications to observe
- Creating observables of distinct items
- Aggregating and quantifying notifications

After a source observable emits a notification, there's often a pipeline the notification goes through before it reaches the destined observer. Almost every example in this book shows how operators are used in some way to manipulate a generated sequence of notifications, which your observers eventually observe. This chapter categorizes and explains the basic operators that you'll use to create queries on the observables at hand. These include transformations and mappings, filtering and flattening, and aggregation operators that generate sums, averages, and other types of quantifiable results, as shown in figure 8.1. Some of the operators shown in this chapter were introduced in previous chapters, but you haven't yet seen how they're defined and the capabilities they provide.

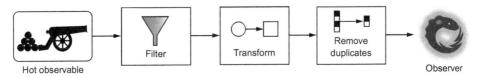

Figure 8.1 Example of an observable pipeline. Each block may or may not be present, and the order of blocks may change as well. Sometimes one type of block may be present more than once.

NOTE For those who speak LINQ as a second language, this chapter might seem trivial at times. But more than once I've found that previous knowledge may lead to false conclusions, so it's better to be on the safe side and make sure that a standard query operator works the way you'd expect it to.

8.1   Selecting what's important (mapping)

Observables emit notifications—so far, so good. Sometimes the notifications you receive aren't exactly what you were looking for, and not always in the form that's the easiest for your program to process. For example, when working with a remote end-point, the object that travels from one side to the other is usually simple and light, containing a minimal amount of data. This is commonly known as a data transfer object (DTO). DTOs carry only the must-have information (for example, identifiers) to your application in order to perform its logic; however, when the DTO enters your application, it's often easier for you to work with your own data type or for you to fetch the corresponding entities from your datastore. For that, you need to create a transforming method with the `Select` operator.

The `Select` operator, illustrated in figure 8.2, lets you transform a notification that's flowing in your observable pipeline (in functional programming, this operator is also called `Map`) to a data format that's more usable for your purposes.

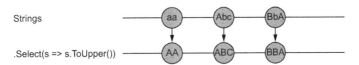

Figure 8.2 The `Select` operator projects each element of an observable sequence into a new form.

TIP Instead of `Select`, you can use the `Map` operator if you feel it's more natural, but you'll need to add NuGet's `System.Reactive.Observable.Aliases` package (www.nuget.org/packages/System.Reactive.Observable.Aliases). Both operators are the same implementation, just with different names.

The next bit of code shows how to use `Select` to transform a received `ChatMessage` that contains the sending user identifier. You load a `User` object from the database

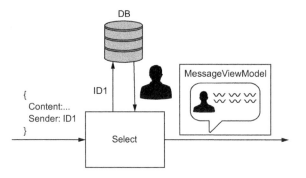

Figure 8.3   Using the `Select` **operator to convert an incoming message DTO to a corresponding** `ViewModel` **with a loaded user object from the database**

and create a `ViewModel` that will be easier to work with in the UI layer. Figure 8.3 illustrates this process.

```
IObservable<ChatMessage> messages = ...                          An observable of chat
                                                                 messages that are pushed
IObservable<ChatMessageViewModel> messagesViewModels =           from a remote server
    messages
        .Select(m => new ChatMessageViewModel
        {                                                        Loads an object from the
                                                                 database based on the identifier
            MessageContent = m.Content,                          received in the notification.
            User = LoadUserFromDb(m.Sender)
        });
```

Extracts a subproperty of the received notification (arrow pointing to `MessageContent = m.Content,`)

The transformation done with the `Select` operator creates a new observable that emits the `ViewModel` you created.

Using `Select`, you can make multiple transformations in a declarative and readable form. The `Select` operator has two overloads—one accepts a simple selector function that receives the notification data, and the second receives the notification index:

```
IObservable<TResult> Select<TSource, TResult>(            Emits notifications
    IObservable<TSource> source,                          of type TSource
    Func<TSource, TResult> selector);
                                                          Receives the source notification
                                                          and transforms it to a
                                                          notification of type TResult
IObservable<TResult> Select<TSource, TResult>(
    IObservable<TSource> source,
    Func<TSource, int, TResult> selector);               Receives the source notification and its
                                                         index in the sequence and transforms
                                                         it to a notification of type TResult
```

The transformation function (the selector) that the `Select` operator receives is free to do whatever transformations you like. It can create an object based on the notification values, extract a subproperty of the received notification and return it, or ignore the notification and return a different value altogether (although this probably won't be that helpful).

An interesting scenario occurs when you want to select a subproperty that's an enumerable or an observable. This creates an observable of enumerables (or observables).

If you want to apply more operators to the enumerables (or observables), you'll have to do that independently for each enumerable (or observable). For these cases, it's better to work with the `SelectMany` operator. As you'll see in a short while, overloads let you keep track of the source object (the event) that created the enumerable.

8.2 Flattening observables

Observables that carry observables (or enumerables) as their notification objects make it harder to apply operators that need to work on each one of the inner elements. Let's say an observable carries collections of numbers, and you want to filter all the odd numbers. What's the best way to filter the collection? Adding a `Where` operator for every inner collection is possible but makes your code less readable. A better approach is to flatten the observable with `SelectMany` and use the `Where` operator on the resulting observable. Now, let's see it in action.

8.2.1 Flattening observables of enumerables

The `SelectMany` operator is used to flatten an observable. If each element in the observable sequence is a collection, as shown in figure 8.4, the resulting observable will emit all the elements from each collection.

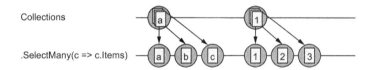

Figure 8.4 The `SelectMany` operator flattens an observable of collections to an observable of items.

`SelectMany` is also called `FlatMap` (as an alias) because it maps each item to a collection and then flattens those collections into one stream. Suppose you have an observable of news items and every item has a collection of images that you want to show on the screen, but only if they're rated PG-13 (child friendly). You can write the Rx query like this:

```
IObservable<NewsItem> news = ...

news.SelectMany(n => n.Images)          ← Extracts the images collection
    .Where(img => img.IsChildFriendly)     from every news item
    .Subscribe(img => AddToHeadlines(img));   ← Filters the images so only
                                                those that are child
                                                friendly are observed
```

Adds the images to the UI

The `SelectMany` operator used here has the following signature:

```
IObservable<TResult> SelectMany<TSource, TResult>(
    this IObservable<TSource> source,
    Func<TSource, IEnumerable<TResult>> selector)
```

It receives the source observable and, using a selector function, generates an enumerable of type TResult for each item in the observable sequence. The resulting observable flattens all the generated enumerables, so that's why the return type is IObservable<TResult>.

You can see in this example that the selector function of SelectMany returns the Images collection. The resulting observable of SelectMany emits all the images from all the news items; therefore, you can write the Where clause at the same level as the SelectMany operator. You don't need to add the Where clause to each collection.

Figure 8.5 shows an example of news items that your application might receive, followed by the application's output for those news items.

The program output is:

```
News headline image: Item1Image1
News headline image: Item2Image1
```

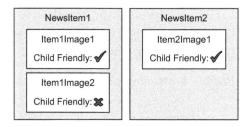

Note that when SelectMany is applied to an observable of enumerables, the items' order is kept; so, in this scenario, all the images of the first news item will be processed before any images of the second news item.

Figure 8.5   The test news items. The first news item contains two images, but only one that is child friendly, and the second news item contains a single image.

SelectMany also has an overload that lets you receive the index of each notification from the source observable:

```
IObservable<TResult> SelectMany<TSource, TResult>(
    this IObservable<TSource> source,
    Func<TSource, int, IEnumerable<TResult>> selector)
```
◁——— **Receives each item in the source observable, together with its index**

You can use this overload to change the way you generate the enumerable, based on the position of the source item in the observable sequence. Next, I'll show you how to keep track of the source notifications that create the enumerable to which the observed items belong.

PROCESSING THE SOURCE AND THE RESULT

SelectMany does a great job flattening the observable, but each inner item that's now emitted loses its connection to the source object that generated the collection. For example, the images generated from the news items are separated from that news item object. Luckily, SelectMany offers another overload that can be helpful.

Suppose for each image in the headline view you want to add a link to the news item it belongs to. This is how you'd use SelectMany now:

```
IObservable<NewsItem> news = ...

news.SelectMany(n => n.Images,
```
◁——— **Extracts the images collection from every news item**

```
(newsItem, img) => new NewImageViewModel
{
    ItemUrl = newsItem.Url,
    NewsImage = img
})
.Where(vm => vm.NewsImage.IsChildFriendly)
.Subscribe(img => AddToHeadlines(img));
```

Takes as an argument the newsItem that generates the collection from which the img comes. Based on the object pair, an ImageViewModel is created.

The overloads for the `SelectMany` operator that accept a `resultSelector` function are shown in the following code snippet. For each item in every collection, the `resultSelector` function is invoked, together with the source element that generates the collection. The value returned from `resultSelector` is the value that the resulting observable emits. The `resultSelector` in the second overload also receives the index of the emitted notification.

Invoked for each item from every collection, together with the item that generates the collection, and then produces the next value in the resulting observable sequence.

```
IObservable<TResult> SelectMany<TSource, TCollection, TResult>(
    this IObservable<TSource> source,
    Func<TSource, IEnumerable<TCollection>> collectionSelector,
    Func<TSource, TCollection, TResult> resultSelector)
IObservable<TResult> SelectMany<TSource, TCollection, TResult>(
    this IObservable<TSource> source,
    Func<TSource, int, IEnumerable<TCollection>> collectionSelector,
    Func<TSource, int, TCollection, int, TResult> resultSelector)
```

Invoked for each item from every collection, together with the item's index and the source item that generates the collection.

A nice feature that the C# compiler provides is the ability to add the `SelectMany` operator to the query without a plethora of code when done manually. To achieve this, use the `Let` operator when writing the query. Here's how to manually create the view models of the child-friendly news images with query syntax:

```
IObservable<NewsItem> news = ...
var newsImages =
    from n in news
    from img in n.Images
    where img.IsChildFriendly
    select new NewImageViewModel
    {
        ItemUrl = n.Url,
        NewsImage = img
    };
```

The two `from` statements (and you can use as many `from` statements as you like) will cause the compiler to generate a `SelectMany` that will wrap the news item and the news image inside an object. Thereafter, all references to the news item and news image will take its value from that object behind the scenes.

`SelectMany` works not only on observables of enumerables but on observables of observables as well.

8.2.2   *Flattening observables of observables*

The same difficulty of applying operators to each emitted observable applies to observables that carry other observables as well (as in figure 8.6).

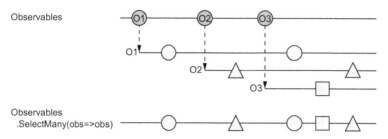

Figure 8.6   The `SelectMany` operator flattens an observable of observables to an observable of emitted items from all the observables.

Suppose your Chat application supports different chat rooms that can be opened by you or by other users that add you as a participant. Each chat room is represented as the type `ChatRoom`, which holds an observable for the messages sent in each room. In the application, you want to show a dashboard view with the recent messages (no matter from which room they were sent). This is shown in figure 8.7.

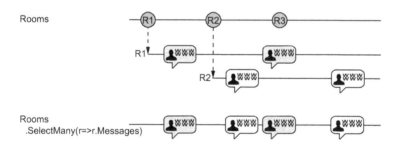

Figure 8.7   Flattening messages from various chat rooms to one stream of messages

Here's how you can do this with Rx:

```
IObservable<ChatRoom> rooms = ...

rooms
    .Log("Rooms")                                  Adds a log message for
    .SelectMany(r => r.Messages)                   every emitted chat
    .Select(m => new ChatMessageViewModel(m))      room notification
    .Subscribe(vm => AddToDashboard(vm));
```

Adds a log message for every emitted chat room notification

Extracts the messages observable from each chat room

Adds each message view model to the application's dashboard

Transforms each ChatMessage to a UI-suitable object

To simulate a situation in which two chat rooms are opened and messages are sent, I created this simple code where the `rooms` observable and each `Messages` observable is a `Subject`.

Listing 8.1 Test program to simulate the creation of chat rooms and message emissions

```
var roomsSubject = new Subject<ChatRoom>();
IObservable<ChatRoom> rooms = roomsSubject.AsObservable();

var room1 = new Subject<ChatMessage>();
roomsSubject.OnNext(new ChatRoom {Id = "Room1", Messages = room1Messages});
room1.OnNext(new ChatMessage{Content = "First Message", Sender = "1"});
room1.OnNext(new ChatMessage{Content = "Second Message", Sender = "1"});

var room2 = new Subject<ChatMessage>();
roomsSubject.OnNext(new ChatRoom{Id = "Room2", Messages = room2Messages});
room2.OnNext(new ChatMessage{Content = "Hello World", Sender = "2" });

room1.OnNext(new ChatMessage{Content = "Another Message", Sender = "1" });
```

Running this test program against the query produces this output:

```
Rooms - OnNext(ChatRoom: Room1)
Room: Room1 , Message: "First Message" was sent by Id=1 Name:User1
Room: Room1 , Message: "Second Message" was sent by Id=1 Name:User1
Rooms - OnNext(ChatRoom: Room2)
Room: Room2 , Message: "Hello World" was sent by Id=2 Name:User2
Room: Room1 , Message: "Another Message" was sent by Id=1 Name:User1
```

In chapter 6, you created the `Log` operator that, when called, prints a message for every `OnNext`, `OnError`, and `OnCompleted` method. `Log` is used here to display a message when a new room is opened (the bolded lines in the output). You can see in the output that all the messages that were sent, no matter from which room, are displayed in a centralized fashion. The view model created for each message is the one that formats the output line for each message, and the `AddToDashboard` method simply writes it to the console.

PROCESSING THE SOURCE AND THE RESULT

As with observables of enumerables, when applying the `SelectMany` operator on an observable of observables, you can specify a `resultSelector` function that will be invoked for each notification (regardless of which observable originates the notification), together with the source item that creates the observable that emits the notification (figure 8.8). This allows you to track the connection between the notifications and their origin and to produce a value based on the results. For example, for chat messages that are emitted concurrently from multiple chat rooms, it's important to know what the source chat room is so you can show it on screen or highlight it if it's a room of importance to the user.

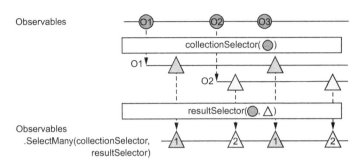

Figure 8.8 When the `SelectMany` operator is applied to an observable of observables, the `resultSelector` will be invoked for each notification, together with the source item that created the observable it was emitted from.

Here's how to use `SelectMany` to add the `ChatRoom` identifier to the chat message `ViewModel`:

```
IObservable<ChatRoom> rooms = roomsSubject.AsObservable();

rooms
    .Log("Rooms")
    .SelectMany(r => r.Messages,
                (room, msg) => new ChatMessageViewModel(msg)
{Room = room.Id})
    .Subscribe(vm => AddToDashboard(vm));
```

> **Receives the chat message and the chat room it belongs to and produces a ChatMessageViewModel that also includes the room identifier**

Unlike enumerables, observables can emit asynchronous notifications, so the order in which the `resultSelector` is invoked is nondeterministic. This means that `SelectMany` will have to cache all the items from the source observable in order to pass them with each notification emitted by the observable they created. This is, of course, only until the observables have completed. Consequently, using `SelectMany` may affect the memory footprint of your application.

> **NOTE** The `SelectMany` operator is powerful when adding asynchronous method invocations as part of the observable pipeline. Chapter 5 discusses this technique, along with other techniques for working with asynchronous operations.

8.3   *Filtering an observable*

Not all notifications emitted by an observable are meaningful to your application; therefore, they need to be filtered out of the observable sequence. These might be notifications whose values are higher than a specific threshold, or chat messages sent from a user you blocked, or news items already received from another news source.

8.3.1   *Filtering with the Where operator*

I've used the `Where` operator in almost every example in this book; it's one of the fundamental operators for most query languages. `Where` receives a predicate function

Figure 8.9   The `Where` operator takes a predicate function and filters the elements of an observable sequence.

that's invoked for each emitted value and returns a Boolean, which indicates whether the value is allowed to proceed in the pipeline and be observed by the observer. The `Where` operator, depicted in figure 8.9, is also known as the `Filter` operator.

The next example filters an observable of strings, so only the strings that start with a capital *A* are emitted:

```
var strings = new[] {"aa", "Abc", "Ba", "Ac"}.ToObservable();

strings.Where(s => s.StartsWith("A"))
    .SubscribeConsole();
```

This produces the following output:

```
- OnNext(Abc)
- OnNext(Ac)
- OnCompleted()
```

The `Where` operator checks each emitted notification solely; it doesn't hold a view of the entire observable sequence generated before the current notification. This makes it harder to create predicate functions that make decisions based on past events. Therefore, it's the developer's responsibility to keep track of that information and to use it. For example, you may need a view of what happened previously if you need to get a distinct observable sequence (where each value is emitted at most once). Luckily, Rx provides this kind of operator for your use.

8.3.2   *Creating a distinct sequence*

The `Distinct` operator permits a restrictive policy on the resulting observable, so values appear only once in the sequence. If the observable emits news items that come from multiple news sources, but you want to see a news item only once, for example, the `Distinct` operator makes this easy to achieve, assuming the news item has an identifier. Figure 8.10 shows a marble diagram of `Distinct`.

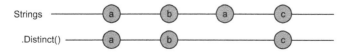

Figure 8.10   The `Distinct` operator suppresses duplicate items emitted by an observable.

Note that the `Distinct` operator emits values as they come (and not when the source observable completes), unless they were already emitted:

```
var subject = new Subject<NewsItem>();
subject.Log()
    .Distinct(n=>n.Title)
    .SubscribeConsole("Distinct");
subject.OnNext(new NewsItem() {Title = "Title1"});
subject.OnNext(new NewsItem() {Title = "Title2"});
subject.OnNext(new NewsItem() {Title = "Title1"});
subject.OnNext(new NewsItem() {Title = "Title3"});
```

Displays the emitted values with Log before they're observed by Distinct

Determines the equality between values using a selector function and Distinct; here items with the same Title are equals.

Emits a NewsItem with a Title that was already emitted

In the output of this program the lines prefixed with `Distinct` are emitted by the observable after removing the duplicates (with the `Distinct` operator):

```
- OnNext(Title1)
Distinct - OnNext(Title1)
 - OnNext(Title2)
Distinct - OnNext(Title2)
 - OnNext(Title1)
 - OnNext(Title3)
Distinct - OnNext(Title3)
 - OnCompleted()
Distinct - OnCompleted()
```

As you can see, the second time the `Title1` news item is emitted, it's filtered out.

The `Distinct` operator has several overloads. If the emitted data type overrides the `Equals` method, you can leave the `Distinct` operator empty (with no arguments), and it'll check equality based on the implementation of `Equals`. Alternatively, you can provide an `EqualityComparer` that determines the equality between the items:

```
IObservable<TSource> Distinct<TSource>(this IObservable<TSource> source)

IObservable<TSource> Distinct<TSource>(
    this IObservable<TSource> source,
    IEqualityComparer<TSource> comparer)

IObservable<TSource> Distinct<TSource, TKey>(
    this IObservable<TSource> source, Func<TSource, TKey> keySelector,
    IEqualityComparer<TKey> comparer)

IObservable<TSource> Distinct<TSource, TKey>(
    this IObservable<TSource> source, Func<TSource, TKey> keySelector,
    IEqualityComparer<TKey> comparer)
```

Returns observable sequence containing only distinct elements

Returns observable sequence containing only distinct elements according to the comparer

Returns observable sequence containing only distinct elements according to the keySelector

Returns observable sequence containing only distinct elements according to the keySelector and the comparer

NOTE In order for the `Distinct` operator to behave as expected, it must save the entire emitted distinct sequence internally. This affects the memory footprint of your application, so you must use it with care.

8.3.3 Removing duplicate contiguous values

Suppose you have a search form, and every time the user changes a search term, a search request is sent to the search service. Because the search request is expensive in terms of time and service load, you want to reduce the number of calls made if they're duplicate queries, as shown in figure 8.11.

Figure 8.11 To reduce load on the service, avoid sending the same term more than once contiguously.

The `DistinctUntilChanged` operator returns an observable sequence that emits only distinct contiguous elements. If the source observable emits the same element consecutively, the value is emitted only once (the first appearance) by the observable returned from `DistinctUntilChanged`. But, unlike `Distinct`, if the value is emitted again after other values are emitted in between, the value is emitted again. Figure 8.12 shows the marble diagram for this operator.

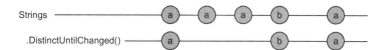

Figure 8.12 The `DistinctUntilChanged` operator filters consecutive duplicate items from the observable.

The next example uses `DistinctUntilChanged` to prevent the same search term from being sent to the search service if it has already been sent. To make this approach more realistic, I'm using another important operator called `Throttle`. This operator emits a value only if a particular timespan has passed without another value being emitted. In this case, a search term is sent only if no other search term is provided within 400 milliseconds:

Emits a notification every time the text in the SearchTerm text box changes

Takes the text from the text box whenever there's a notification

```
Observable.FromEventPattern(SearchTerm, "TextChanged")
    .Select(_ => SearchTerm.Text)
    .Throttle(TimeSpan.FromMilliseconds(400))
    .DistinctUntilChanged()
    .Subscribe(s => /* Sending the search term to the WebService */);
```

Waits 400 ms before allowing the search term to be emitted

You can find a sample WPF application that uses this code at http://mng.bz/84bh. In the sample application, I added all the search terms to a list instead of querying a real

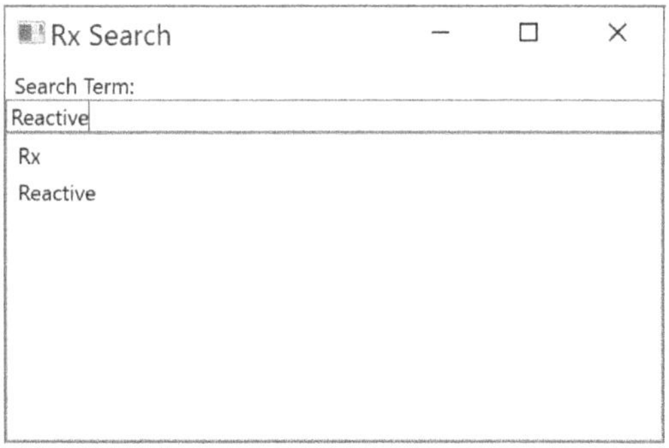

Figure 8.13   With `DistinctUntilChanged`, the word *Reactive* appears only once, even though it was provided twice.

web service. Figure 8.13 shows the output when I wrote Rx, *Reactive* and then wrote ReactiveX but deleted the *X* in less than 400 ms. Note that the list isn't cleared between search terms and, with each term, grows over time.

Just like the `Distinct` operator, `DistinctUntilChanged` provides a few overloads that let you specify the way equality is determined by `keySelector` and/or `EqualityComparer` between values emitted by the observable:

```
IObservable<TSource> DistinctUntilChanged<TSource>(
    this IObservable<TSource> source,
    IEqualityComparer<TSource> comparer)
IObservable<TSource> DistinctUntilChanged<TSource, TKey>(
    this IObservable<TSource> source,
    Func<TSource, TKey> keySelector)
IObservable<TSource> DistinctUntilChanged<TSource, TKey>(
    this IObservable<TSource> source,
    Func<TSource, TKey> keySelector,
    IEqualityComparer<TKey> comparer)
```

The result of an Rx query isn't always an observable sequence of items. Occasionally, you may want a single result, such as the sum of the items or a count of them. The Rx aggregation operators let you do that.

8.4   *Aggregating the observable sequence*

Rx lets you take an observable sequence and reduce it to an aggregated value from the entire sequence or from the sequence up to the current point. This type of aggregation includes summing the sequence, averaging, and finding maximum and minimum values, depending on your aggregation algorithm.

8.4.1   *Using basic aggregation operators*

Those who are familiar with SQL and LINQ know that you can easily include basic aggregate functions in the query, and the underlying system will do the work for you. Rx operators let you utilize the same technique.

SUM

The Sum operator sums all values in the source observable sequence and emits the summation on the resulting observable when the source completes. Figure 8.14 shows a marble diagram of Sum.

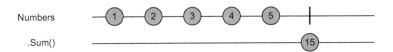

Figure 8.14 The Sum operator calculates the sum of numbers emitted by an observable and then emits the sum.

The Sum operator supports the summation of all primitive number types (integers, floats, and so on), as well as their nullable forms, where the null values will be discarded. Here's an example that sums integers from an observable sequence containing the numbers 1 to 5:

```
Observable.Range(1, 5)
    .Sum()
    .SubscribeConsole("Sum");
```

The output is as follows:

```
Sum - OnNext(15)
Sum - OnCompleted()
```

You can see that sum (15) was emitted when the source observable completed. Using a selector function and overloads for the Sum operator, you can specify which operand to use for the summation. This allows you to select a subproperty of the emitted object. Here's the signature of the overload that accepts integers (int); the same signature exists for the other primitive types as well:

```
IObservable<int> Sum<TSource>(this IObservable<TSource> source,
    Func<TSource, int> selector)
```

COUNT

To count the number of values emitted by an observable, apply the Count operator, depicted in figure 8.15.

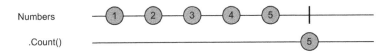

Figure 8.15 The Count operator counts the number of items emitted by the source observable and emits this value.

The observable returned from `Count` emits the count when the source observable completes:

```
Observable.Range(1, 5)
    .Count()
    .SubscribeConsole("Count");
```

The output is as follows:

```
Count - OnNext(5)
Count - OnCompleted()
```

The `Count` operator also lets you specify a predicate that determines which emitted value will be counted. This is equivalent to using a `Where` operator followed by the parameterless `Count` operator. This is how you count only the even numbers in an observable sequence:

```
Observable.Range(1, 5)
    .Count(x => x % 2 == 0)
    .SubscribeConsole("Count of even numbers");
```

Here's the output:

```
Count of even numbers - OnNext(2)
Count of even numbers - OnCompleted()
```

AVERAGE

The `Average` operator, illustrated in figure 8.16, creates an observable that emits the average of the values emitted from the source observable when it completes.

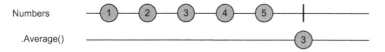

Figure 8.16   The `Average` operator calculates the average of numbers emitted by an observable and emits this average.

`Average` supports averaging all primitive number types (integers, floats, and so on), as well as their nullable forms, where the null values will be discarded:

```
Observable.Range(1, 5)
    .Average()
    .SubscribeConsole("Average");
```

The output is as follows:

```
Average - OnNext(3)
Average - OnCompleted()
```

Using a `selector` function and overloads for the `Average` operator, you can specify which operand to use for averaging. This allows you to select a subproperty of the emitted object. Here's the signature of the overload that accepts integers (`int`); the same signature exists for the other primitive types as well:

```
IObservable<double> Average<TSource>(this IObservable<TSource> source,
Func<TSource, int> selector)
```

MAX AND MIN

The `Max` and `Min` operators let you find the maximum and minimum values in an observable sequence and emit them when it completes, as shown in figure 8.17.

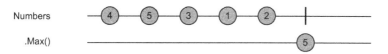

Figure 8.17 The `Max` operator emits the maximum value in an observable sequence.

Here's an example of finding the maximal and minimal values:

```
Observable.Range(1, 5)
    .Max()
    .SubscribeConsole("Max");
Observable.Range(1, 5)
    .Min()
    .SubscribeConsole("Min");
```

The output is as follows:

```
Max - OnNext(5)
Max - OnCompleted()
Min - OnNext(1)
Min - OnCompleted()
```

.NET provides the default comparer that `Max` and `Min` use for your data type; however, if the default comparison condition isn't suitable for your needs, you can provide an `IComparer` and/or a selector function. The following shows the list of overloads for the `Max` operator; the `Min` operator provides the same overloads:

```
IObservable<TSource> Max<TSource>(
    this IObservable<TSource> source,
    IComparer<TSource> comparer)
IObservable<TResult> Max<TSource, TResult>(
    this IObservable<TSource> source,
    Func<TSource, TResult> selector)
IObservable<TResult> Max<TSource, TResult>(
    this IObservable<TSource> source,
    Func<TSource, TResult> selector,
    IComparer<TResult> comparer)
```

Note that the values returned by the `selector` are the ones from which the maximum/minimum values will be chosen and subsequently emitted. The source item (the containing object, for example) producing the values won't be emitted.

If you have an observable sequence of students' grades, and you want to find the student with the maximum grade, for example, the Max operator won't help because you receive the maximum grade only as a number and not the contained object. This is shown in the following example:

```
Subject<StudentGrade> grades = new Subject<StudentGrade>();
grades.Max(g => g.Grade)
    .SubscribeConsole("Maximal grade");

grades.OnNext(new StudentGrade() {Id = "1",Name = "A", Grade = 85.0});
grades.OnNext(new StudentGrade() {Id = "2",Name = "B", Grade = 90.0});
grades.OnNext(new StudentGrade() {Id = "3",Name = "C", Grade = 80.0});
grades.OnCompleted();
```

This example generates the following output:

```
Maximal grade - OnNext(90)
Maximal grade - OnCompleted()
```

As you can see, the Max operator (and selector) emits the value 90 and not the StudentGrade object that contained the maximum values. If you want to print the name of the student with the maximum grade, you won't be able to do that. To reach the behavior you want (emitting the maximum/minimum object and not just the maximum/minimum value), you need to use the MaxBy/MinBy operator.

8.4.2 *Finding the maximum and minimum items by condition*

The operators MaxBy and MinBy let you search an observable sequence to find the items containing the maximum and the minimum values, respectively, and then emit that value when the search completes, as shown in figure 8.18. You set the maximum or minimum values by invoking a keySelector function on each item emitted by the source observable.

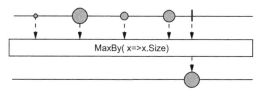

Figure 8.18   The MaxBy operator, based on the values provided by the keySelector function, emits the maximum value as an item when the source observable completes.

Because multiple items might have the same maximum or minimum value, the operators MaxBy or MinBy return an observable of lists:

```
IObservable<IList<TSource>> MaxBy<TSource, TKey>(
    this IObservable<TSource> source,
    Func<TSource, TKey> keySelector)
```

The following example finds the StudentGrade object that has the maximum Grade property:

```
Subject<StudentGrade> grades = new Subject<StudentGrade>();
grades.MaxBy(s => s.Grade)
    .SelectMany(max => max)
    .SubscribeConsole("Maximal object by grade");
```

Emits each maximum item that MaxBy found

```
grades.OnNext(new StudentGrade() { Id = "1", Name = "A", Grade = 85.0 });
grades.OnNext(new StudentGrade() { Id = "2", Name = "B", Grade = 90.0 });
grades.OnNext(new StudentGrade() { Id = "3", Name = "C", Grade = 80.0 });
grades.OnCompleted();
```

After running the example, this is the output:

```
Maximal object by grade - OnNext(Id: 2, Name: B, Grade: 90)
Maximal object by grade - OnCompleted()
```

This example and its output show that you succeeded in finding the student object with the maximum grade—student B with grade 90.

8.4.3 *Writing your aggregation logic with Aggregate and Scan*

In Rx, you can create your own aggregation functions and apply them to an observable sequence. The aggregate functions are invoked for each item that's emitted, together with the aggregated value up to that point. The computed value is the input for the next invocation with the next item.

You can use two operators with aggregate functions:

- Aggregate—Applies a function to each item emitted by an observable, and then emits the computed value upon the source observable completion.
- Scan—Applies a function to each item emitted by a sequential observable, and then emits each successive value.

Figure 8.19 depicts the Aggregate operator, and figure 8.20 depicts the Scan operator.

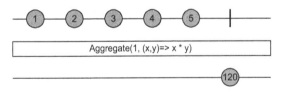

Figure 8.19 The Aggregate operator applies a function to each item emitted by an observable, and then emits the computed value upon the source observable completion.

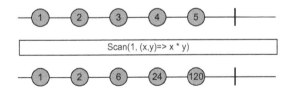

Figure 8.20 The Scan operator applies a function to each item emitted by sequential observables and emits each successive value.

Here's an example that creates the multiplication of all values in an observable sequence, first with Aggregate and then with Scan:

```
Observable.Range(1, 5)
    .Aggregate(1,                          ◁─┘ Sets a seed value
```

```
                (accumulate, currItem) => accumulate * currItem)    ◁─────┐
        .SubscribeConsole("Aggregate");                                   │
                                                                          │
Observable.Range(1, 5)                                                    │
    .Scan(1,                          ◁──┐ Sets a seed value              │
            (accumulate, currItem) => accumulate * currItem)   ◁──────────┘
    .SubscribeConsole("Scan");
```

For each item, receives the accumulator (the
computed value up to this point) and the current item.
The value returned is the new accumulator value.

This is the output produced:

```
Aggregate - OnNext(120)
Aggregate - OnCompleted()
Scan - OnNext(1)
Scan - OnNext(2)
Scan - OnNext(6)
Scan - OnNext(24)
Scan - OnNext(120)
Scan - OnCompleted()
```

In this example, the input observable emits a sequence of values 1 to 5, the Aggregate operator emits the factorial value 120, and Scan emits the factorials 1! 2! 3! 4! 5!

Beside the seed value and the accumulator function, the Aggregate operator provides an overload that you can use to pass a resultSelector function that's invoked for the last value—the aggregate result:

```
IObservable<TResult> Aggregate<TSource, TAccumulate, TResult>(     │ Accumulator
    this IObservable<TSource> source,                              │ function to be
    TAccumulate seed,                  ◁──┐ Initial accumulator value │ invoked on
    Func<TAccumulate, TSource, TAccumulate> accumulator,   ◁──────────┘ each element
    Func<TAccumulate, TResult> resultSelector)   ◁──┐
```

A function to transform the final
accumulator value into the result value

Suppose you need to retrieve the second largest item in an observable. Instead of creating your own variables to store the relevant state and use them inside the aggregate operators by capturing them as closures (mutating state as part of the observable is usually a code smell), you can use the Aggregate operator to encapsulate the mutated state for you. The next example retains the two largest items emitted by an observable (so far) in a sorted collection. And, when the observable is complete, it emits the second largest item.

Listing 8.2   Creating observable with Aggregate operator emitting second-largest item

```
Subject<int> numbers = new Subject<int>();

numbers.Aggregate(
    new SortedSet<int>(),          ◁──┐ Passes a sorted set that'll be
                                       │ used to hold the largest items
```

```
        (largest, item) =>
        {
            largest.Add(item);
            if (largest.Count > 2)
            {
                largest.Remove(largest.First());
            }
            return largest;
        },
        largest => largest.FirstOrDefault())
        .SubscribeConsole();
numbers.OnNext(3);
numbers.OnNext(1);
numbers.OnNext(4);
numbers.OnNext(2);
numbers.OnCompleted();
```

Keeps only the first two largest items by adding them to the sorted collection and removes the first item (the smallest) if needed

Returns collection that contains the two largest items

Because the collection is sorted and contains two items at most, the first item is the second-largest one.

This example uses an empty `SortedSet` as a seed. This class helps keep the items sorted and ensures that there won't be duplicate items in the set. For each item emitted from the source observable, the accumulator function adds an item to the set, and then compacts it to hold two items at most.

When the source observable is complete, the `resultSelector` function takes the first item in the set (if it exists) and returns it. Because `SortedSet` is sorted, and you want to make sure there will be two items at most, the first item is the second greatest that you want to find.

The output from the preceding example is shown here:

```
- OnNext(3)
- OnCompleted()
```

Using `Aggregate` and `Scan` allows you to create your own powerful aggregation functions. In a way, they're the reactive equivalent to a loop, which you would've used for collections in order to produce a single value from it.

8.5   Summary

The querying abilities that Rx provides are rich and extensive. This can sometimes be overwhelming and complex to understand, so I made this chapter easy to digest in order to teach you the fundamentals of writing an Rx query by using some of the most used operators. Here's what I covered:

- The `Select` operator transforms the emitted notification to another form. This includes taking only a subproperty or creating a new object (for example, a `ViewModel`).
- Observables emit other observables or other collections (or items that contain them). The `SelectMany` operator merges the inner observables (or collections) to a flat stream; pass a `collectionSelector` function and you're done.

- The `SelectMany` operator also takes a `resultSelector` function that you can call for every emitted item, together with its source item.
- `SelectMany` is the power force behind the `Let` operator that you can use when manually writing a query.
- The `Where` operator filters emitted notifications, which receive a predicate function to test each notification.
- The `Distinct` operator gets an observable of distinct items.
- The `DistinctUntilChanged` operator gets an observable of distinct consecutive items.
- Rx provides the common statistical aggregation functions that you can apply to an observable. These are `Sum`, `Count`, `Average`, `Max`, and `Min`.
- The `MaxBy` and `MinBy` operators get the maximum and minimum item, respectively, based on a subproperty.
- You can use the `Aggregate` and `Scan` operators to customize the aggregation logic.
- The `Aggregate` operator emits the aggregated result only when the source observable completes.
- The `Scan` operator emits a sequential aggregated result each time a notification is emitted by the source observable.

In this chapter, we dealt only with operators that act in the scope of a single observable. The next chapter describes the operators used to break the observable into finer observables (groups) and to combine multiple observables.

Partitioning and
combining observables

This chapter covers

- Partitioning observables into groups of related notifications
- Emitting chunks of notifications by sliding windows and buffers
- Combining multiple observables into one
- Reacting to patterns of coincidence

A typical application is usually composed of multiple workflows that structure its behavior. In many cases, the application needs to handle and react to more than one data source, UI events, push notifications, remote procedure calls, and so on. Suppose your application needs to consume messages from various sources (such as social networking) and react to all of them in the same way. Or, say your application deals with a source that emits a stream of various kinds of notifications (such as stock prices), and it needs to look at each subgroup of notifications (for each stock) separately and independently. How do you do that?

There are many ways to combine observables and react to a combination of the notifications emitted by them (for example, taking only the latest, pairing, or joining by condition). And, there are different ways to create subgroups from an observable (for example, by time or condition). This chapter takes you to the next level by using concepts you already know from enumerables and applying those to the world of observables.

9.1   Combining observables

Working with a single observable has its benefits; however, the internet is composed of multiple events occurring independently. To react to notifications emitted from multiple observables, Rx provides operators that make it easy to combine the observables.

9.1.1   Pairing items from observables (zipping)

When you need to combine values that are in the same index in two (or more) observables, the `Zip` operator should be your answer. It takes the observables you want to pair and a selector function that describes how to do that. The first item of each observable is zipped together, the second item of each observable is zipped together, and so on.

The arguments for the selector function are the set of values, emitted at the same index (each in its source observable), from the items emitted by the observables you want to zip. The selector function then returns the calculated result from those values.

Suppose you have two temperature sensors in a room that emit values roughly at the same time and you want to show the average temperature from both readings. Here's how to do that with the `Zip` operator:

```
IObservable<double> temp1 = ...
IObservable<double> temp2 = ...

temp1
    .Zip(temp2, (t1, t2) => (t1 + t2)/2)
    .SubscribeConsole("Avg Temp.");
```

A sample output of this program is shown in figure 9.1.

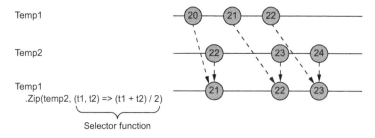

Figure 9.1   The `Zip` operator lets you zip values with the same index from two (or more) observables by using a selector function.

The problem with the Zip operator is that it relies on the index of the values emitted by both observables. If the rate of one of the observables is higher than the other, Zip accumulates the emitted values in memory until the next value is emitted from the second observable (this also means that if the second observable never emits or completes, the values from the first observable will never be used, but still remain in memory). In many cases, you'll want to combine only the latest values emitted by the observables.

9.1.2 Combining the latest emitted values

To combine the set of values last emitted by the observables, use the CombineLatest operator (figure 9.2). Unlike the Zip operator, when one of the observables returns a value, CombineLatest also returns a value, even if a second observable doesn't emit for a long time.

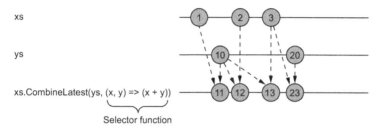

Figure 9.2 The CombineLatest **operator combines the latest emitted values from each observable by using a selector function.**

Consider this example: you have a sensor that monitors heart rate and one that monitors speed. You want to display the most up-to-date value, regardless of the update rate of each sensor. To simulate this case, you'll create the observables as subjects you can control:

```
Subject<int> heartRate = new Subject<int>();
Subject<int> speed = new Subject<int>();

speed.CombineLatest(heartRate,
            (s, h) => String.Format("Heart:{0} Speed:{1}", h, s))
   .SubscribeConsole("Metrics");
```

> **Combines two observables into a string that contains the values from each**

Now you can emit the values from each observable and see what happens:

```
heartRate.OnNext(150);
heartRate.OnNext(151);
heartRate.OnNext(152);
speed.OnNext(30);
speed.OnNext(31);
heartRate.OnNext(153);
heartRate.OnNext(154);
```

The output from this sequence is shown here:

```
Metrics - OnNext(Heart:152 Speed:30)
Metrics - OnNext(Heart:152 Speed:31)
Metrics - OnNext(Heart:153 Speed:31)
Metrics - OnNext(Heart:154 Speed:31)
```

Two things are of note here. First, you can see that the heart-rate value of 152 is emitted twice at the beginning. This is because the `speed` observable emits two values, one after the other, and 152 is the latest value emitted by the `heartRate` observable. The same thing happens when the `heartRate` observable emits its values while the latest speed value is 31 (shown in the last two lines).

The second thing to notice is that when the `heartRate` observable initially produces the values 150 and 151, nothing is emitted by the combined observable. Indeed, `CombineLatest` emits values only if all observables emit a value at least once; otherwise, there isn't a *latest* value from all observables.

One way to overcome *dropped values*, making sure the combined observable emits a value even if all observables haven't yet emitted a value, is to add a value at the beginning of each observable by using the `StartWith` operator. For example, changing the previous snippet to the following prints the heart-rate values of 150 and 151 as well:

```
speed.StartWith(0)
    .CombineLatest(heartRate.StartWith(0),
                    (s, h) => String.Format("Heart:{0} Speed:{1}", h, s))
    .SubscribeConsole("Metrics");
```

> **NOTE** Currently, the Rx codebase also includes the operator `WithLatestFrom`, which is like a one-way `CombineLatest`. `WithLatestFrom` combines each value from the first observable with the latest value from the second observable, but not the other way around. This operator isn't included in Rx versions prior to 3.0, which this book is using.

Combining observables isn't restricted only to taking a value from each observable and creating a unified result from them. As you'll see next, another combination includes creating a unified observable and placing the values emitted from each observable into a single stream.

9.1.3 *Concatenating observables*

The `Concat` operator connects two or more observables of the same type into a single stream (figure 9.3). When the first observable completes, `Concat` links the values from the second observable to the resulting observable, even if they were emitted long

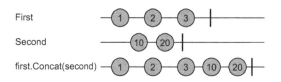

Figure 9.3 The `Concat` **operator concatenates the second observable sequence to the first observable sequence upon successful termination of the first.**

before the first observable completes. It's important to note that the `Concat` operator subscribes itself to the second observable only after the first observable completes, so if the second observable is *hot* and notifications were emitted before subscribing, they won't be part of the resulting observable emissions.

Confusion about hot and cold observables and the `Concat` operator may arise when you use it in asynchronous operations. For example, say you use `Concat` to ensure that the results from two asynchronous operations are emitted in an order that isn't the expected order returned by asynchronous operations. Remember, when tasks are converted to observables, an `AsyncSubject` is created so the value of the asynchronous computation won't get dropped, which turns a hot operation into a cold observable.

The following example simulates two asynchronous operations that load messages from Facebook and Twitter. Facebook is slower in this case (due to the use of the `Delay` operator), but because I'm using `Concat`, the Facebook messages appear first in the output:

```
using System.Reactive.Threading.Tasks;

Task<string[]> facebookMessages = Task.Delay(10).ContinueWith(_=>new[]
    {"Facebook1", "Facebook2"});
Task<string[]> twitterStatuses =
    Task.FromResult( new[] {"Twitter1", "Twitter2"});
Observable.Concat(facebookMessages.ToObservable(),
                  twitterStatuses.ToObservable())
    .SelectMany(messages=>messages)
    .SubscribeConsole("Concat Messages");
```

> **Simulates an asynchronous operation that's slow (takes 10 ms to complete)** — (points to `Task.Delay(10).ContinueWith(_=>new[]`)
>
> **Simulates an asynchronous operation that's fast** — (points to `Task.FromResult( new[] {"Twitter1", "Twitter2"});`)

Running this example shows this output:

```
Concat Messages - OnNext(Facebook1)
Concat Messages - OnNext(Facebook2)
Concat Messages - OnNext(Twitter1)
Concat Messages - OnNext(Twitter2)
Concat Messages - OnCompleted()
```

Even though the results from Facebook take longer to arrive (due to the use of `Delay`), they're still present first. At times, however, that order between the observables has no meaning, and you want to react to the notifications emitted by the observables the moment they're pushed. For this, you need the `Merge` operator.

9.1.4   *Merging observables*

Merging observables means you want to route the notifications from the source observables into a single observable, so that when a notification is emitted by one of the sources, it's also emitted by the merged observable (figure 9.4). This allows

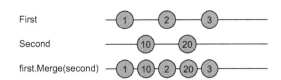

Figure 9.4   The `Merge` operator merges the notifications from the source observables into a single observable sequence.

you to react to the notifications as fast as possible, no matter what source observable emitted them.

The following example simulates two asynchronous operations that load messages from Facebook and Twitter. Facebook is slower in this case (due to the use of the `Delay` operator), but because I'm using `Merge`, the Twitter messages are shown first and only then. When the Facebook operation completes, its messages are then shown:

```
Task<string[]> facebookMessages =
    Task.Delay(10)
        .ContinueWith(_ => new[] { "Facebook1", "Facebook2" });
Task<string[]> twitterStatuses =
    Task.FromResult(new[] { "Twitter1", "Twitter2" });

Observable.Merge(
        facebookMessages.ToObservable(),
        twitterStatuses.ToObservable())
    .SelectMany(messages => messages)
    .SubscribeConsole("Merged Messages");

Console.ReadLine();
```

Simulates a slow asynchronous operation (takes 10 ms to complete)

Simulates a fast asynchronous operation

Now, even though the Facebook asynchronous operation is passed first to the `Merge` operator, the first values you'll see printed are those from Twitter because this operation completes first:

```
Merged Messages - OnNext(Twitter1)
Merged Messages - OnNext(Twitter2)
Merged Messages - OnNext(Facebook1)
Merged Messages - OnNext(Facebook2)
Merged Messages - OnCompleted()
```

`Concat` and `Merge` are useful for combining a fixed set of observables when you write your code, but your application might create observables in a more dynamic way (based on user usage, for example). You'll want those operators to be more dynamic with their inputs because, as mentioned in chapter 1, everything is a stream.

9.1.5   *Dynamic concatenating and merging*

Both `Concat` and `Merge` let you pass not only a fixed collection of observables you want to combine, but also an observable of the observables to combine. This is the construct:

```
IObservable<TSource> Concat<TSource>(
    this IObservable<IObservable<TSource>> sources)
IObservable<TSource> Merge<TSource>(
    this IObservable<IObservable<TSource>> sources)
```

These overloads let you add `Merge` or `Concat` as part of a broader pipeline; for example, when a source observable emits a value that'll be transformed into another observable (like one that represents an asynchronous operation). Suppose you want to create an observable from the text-changed event of a text box, and when the text changes, you want to make a call to a remote search service and show all the results from all the searches.

Simulates an observable that emits the text in a text box when it changes

```
IObservable<string> texts = new[] {"Hello", "World"}.ToObservable()
texts
    .Select(txt => Observable.Return(txt + "-Result"))
    .Merge()
    .SubscribeConsole("Merging from observable");
```

Transforms the text into an observable, simulating a call to a remote search service. resulting in an observable of observables.

Running the example yields this output:

```
Merging from observable - OnNext(Hello-Result)
Merging from observable - OnNext(World-Result)
Merging from observable - OnCompleted()
```

NOTE Conceptually, the operator `SelectMany` (described broadly in chapter 8) operates the same as calling `Select` and `Merge`.

As with dynamic allocations, without dynamic operations, you sometimes need to set a limit; otherwise, performance decreases (just like overallocations that may cause `Out-OfMemoryException` or responsiveness degradation). Luckily, Rx provides control over this.

CONTROLLING THE CONCURRENCY

`Concat` subscribes itself to an observable only when the previous observable completes, but `Merge` needs to subscribe to all the observables at the beginning of its operation. Subscribing to many observables might pose a performance problem for your application or a heavy load on the observable source (such as a remote service). For those reasons, you might need to restrict the amount of concurrent subscriptions that `Merge` is allowed to make. Here's an example that shows how to do this:

```
IObservable<string> first =
    Observable.Interval(TimeSpan.FromSeconds(1))
        .Select(i=>"First"+i)
        .Take(2);
IObservable<string> second =
    Observable.Interval(TimeSpan.FromSeconds(1))
        .Select(i=> "Second" + i)
        .Take(2);
IObservable<string> third = Observable.Interval(TimeSpan.FromSeconds(1))
        .Select(i=> "Third" + i).Take(2);
new[] {first,second,third}.ToObservable()
    .Merge(2)
    .SubscribeConsole("Merge with 2 concurrent subscriptions");
 Console.ReadLine();
```

Creates three observables that emit a value every second, stopping them after two emissions

Restricts the Merge operator to two concurrent subscriptions

Creates an observable that emits the observables created previously

In this case, you have three observables that can emit notifications concurrently. If `Merge` subscribes to all of them, you'd see the messages generated from the three observables intertwined. Instead, you get the following:

```
Merge with 2 concurrent subscriptions - OnNext(Second0)
Merge with 2 concurrent subscriptions - OnNext(First0)
Merge with 2 concurrent subscriptions - OnNext(Second1)
Merge with 2 concurrent subscriptions - OnNext(First1)
Merge with 2 concurrent subscriptions - OnNext(Third0)
Merge with 2 concurrent subscriptions - OnNext(Third1)
Merge with 2 concurrent subscriptions - OnCompleted()
```

Note that the notifications emitted by the third observable are separate from the others. This is because it's subscribed to only when one of the first two observables completes (after 2 seconds). If after the first observable completes, the second observable still emits notifications, you'd see the merged result from the second and third observables.

9.1.6 *Switching to the next observable*

Consider the preceding example in which for every text change, you make a call to a remote search service and then display *all* the results onscreen. A more realistic approach is that you'd show only the latest results.

Now imagine that while waiting for the search results to arrive from the back end, another search is executed (the text has changed again). In this case, you'd unsubscribe from the previous asynchronous search operation and start a new search to which you'd now be subscribed.

To accomplish the task of switching to a new observable when it's available, you need to use the `Switch` operator, depicted in figure 9.5.

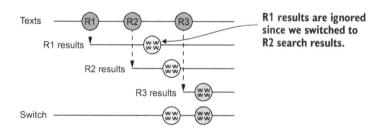

Figure 9.5 The `Switch` operator takes an observable that emits observables and creates a single observable that emits the notifications from the most recent observable.

Here's a simple program that simulates the text changes shown in the marble diagram. You use the `Delay` operator to add a little delay to R1 emissions so the system will switch to the R2 observable before the R results are available.

Listing 9.1 Switching to the most recent search results with the `Switch` operator

```
var textsSubject = new Subject<string>();
IObservable<string> texts = textsSubject.AsObservable();
texts
    .Select(txt => Observable.Return(txt + "-Result")
                .Delay(TimeSpan.FromMilliseconds(txt == "R1" ? 10 : 0)))
    .Switch()
    .SubscribeConsole("Merging from observable");

textsSubject.OnNext("R1");
textsSubject.OnNext("R2");
Thread.Sleep(20);
textsSubject.OnNext("R3");
```

Adds a delay to R results so the next search term will be switched to before the results return

Adds a short delay so the system will have time to process R2 results before R3 retakes control

---

SWITCHING TO THE FIRST OBSERVABLE TO EMIT

Imagine you have multiple observables that represent options to receive the same sequence of notifications (for example, multiple service representatives in real life), but you need to select only one of them—the one that's the fastest (the first to emit).

This can be a selection between servers or a selection between a computed result and a cached one. `Switch` won't help here because it'll bind to the first observable to emit and then switch to the slower one.

The `Amb` (short for *ambiguity*) operator works similarly to the `Switch` operator, but instead of switching to a new observable each time a new one is emitted, `Amb` switches only to the first observable to emit. Think of it this way: if all the observables are considered equally fit as the source, you want them to duel, and the first one to shoot wins.

Here's an example:

```
var server1 =
    Observable.Interval(TimeSpan.FromSeconds(2))
            .Select(i => "Server1-" + i);
var server2 =
    Observable.Interval(TimeSpan.FromSeconds(1))
            .Select(I => "Server2-" + i);

Observable.Amb(server1, server2)
    .Take(3)
    .SubscribeConsole("Amb");
Console.ReadLine();
```

In this case, the `server2` observable emits first, so you'll see only the values with the prefix `Server2-`.

> **TIP** You can also write the example like this:
> `server1.Amb(server2).Take(3).SubscribeConsole("Amb");`.

So far, you've learned how to combine and pair observables. Next, you'll get to know techniques for breaking an observable into subobservables.

9.2 Grouping elements from the observable

The elements that observables emit can be grouped based on a particular condition. Unlike collections or datasets, grouping elements from observables creates a group with an unfixed size, in which the number of elements is unknown and can be infinite. This is because you can't predict what elements will be emitted by the observable in the future.

To group elements from an observable, you need to generate the group as an observable by itself; that is, an observable that emits a notification for every element that's part of the group. For example, using the `GroupBy` operator, you can split an information stream of people into a group of males and a group of females (figure 9.6).

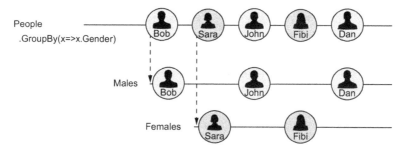

Figure 9.6 The `GroupBy` operator groups the elements of an observable sequence according to a specified key selector function (for example, splitting a stream of people into a group of males and a group of females). Each group is an observable of the group elements.

The basic `GroupBy` signature looks like this:

```
IObservable<IGroupedObservable<TKey, TSource>> GroupBy<TSource, TKey>(
    this IObservable<TSource> source,
    Func<TSource, TKey> keySelector)
```

Note that the return type is an observable of grouped observables. The grouped observable is itself an observable that also includes the property `Key`, which holds the key that describes each element it emits.

GroupBy also includes overloads that let you pass an elementSelector (to decide how each element will be transformed before being emitted by the grouped observable) and a capacity (to control the maximum number of groups that can live concurrently).

By separating the elements into different observables, you can create separate queries for each group. For example, you can now get the average age for females and for males:

```
var genderAge =
    from gender in people.GroupBy(p => p.Gender)      ⟵  Groups the elements in the
    from avg in gender.Average(p => p.Age)                people observable by gender
    select new {Gender=gender.Key, AvgAge=avg};   ⟵  Averages each
                                                       grouped observable

genderAge.SubscribeConsole("Gender Age");
```

You can also use the GroupBy query syntax clause for the preceding example:

```
var genderAge =
    from p in people
    group p by p.Gender
    into gender
    from avg in gender.Average(p => p.Age)
    select new { Gender = gender.Key, AvgAge = avg };
```

Next, you'll look at another concept that's clear in the world of collections but is a little tricky in the world of observables: joins.

9.3 *Joining observables (coincidence-based combining)*

Combining observables isn't restricted to only using the elements emitted to create a new type of result. Another interesting combination is to find relationships and logical correlations between elements—when trying to answer which elements exist in the same time frame, for example.

When querying database tables or collections of items, joining entities is clear—you combine fields from two or more entities by using values that are common to each. How can you apply this definition to the world of reactive streams? Rx bases commonality on the *coincidence of occurrence*, meaning when notifications are occurring in the same time frame.

In short, combining elements from various observables based on the coincidence that they exist in the same time frame is what we call joining. You can join two or more observables in two ways. The first emits joint pairs into a single flat stream. The second creates groups of correlated items and emits an item into a *correlation group*.

9.3.1 *Joining to a flat stream*

Let's start with an example of how joining observables works. Suppose you're running a statistical study and want to get notifications on the occurrence of males and females

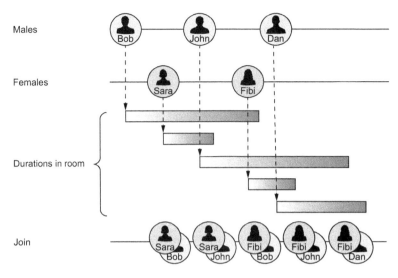

Figure 9.7   The `Join` operator combines items emitted by two observables when an item from one observable is emitted during a time frame of an emitted item from the other observable.

that are in the same room at the same time. This is a classic case for joins, as shown in figure 9.7.

To create joins between observables, you use the `Join` operator, which correlates the elements of two sequences based on overlapping durations. The signature for `Join` is complex and requires some explanation:

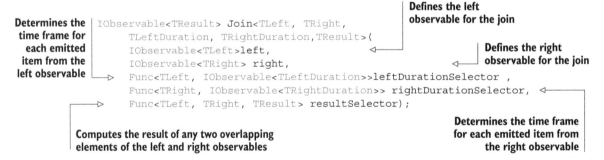

The tricky part of the method signature is the *duration selector functions*. Those functions receive an emitted element and return an observable whose emissions determine the end of the time frame for the element.

Suppose you have a sensor, coded as a hot observable of `DoorEvent` objects, that monitors people who enter and exit a room. You want to emit all the males and females that are in the same room at the same time:

```
IObservable<DoorOpened> doorOpened = doorOpenedSubject.AsObservable();
```

DoorEvent is defined as follows:

```
class DoorOpened
{
    public string Name { get; set; }
    public OpenDirection Direction { get; set; }   ◄──┐  Specifies whether the person is
    public Gender Gender { get; set; }                   entering or leaving the room
}
```

You can extract the observable of the males entering the room and the females entering the room like this:

```
var entrances = doorOpened.Where(o => o.Direction ==
    OpenDirection.Entering);
var maleEntering = entrances.Where(x => x.Gender == Gender.Male);
var femaleEntering = entrances.Where(x => x.Gender == Gender.Female);
```

In the same way, you can extract the observable of those leaving:

```
var exits = doorOpened.Where(o => o.Direction == OpenDirection.Leaving);
var maleExiting = exits.Where(x => x.Gender == Gender.Male);
var femaleExiting = exits.Where(x => x.Gender == Gender.Female);
```

Now, you'll want to join the occurrence of males in the room with the occurrence of females in the room. For that you need to define for each notification (male or female entering) the time frame that marks the existence in the room. With the reactive approach, defining the time frame means defining an observable that emits (or completes) when the time frame closes. Here's how you bring that into action:

Defines the time frame for each man entering the room. When the man enters the room, the time window closes.

Creates a join operation for the males and females entering the room

```
maleEntering
    .Join(femaleEntering,
        male => maleExiting.Where(exit => exit.Name == male.Name),
        female => femaleExiting.Where(exit => female.Name == exit.Name),  ◄──┐
        (m, f) => new {Male = m.Name, Female = f.Name})
    .SubscribeConsole("Together At Room");
```

Packs the male and female pairs that are in the same room together

Defines the time frame for each woman entering the room. When the woman enters the room, the time window closes.

> **TIP** An interesting type of a time-frame observable is one that uses the same observable that emits the elements as the one that defines the time frame. By doing this, you're expressing that the time frame for an element is the time until the next element is emitted.

To test your code, you'll create a subject that acts as the back end of your observable and then you'll emit notifications that simulate the sequence shown previously in figure 9.7:

```
doorOpenedSubject.OnNext(
    new DoorOpened("Bob", Gender.Male, OpenDirection.Entering));
doorOpenedSubject.OnNext(
```

```
        new DoorOpened("Sara", Gender.Female, OpenDirection.Entering));
doorOpenedSubject.OnNext(
        new DoorOpened("John", Gender.Male, OpenDirection.Entering));
doorOpenedSubject.OnNext(
        new DoorOpened("Sara", Gender.Female, OpenDirection.Leaving));
doorOpenedSubject.OnNext(
        new DoorOpened("Fibi", Gender.Female, OpenDirection.Entering));
doorOpenedSubject.OnNext(
        new DoorOpened("Bob", Gender.Male, OpenDirection.Leaving));
doorOpenedSubject.OnNext(
        new DoorOpened("Dan", Gender.Male, OpenDirection.Entering));
doorOpenedSubject.OnNext(
        new DoorOpened("Fibi", Gender.Female, OpenDirection.Leaving));
doorOpenedSubject.OnNext(
        new DoorOpened("John", Gender.Male, OpenDirection.Leaving));
doorOpenedSubject.OnNext(
        new DoorOpened("Dan", Gender.Male, OpenDirection.Leaving));

// Rest of code that simulates participants leaving the room
```

Running this procedure produces the following output:

```
Together At Room - OnNext({ Male = Bob, Female = Sara })
Together At Room - OnNext({ Male = John, Female = Sara })
Together At Room - OnNext({ Male = Bob, Female = Fibi })
Together At Room - OnNext({ Male = John, Female = Fibi })
Together At Room - OnNext({ Male = Dan, Female = Fibi })
```

WRITING JOINS WITH QUERY SYNTAX

The C# compiler lets you write joins with a LINQ query. The `join` clause is shown here:

```
from [left] in [leftObservable]
join [right] in [rightObservable] on [leftDuration] equals [rightDuration]
select ...
```

With the query syntax approach, finding the male and female pairs that are in the room at the same time looks like this:

```
from male in maleEntering
join female in femaleEntering on maleEntering.Where(exit =>
exit.Name == male.Name) equals
femaleExiting.Where(exit => female.Name == exit.Name)
select new {Male = male.Name, Female = female.Name};
```

The `join` clause creates a single observable on which all the correlations are emitted. Sometimes, however, a divide-and-conquer approach is easier to work with.

In the spirit of this approach, you'd like to receive per each male, all the occurrences of that male with the females in the room with him. So each male becomes a group key for the group of all the associated females, and this group is an observable of those females. So instead of one observable with all the pairs, you'll have multiple observables—one for each group. For this behavior, you need to use the `GroupJoin` operator.

9.3.2 Joining into groups

The `GroupJoin` operator lets you correlate the elements of two observable sequences based on overlapping durations and combines the elements that correlate with each element into a group that's itself an observable (figure 9.8). For example, in a statistical observation experiment, you want to emit, for each male, all the females that were in the same room with him. You'll call this observable of associated females per male a *group*.

The motivation for this group, based on coincidence, is that for each group you can define a finer query in a much easier way. For example, what's the average age of the women group?

The `GroupJoin` operator has a signature similar to `Join`:

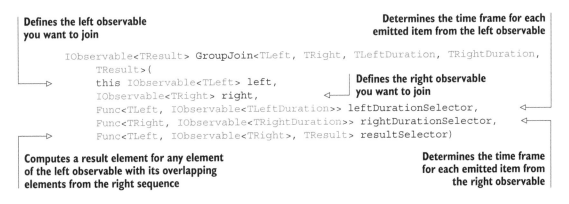

Defines the left observable you want to join

Determines the time frame for each emitted item from the left observable

```
IObservable<TResult> GroupJoin<TLeft, TRight, TLeftDuration, TRightDuration,
    TResult>(
    this IObservable<TLeft> left,
    IObservable<TRight> right,
    Func<TLeft, IObservable<TLeftDuration>> leftDurationSelector,
    Func<TRight, IObservable<TRightDuration>> rightDurationSelector,
    Func<TLeft, IObservable<TRight>, TResult> resultSelector)
```

Defines the right observable you want to join

Computes a result element for any element of the left observable with its overlapping elements from the right sequence

Determines the time frame for each emitted item from the right observable

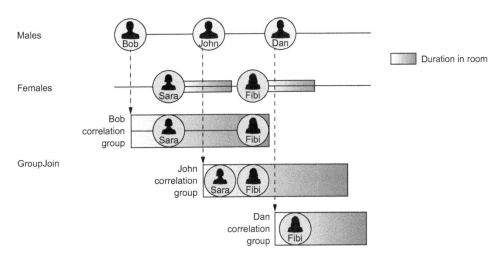

Figure 9.8 The `GroupJoin` operator correlates elements from two observables based on overlapping duration time frames. The elements from the second observable are grouped by the element from the first observable to which they correlate.

Suppose you want to extend your example from the previous section (finding all the pairs of males and females in a room together). Now, you want to add a counter that shows the number of females that each male was in the room with, up to the current point.

As before, you have observables that emit the males and females that enter and exit the room:

```
var maleEntering = entrances.Where(x => x.Gender == Gender.Male);
var femaleEntering = entrances.Where(x => x.Gender == Gender.Female);
var maleExiting = exits.Where(x => x.Gender == Gender.Male);
var femaleExiting = exits.Where(x => x.Gender == Gender.Female);
```

Now you can use `GroupJoin` to create the groups of correlations. For each male, you create an object that contains the male's name and the observable of females that correlate to him:

```
var malesAcquaintances =
    maleEntering
        .GroupJoin(femaleEntering,
            male => maleExiting.Where(exit => exit.Name == male.Name),
            female => femaleExiting.Where(exit => female.Name == exit.Name),
            (m, females) => new {Male = m.Name, Females = females});
```

Then you can create a query for the `malesAcquaintances` observable that computes the number of females each man meets in the room and subscribe to it:

```
var amountPerUser =
    from acquaintances in malesAcquaintances
    from cnt in acquaintances.Females.Scan(0, (acc, curr) => acc + 1)
    select new {acquaintances.Male, cnt};

amountPerUser.SubscribeConsole("Amount of meetings for User");
```

Running this example with the males and females shown in figure 9.8 generates this output:

```
Amount of meetings per User - OnNext({ Male = Bob, cnt = 1 })
Amount of meetings per User - OnNext({ Male = John, cnt = 1 })
Amount of meetings per User - OnNext({ Male = Bob, cnt = 2 })
Amount of meetings per User - OnNext({ Male = John, cnt = 2 })
Amount of meetings per User - OnNext({ Male = Dan, cnt = 1 })
```

Note that a notification emits each time the count changes.

GROUPJOIN WITH QUERY SYNTAX

For simplicity, you can write a `GroupJoin` clause by using the LINQ query syntax. `GroupJoin` has the same format as the clause used in LINQ, but the meaning of its parts is as follows:

```
from [left] in [leftObservable]
join [right] in [rightObservable] on [leftDuration] equals [rightDuration]
    into [correlationGroup]
select ...
```

This is how you'd correlate the males and females in the same room:

```
from male in maleEntering
join female in femaleEntering on maleExiting.Where(e => e.Name == male.Name)
equals femaleExiting.Where(e => female.Name == e.Name)
into maleEncounters
select new { Male = male.Name, Females = maleEncounters };
```

Joins are a powerful tool in the Rx toolbox, as they allow you to find correlations between elements and to capture coincidence.

At this point in the chapter, you already have a good idea of how to connect different observables and a basic understanding of how to split a single observable into sub-observables (groups). Next, you'll learn more useful techniques for breaking the observable into parts.

9.4 *Buffers and sliding windows*

When thinking about observables, you'll look at them in many cases as a representation of an unbounded stream of elements (or notifications). Working with unbounded things, whether they're observables or collections, isn't easy to grasp. As humans, we like to break them into smaller, bounded things to process each separately until, finally, we reflect their result in the "big picture" of the entire unbounded set. This is known as the *divide-and-conquer approach*. With reactive programming, you can do that in two ways:

- Buffering breaks the observable sequence into bounded collections called *buffers*.
- Windowing breaks the observable sequence into finer observables to define their duration.

The important difference between the two is that with windowing, you get the emission as soon as it arrives, and with buffering you get the buffer's emission only when it closes (either because it's full or because the buffering time is over), as shown in figure 9.9.

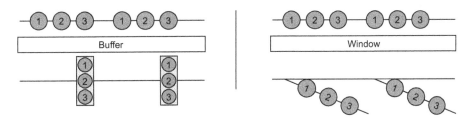

Figure 9.9 Buffering versus windowing: with windowing, you get the emissions as soon as they arrive, and with buffering you get the buffer only when it closes.

Two definitions of window

The word *window* is a little confusing here because it represents two different but related things.

First, *window* is the substream of elements under a certain boundary (duration or amount).

Second, *window* is the logical boundary in which elements are gathered from the stream.

In figure 9.9 you can say that the buffer is created from a *time frame (window)* that spans over the three items, which are emitted and then collected to the buffer.

You can also say that the three items that are emitted in that *time frame* are emitted to an observable that we call a *window*.

You can define three types of windows when you consider them as containers of elements over time:

- *Tumbling windows* are a series of fixed-sized, nonoverlapping, contiguous time intervals.
- *Hopping windows* are a series of windows that "hop" forward in time by a fixed period.
- *Sliding windows* are a type of hopping window in which the window width is larger than the "hop," causing the windows to overlap.

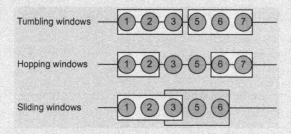

9.4.1   *Buffering*

With buffering, you can wrap consecutive elements emitted by an observable into a buffer and create an observable of collections, but not of single elements. You can buffer by time, number of items, or any logical duration you specify by using an observable whose notifications define when the buffer closes.

Suppose your application connects to your bike's speedometer, which pushes the speed at a constant rate. You want your application to show how your acceleration changes. To do that, you need to get two consecutive readings and calculate the difference between them. You can use Buffer to accomplish that, where the buffering is done with a sliding window of two items.

Figure 9.10 shows the marble diagram of what you're trying to achieve.

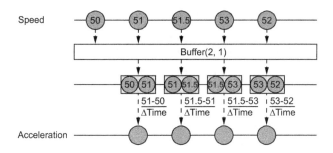

Figure 9.10 A marble diagram of acceleration calculated with the `Buffer` operator

This listing shows the code for the marble diagram in figure 9.10.

Listing 9.2 Using `Buffer` to find the deltas between two speedometer readings

```
IObservable<double> speedReadings = ...                              An observable
                                                                     that emits
Double timeDelta = 0.000277777777777778; //1 second in hours unit    speed in MPH
                                                                     every 1 second
Var accelerations =
    From buffer in speedReadings.Buffer(count: 2, skip: 1)
    Where buffer.Count==2
    Let speedDelta = buffer[1] - buffer[0]
    Select speedDelta/timeDelta;

accelerations.SubscribeConsole("Acceleration");
```

Applies the Buffer operator on the observable to wrap the emitted items into

Specifies the number of items to be buffered (the last item emitted by the observable will be wrapped inside a buffer alone)

Calculates the delta between two speedometer readings that were buffered

In this example, you use the query syntax approach because it allows you to use the `let` keyword to introduce new subcalculations that make your code smaller. After applying the `Buffer` operator on the `speedReadings` observable, you get an observable of buffers with two consecutive items.

> **TIP** Instead of creating a buffer of two consecutive elements to find the speed delta, you could use the `Zip` operator like this: `speedReadings.Zip (speedReadings.Skip(1), (x,y)=> y-x)`. This zips the observable with a shifted version of itself.

You can see in the example that you provide two arguments to the `Buffer` operator by using this overload:

```
IObservable<IList<TSource>> Buffer<TSource>(IObservable<TSource> source,
        int count,
        int skip);
```

The first argument passed is the number of items you want in each buffer, and the second argument (called `skip`) defines the number of notifications that need to be emitted when the first buffer opens, before another buffer will be opened. The combinations of the two arguments create the various types of windows (as a container of elements over time, explained in the beginning of this section), as shown in figure 9.11:

- *Tumbling window.* If `skip` is the same as the number of items in the buffer, a buffer opens the moment the previous one closes.
- *Hopping window.* If `skip` is larger than the number of items in the buffer, then after a buffer is closed, the next buffer opens only after `count-skip` (count minus `skip`) elements have been emitted.
- *Sliding window.* If `skip` is smaller than the number of items a buffer contains, then the buffer overlaps with the next one and shares some of the items.

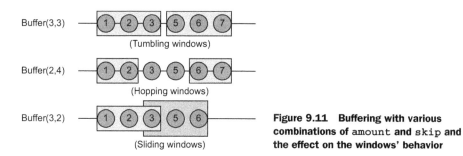

Figure 9.11   Buffering with various combinations of `amount` and `skip` and the effect on the windows' behavior

`Buffer` has overloads that let you make the buffering by time span, or you can set the buffering to be both by time and number of items, whichever happens first:

```
IObservable<IList<TSource>> Buffer<TSource>(IObservable<TSource> source,
    TimeSpan timeSpan);
IObservable<IList<TSource>> Buffer<TSource>(IObservable<TSource> source,
    TimeSpan timeSpan,
    TimeSpan timeShift);
IObservable<IList<TSource>> Buffer<TSource>(IObservable<TSource> source,
    TimeSpan timeSpan,
    Int count);
```

Buffer until timeSpan is reached or until the number in the buffer is equal to the provided count

Interval between creation of consecutive buffers

If you need more control over when the buffer starts and when it closes, you can use the `Buffer` overload that accepts observables as its triggers for starting or closing a buffer.

If the closing of a buffer triggers the opening of the next buffer, use this overload:

```
IObservable<IList<TSource>> Buffer<TSource, TBufferBoundary>(
    IObservable<TSource> source,
    IObservable<TBufferBoundary> bufferBoundaries);
```

Closes the current buffer and opens the next one by emitting a notification

If a single observable for controlling the closing of the buffer (and opening the next one) isn't enough for your needs, and you need to create a specific duration for each buffer that's opened, consider using this overload:

```
IObservable<IList<TSource>> Buffer<TSource, TBufferClosing>(
    IObservable<TSource> source,
    Func<IObservable<TBufferClosing>> bufferClosingSelector);
```

> Called when a buffer is opened and returns an observable that triggers the buffer closure by emitting a notification

If buffers can open and close independently, consider using this overload:

```
IObservable<IList<TSource>> Buffer<TSource, TBufferOpening,
                                    TBufferClosing>(
    IObservable<TSource> source,
    IObservable<TBufferOpening> bufferOpenings,
    Func<TBufferOpening, IObservable<TBufferClosing>>
    bufferClosingSelector);
```

> Triggers the opening of a buffer by emitting a notification

> Returns an observable that triggers the buffer closure by emitting a notification

Suppose you're writing a chat messaging application that can receive messages at a rapid rate. Because you don't want to block your UI, you need to protect it from too many updates in a short period of time. What you want is to wait until there's a short pause between the messages and then put all the messages on the screen at once. To do that, you can buffer the chat messages and control the buffering with another observable that emits when there's a short pause:

```
IObservable<string> messages = ...
```

> Emits messages; some may be received at a high rate.

```
messages.Buffer(messages.Throttle(TimeSpan.FromMilliseconds(100)))
    .SelectMany((b, i) =>
b.Select(m => string.Format("Buffer {0} - {1}", i, m)))
    .SubscribeConsole("Hi-Rate Messages");
Console.ReadLine();
```

> Buffering messages into buffers that are closed when there's a delay of 100 ms between the messages

To simulate the situation of high-rate messages, you'll create an observable that emits four messages, one every 50 ms, and then pauses for 200 ms before it emits four more messages. (Note that I'm converting the cold observable into a hot one in order to get realistic results):

```
var coldMessages = Observable.Interval(TimeSpan.FromMilliseconds(50))
    .Take(4)
    .Select(x => "Message " + x);

IObservable<string> messages =
    coldMessages.Concat(
        coldMessages.DelaySubscription(TimeSpan.FromMilliseconds(200)))
```

```
        .Publish()
        .RefCount();

//Rest of the example as it is shown in the snippet and use the Buffer
    operator
```

Running this example displays these results:

```
Hi-Rate Messages - OnNext(Buffer 0 - Message 0)
Hi-Rate Messages - OnNext(Buffer 0 - Message 1)
Hi-Rate Messages - OnNext(Buffer 0 - Message 2)
Hi-Rate Messages - OnNext(Buffer 0 - Message 3)
Hi-Rate Messages - OnNext(Buffer 1 - Message 0)
Hi-Rate Messages - OnNext(Buffer 1 - Message 1)
Hi-Rate Messages - OnNext(Buffer 1 - Message 2)
Hi-Rate Messages - OnNext(Buffer 1 - Message 3)
Hi-Rate Messages - OnCompleted()
```

With the different overloads of the `Buffer` operator, you can control when a buffer is opened and when it's closed. Still, your observer receives the elements inside the buffer only when the buffer closes, which can take some time (depending on your logic).

If you need to perform any operations on the elements inside the buffer (such as summing or filtering them), you can do that only at the end of each buffer. For cases like this, requiring a more "live" operation, you should use the `Window` operator.

9.4.2   *Windowing the observable sequence*

The `Window` operator lets you fragment the observable sequence into windows along temporal boundaries or capacity. A window is an observable that emits the elements in that temporal boundary (figure 9.12). The `Window` operator looks similar to the `Buffer` operator, but instead of wrapping all the elements of the buffer inside a collection that emits when the buffer closes, a window emits the items as soon as they arrive.

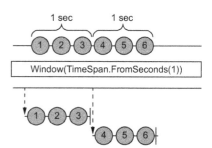

Figure 9.12   The `Window` operator splits the observable sequence into sub-observables based on temporal boundaries or capacity.

Suppose you have an application for a call center that collects donations. The work is done in shifts of 1 hour, and you want to see how many donations were collected in each shift.

In this case, working with `Buffer` isn't sufficient because you'll get the sum of the donations only at the end of the 1-hour window. Instead, you'll use the `Window` operator so that values are summed and displayed immediately onscreen:

```
IObservable<decimal> donations = ...

var windows = donations.Window(TimeSpan.FromHours(1));

var donationsSums =
    from window in windows.Do(_ => Console.WriteLine("New Window"))
```

Prints a message when a new window is opened (and the previous one closed).

```
from sum in window.Scan((prevSum, donation) => prevSum+donation)
select sum;

donationsSums.SubscribeConsole("donations in shift");
```

Creates an aggregated computation and emits the value when the computation changes

The donations observable is broken into non-overlapping windows of 1 hour each. Then, you take each window and apply the `Scan` operator to sum all the values of the donations made. `Scan` emits the summation when the values change (as opposed to `Aggregate`, which emits when the observable completes).

The `donationsSums` observable is a flat observable that emits the summations from all the windows. Because you've added the `Do` operator to the `windows` observable, you'll see a message between each window. Here's the output I received when running the example for two shifts with the sample donation values:

```
Shift 1—50$, 55$, 60$
Shift 2—49$, 48$, 45$
Output:
New Window
donations in shift - OnNext(50)
donations in shift - OnNext(105)
donations in shift - OnNext(165)
New Window
donations in shift - OnNext(49)
donations in shift - OnNext(97)
donations in shift - OnNext(142)
donations in shift - OnCompleted()
```

The `Window` operator has some overloads that let you control when the window is opened and when it closes. Windows can be opened and closed based on the number of items they contain or by the duration of time they should be opened. You can also specify the number of items to be skipped between them or the duration of a pause between closing a window and opening another.

Here's a small subset of these overloads (you'll find them similar to the ones that the `Buffer` operator provides):

```
IObservable<IObservable<TSource>> Window<TSource>(
    IObservable<TSource> source,
    int count,
    int skip);
IObservable<IObservable<TSource>> Window<TSource>(
    IObservable<TSource> source,
    TimeSpan timeSpan,
    TimeSpan timeShift);
IObservable<IObservable<TSource>> Window<TSource>(
    IObservable<TSource> source,
    TimeSpan timeSpan,
    int count);
```

Figure 9.13   Fixed windows versus sliding windows

If the number of items to skip (or the time shift) is less than the number of items in the window (or the window duration), a sliding window is created, and there will be an overlap between the two windows, as shown in figure 9.13.

DYNAMIC WINDOWS

Windows can open and close dynamically, based on your own logic that might depend on other observables. You can define the window closure strategy differently for each window by providing a function that creates an observable per window. This observable determines when the window closes by emitting a notification on completion:

```
IObservable<IObservable<TSource>> Window<TSource, TWindowClosing>(
    IObservable<TSource> source,
    Func<IObservable<TWindowClosing>> windowClosingSelector);
```

Opening a window can be controlled in a similar fashion. You can provide an observable to the `Window` operator that triggers the opening of a window by emitting a notification:

```
IObservable<IObservable<TSource>> Window<TSource, TWindowOpening, TWindow-
    Closing>(
    IObservable<TSource> source,
    IObservable<TWindowOpening> windowOpenings,        ← Triggers the opening of a window
    Func<TWindowOpening, IObservable<TWindowClosing>> windowClosingSelector);
                                                            by emitting a notification
```

Executes when a window opens and returns an
observable that triggers the window closure by emitting

If you want to create nonoverlapping windows and control the window boundaries by your own logic, you can use this overload:

```
IObservable<IObservable<TSource>> Window<TSource, TWindowBoundary>(
    IObservable<TSource> source,
    IObservable<TWindowBoundary> windowBoundaries);
```

`windowBounderies` is an observable that you provide to close the previous window and open the next by emitting a notification.

Windows and buffers are two ways you can split a big problem into many small ones and solve each one independently. By splitting your observable into parts, you can gain insight into the different parts that later can be reflected overall. This is ideal for aggregations or other operations over subsets of elements that fall within a certain period of time.

This concludes your journey into the ways to combine observables and the ways to split them. You accomplished quite a lot in this chapter, which presented advanced techniques in reactive logic. It's time to summarize what you've learned so you'll have a future reference to use for refreshing your memory.

9.5   Summary

In this chapter, you've learned that building reactive queries isn't restricted to a single observable and that you can create queries that rely on the relationship and combinations of multiple observables:

- The `Zip` operator pairs elements from two or more observables that share the same index.
- The `CombineLatest` operator combines the latest values emitted from each of the observables.
- The `Concat` operator emits the elements from the next observable when the previous observable completes.
- `Concat` subscribes to the observable only when the previous one completes.
- The `Merge` operator subscribes to all of the observables and emits their notifications as they arrive.
- You can restrict the number of concurrent subscriptions for the `Merge` operator by passing the number of allowed concurrent subscriptions as an argument.
- The `Switch` operator creates a single observable that emits the notifications from the most recent observable.
- The `Amb` operator works similarly to `Switch`, but switches to the first observable that emits.
- In Rx, grouping means to create observables of elements that share the same key. This is done with the `GroupBy` operator.
- In Rx, joining two observables means to emit pairs of elements that exist in the same time frame.
- The `Join` operator combines items emitted by two observables in the same time frame and emits the pairs into a single flat observable.
- The `GroupJoin` operator correlates the elements of two observable sequences based on overlapping durations, and then groups all elements that correlate with each element, which is an observable itself.
- You can write your `Join` and `GroupJoin` queries using both query syntax and method chaining.
- The `Buffer` operator breaks an observable sequence into bounded collections and creates an observable of those collections.
- The `Window` operator breaks an observable sequence into finer observables.

- Both `Buffer` and `Window` allow you to control the duration or capacity of the buffer or windows and allow the creation of sliding windows.

In the many examples you've seen in this book, from creating observables through querying and combining, we've added the element of time and of execution context (threads, tasks, and so on). The next chapter teaches you how Rx models time and concurrency and how to use that to control the execution of your queries.

Working with
Rx concurrency and
synchronization

This chapter covers

- Rx schedulers
- Time-based operators
- Synchronization in the observable pipeline

Timing is everything, or at least that's what some say. Unlike collections (enumerables), timing plays a big part in the observables world. The time between notifications can be long or short, and it can affect how you process them. In chapter 9, you saw examples of buffering elements or creating sliding windows over time. There's also the matter of where the execution takes place (for example, threads, tasks, dispatchers, and so on). The concepts of time and execution context are related and provide the foundation for the Rx concurrency model. The scheduler type and its derivations express this model. This chapter explains the scheduler's layer in Rx and how to use it to control concurrency inside the Rx observable pipeline, as well as how to use it with Rx time-based operators.

10.1 Controlling concurrency with schedulers

In computer science, *concurrency* is a property of those systems in which several computations are executing simultaneously and, potentially, interacting with each other. I talked a bit about concurrency in chapter 5, where I mentioned the different .NET

231

asynchronous types. Until now, I've avoided talking directly about how concurrency is handled inside the observable pipeline. If you use the `Interval` operator to create an observable that emits every 10 seconds, for example, on what thread will the notifications be received? On what thread will the observer's subscription take place? In some cases, such as when working with UI frameworks, controlling those execution contexts is important because you may have restrictions on which thread executes the code that performs an operation. Usually UI controls can be mutated only on the UI thread; otherwise, you get an exception.

Rx follows this design guideline: everything that introduces concurrency must do so by using a `Scheduler` type, which is the abstraction layer Rx uses for concurrency and time.

10.1.1 *Defining the scheduler*

In simple terms, a *scheduler* is a unit that represents a clock and an execution context. The clock maintains the current time and allows for scheduling work at a specific time (such as a timer). The execution context determines where to process the work (for example, in the current thread or in the current `SynchronizationContext` object). This is shown in figure 10.1. All schedulers in Rx implement the `IScheduler` interface, shown in listing 10.1.

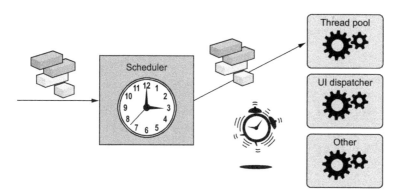

Figure 10.1   **The Rx schedulers are like timers: you assign specific actions or tasks to the scheduler, and when a preset time expires, the scheduler posts the work to the execution context it's bound to.**

Listing 10.1   The `IScheduler` interface

```
public interface IScheduler
{
    DateTimeOffset Now { get; }

    IDisposable Schedule<TState>(
                    TState state,
                    Func<IScheduler, TState, IDisposable> action);
```

Returns the scheduler's notion of current time

Schedules an action to be executed. Returns a disposable that's used to cancel the scheduled action.

Schedules an action to be executed at the given dueTime. Returns a disposable that's used to cancel the scheduled action.

Schedules an action to be executed after the given TimeSpan. Returns a disposable that's used to cancel the scheduled action.

```
IDisposable Schedule<TState>(
        TState state,
        TimeSpan dueTime,
        Func<IScheduler, TState, IDisposable> action);

IDisposable Schedule<TState>(
        TState state,
        DateTimeOffset dueTime,
        Func<IScheduler, TState, IDisposable> action);
}
```

The scheduler contains the property Now, which returns the scheduler's notion of the current time. Most scheduler implementations return DateTimeOffset.UtcNow, but in more advanced cases, as you'll see in appendix C, the scheduler's time abstraction lets you control the time for testing and for revisiting past events.

Along with the Now property, the Scheduler interface provides a couple of overloads to the Schedule methods. Those overloads let you schedule actions to run at an absolute or relative time, or immediately. To schedule actions, you pass a state object of your choice, the scheduling time, and an action of type Func<IScheduler, TState, IDisposable>.

When the preset time arrives and the action is invoked, it receives the scheduler that invoked it and the state object you provided. The state object lets you maintain context from the caller that made the scheduling to the action that'll be running at a later time. There's no restriction on the type of the state object, and it can be any data type you choose.

The action you schedule must return a Disposable object, which acts as a cancellation token. Disposing of it is meant to trigger the cancellation of the running operation as well as to clean any resources that were created as part of it.

Let's see an example of what working with the scheduler looks like. You'll use NewThreadScheduler (which resides in System.Reactive.Concurrency) to schedule an action that prints the current time on-screen. You'll want to schedule this action 2 seconds in the future and, instead of being coupled to the environment clock or the platform-specific timers, you'll rely on the Rx scheduler to do the wiring for you, as shown in figure 10.2.

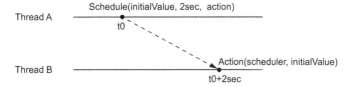

Figure 10.2 Scheduling work with NewThreadScheduler

```
IScheduler scheduler = NewThreadScheduler.Default;

IDisposable scheduling =
    scheduler.Schedule(
        Unit.Default,
        TimeSpan.FromSeconds(2),
        (scdlr, _) =>
        {
            Console.WriteLine("Hello World, Now: {0}", scdlr.Now);
            Return Disposable.Empty;
        });
```

The state object isn't used in this example; Unit.Default is used, which acts like a null object.

The execution time is 2 seconds from when the scheduling takes place.

Receives the scheduler that's used for recursive scheduling and the state object. Disposable.Empty is returned because there is no specific resource handling or cancellation object.

Running this example (and waiting 2 seconds) displays this output:

```
Hello World, Now: 22/12/2015 13:45:00 +00:00
```

In this example, the state object and the returned disposable aren't used, but often those objects are used to control what's going on inside the scheduled action.

Let's see a more advanced example of a recurring event (every 2 seconds) that needs to count how many times it happened. You'll use the state object and also create recursive scheduling to run an action every 2 seconds, which can be canceled with the returned disposable:

```
IScheduler scheduler = NewThreadScheduler.Default;
Func<IScheduler, int, IDisposable> action = null;
action = (scdlr, callNumber) =>
  {
      Console.WriteLine("Hello {0}, Now: {1}, Thread: {2}",
          callNumber,
          scdlr.Now,
          Thread.CurrentThread.ManagedThreadId);
      return scdlr.Schedule(callNumber + 1, TimeSpan.FromSeconds(2),
                            action);
  };

IDisposable  scheduling =
    scheduler.Schedule(
        0,
        TimeSpan.FromSeconds(2),
        action);
```

The C# compiler doesn't allow use of a variable until it's declared, so you separate the action declaration from its definition (where it's being used).

Reschedules the action for another 2 seconds, incrementing the state object (that acts as the calls counter). The disposable returned from the Schedule method is also returned.

The first scheduling passes the initial state object. Because it's the first call, you pass 0.

Figure 10.3 shows the conceptual sequence of the periodic behavior you just created.

If you run this example now, it'll keep on running and writing messages on-screen. When the time comes, and you want to stop it, you can simply dispose of the scheduling object.

Internally, the scheduler connects all disposables that are created downstream of the disposable returned from the initial call to the Schedule method, so even if an inner-level scheduling has already happened, disposing of the top disposable will

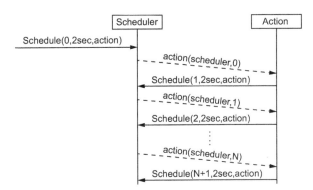

Figure 10.3   You can use schedulers to create a periodic behavior. You can also use the state parameter for passing information to the next iteration.

affect the innermost one. (Appendix A delves deeper into the Rx Disposables library that enables this kind of disposable chain.)

Some schedulers, in addition to implementing the `IScheduler` interface, implement two more interfaces that Rx provides:

- `ISchedulerPeriodic` declares the `SchedulePeriodic` method for scheduling actions to run periodically.
- `ISchedulerLongRunning` declares the `ScheduleLongRunning` method for scheduling actions that'll run for a long period of time.

In most cases, you won't use the scheduler directly. Instead, you'll pass it to Rx operators only to control concurrency.

10.1.2 *Parameterizing concurrency*

The `IScheduler` interface provides an abstraction over the concurrency that you introduce in your application. `IScheduler` allows the operators that perform a concurrent operation to be agnostic to the real implementation of the concurrency simply by providing it with the scheduler you want it to use as a parameter. To create an observable that emits a notification every second but ensures that the emissions happen on the current thread, you can write this code:

```
Console.WriteLine("Before - Thread: {0}",
    Thread.CurrentThread.ManagedThreadId);
Observable.Interval(TimeSpan.FromSeconds(1), CurrentThreadScheduler.Instance)
    .Take(3)
    .Subscribe(x => Console.WriteLine("Inside - Thread: {1}",
                    x,
                    Thread.CurrentThread.ManagedThreadId));
```

Note that I passed the `CurrentThreadScheduler.Instance` to the `Interval` operator. This ensures that the internal timer that `Interval` is using will use the current thread. The code yields this output (thread numbers could differ):

```
Before - Thread: 1
Inside - Thread: 1
```

```
Inside - Thread: 1
Inside - Thread: 1
```

`Interval` creates a cold observable. Because `CurrentThreadScheduler` is used in this example, an observable runs *synchronously* for each observer that subscribes, so the subscription call turns into a blocking operation that continues only after the entire observable sequence completes.

If no scheduler is passed to the `Interval` operator, it'll use the default scheduler that runs the timer on another thread and, therefore, the emissions will happen on that thread, yielding this output (thread numbers could differ):

```
Before - Thread: 1
Inside - Thread: 4
Inside - Thread: 4
Inside - Thread: 4
```

In this case the thread in which the `OnNext` method was called is 4 and is different from the thread that the application was executed on before the subscription took place. In other words, the observable now runs asynchronously.

Like the `Interval` operator, all Rx operators that introduce concurrency in their operations receive a scheduler (a default scheduler is used otherwise). I'll confess I wasn't completely honest in the previous chapters, and I intentionally hid all the operators' overloads that receive the `IScheduler`.

Many developers that approach Rx have a false assumption that everything in Rx is running in the background. This isn't true. In fact, Rx operators are clear about their intentions to execute the so-called background operation by providing an overload that accepts `IScheduler`. Consider the next example of the `Range` operator that creates an observable that emits a sequence of numbers together with the `Repeat` operator that resubscribes to the observable. Try to predict what will be printed:

```
var subscription =
    Observable.Range(1, 5)
        .Repeat()
        .SubscribeConsole("Range on another thread");

subscription.Dispose();
```

Unlike what many developers falsely believe, this writes the sequence 1–5 indefinitely on the console and doesn't *immediately* dispose of the subscription. Because when the observable that emits the sequence completes, the `Repeat` operator resubscribes to it. This happens over and over on the *calling thread*, so the `Dispose` method of the subscription will never be reached.

To overcome this, you can change the `Range` emissions to take place on another thread by doing this:

```
Observable.Range(1, 5, NewThreadScheduler.Default)
```

Now the calling thread won't be blocked, and the call to the `Dispose` method will happen as quickly as possible.

Rx also provides a few implementations of the `IScheduler` interface that's suited for different purposes.

10.1.3 Types of schedulers

To help you set the concurrency of your observable pipeline, Rx provides a couple of schedulers. All the standard Rx schedulers sit under the `System.Reactive.Concurrency` namespace. To demonstrate the different effect each scheduler has, I'll use the test method shown here.

> **Listing 10.2 A test method to show the behavior of various schedulers**

```
public static void TestScheduler(IScheduler scheduler)
{
    scheduler.Schedule(Unit.Default,
        (s, _) => Console.WriteLine("Action1 - Thread:{0}",
                        Thread.CurrentThread.ManagedThreadId));
    scheduler.Schedule(Unit.Default,
        (s, _) => Console.WriteLine("Action2 - Thread:{0}",
                        Thread.CurrentThread.ManagedThreadId));

}
```

NEWTHREADSCHEDULER

Just as the name suggests, `NewThreadScheduler` runs the scheduled action on a new thread. By default, `NewThreadScheduler` creates a new `Thread` object for every scheduling operation, but you can also pass it a `threadFactory` of type `Func<ThreadStart, Thread>`, which is responsible for the way threads are created.

Most of the time, you won't instantiate the scheduler, but will use the `NewThreadScheduler.Default` static property to receive a shared instance.

```
TestScheduler(NewThreadScheduler.Default);
```

Running the code displays this output (thread numbers could differ):

```
Action1 - Thread:7
Action2 - Thread:8
```

One issue usually confuses developers who use `NewThreadScheduler` with a recursive call to the scheduler—it won't open a new thread. Internally, it will use the `EventLoopScheduler` that uses the same thread.

Because creating a new thread for every scheduling isn't efficient,[1] you should use the `NewThreadScheduler` primarily for making long-running operations. For short-lived operations, it's recommended to work with `ThreadPool`.

THREADPOOLSCHEDULER

Creating a new thread for every scheduled action isn't efficient; opening and closing a thread in the OS is time and memory expensive. Instead, the .NET Framework

---

[1] This issue is discussed in chapter 5.

provides the `ThreadPool` class that reuses threads instead of opening a new one each time. `ThreadPoolScheduler` works similarly to `NewThreadScheduler`, but uses the thread pool instead of creating new threads:

```
TestScheduler(ThreadPoolScheduler.Instance);
```

The output is as follows (thread numbers could differ):

```
Action1 - Thread:9
Action2 - Thread:10
```

You can see from the output that two actions are scheduled independently of one another, and on different threads.

Unlike `NewThreadScheduler`, recursive scheduling is also queued on the thread pool, so different scheduled actions might run on different threads. `Thread-PoolScheduler` should be your first choice when you specifically need to schedule on threads.

TASKPOOLSCHEDULER

`TaskPoolScheduler` works similarly to `ThreadPoolScheduler` except, instead of working with `ThreadPool`, it uses the Task Parallel Library (TPL) task pool. In some platforms (such as WinRT), the thread pool isn't accessible, so `TaskPoolScheduler` is the perfect replacement.

CURRENTTHREADSCHEDULER

`CurrentThreadScheduler` schedules the actions on the same thread where the caller of the `Schedule` method runs. Any recursive scheduling that happens inside a scheduled action is put into an ordered-by-time queue maintained by the scheduler. After a scheduled operation completes, the scheduler picks the next operations from the queue and runs it when its `dueTime` comes, or immediately if it has already passed.

```
TestScheduler(CurrentThreadScheduler.Instance);
```

The output is as follows (thread numbers could differ):

```
Calling thread: 1
Action1 - Thread:1
Action2 - Thread:1
```

The example shows that each scheduled action runs on the same thread, and that this thread is the same one the caller is running on. When you program recursive schedulings, they'll also run on the same thread.

IMMEDIATESCHEDULER

Like `CurrentThreadScheduler`, `ImmediateScheduler` schedules the action on the current thread. But unlike `CurrentThreadScheduler` that queues the scheduled actions and then runs them one after the other, `ImmediateScheduler` runs each action immediately or blocks it until the `dueTime` comes:

```
var immediateScheduler = ImmediateScheduler.Instance;

Console.WriteLine("Calling thread: {0} Current time: {1}",
Thread.CurrentThread.ManagedThreadId, immediateScheduler.Now);

immediateScheduler.Schedule(Unit.Default,
    TimeSpan.FromSeconds(2),                    ←─┐  Schedules the action to
    (s, _) =>                                      │  run after 2 seconds
    {
        Console.WriteLine("Outer Action - Thread:{0}",
                    Thread.CurrentThread.ManagedThreadId);
        s.Schedule(Unit.Default,
            (s2, __) =>
            {
                Console.WriteLine("Inner Action - Thread:{0}",
                        Thread.CurrentThread.ManagedThreadId);
                return Disposable.Empty;
            });
        Console.WriteLine("Outer Action - Done");
        return Disposable.Empty;
    });
Console.WriteLine("After the Schedule, Time: {0}",immediateScheduler.Now);
```

The output is as follows (thread numbers could differ):

```
Calling thread: 1 Current time: 24/12/2015 18:00:47 +00:00
Outer Action - Thread:1
Inner Action - Thread:1
Outer Action - Done
After the Schedule, Time: 24/12/2015 18:00:49 +00:00
```

There are a few things to note in this example output. First, all the actions run on the same thread that the initial caller runs on. Second, the inner action is scheduled immediately and not when the outer action completes. Third, the message `After the Schedule` prints 2 seconds after the call to the `Schedule` method. This is because you pass the `TimeSpan.FromSecond(2)` as an argument to the `Schedule` method that causes it to block until the `dueTime` arrives. You should use `Immediate-Scheduler` when you need to schedule actions that involve a small amount of work that can be viewed as constant time operations.

EVENTLOOPSCHEDULER

`EventLoopScheduler` is a scheduler bound to a single thread that runs all the actions. When `EventLoopScheduler` is created, it creates a thread (or you can provide a thread factory of your own) to run all the actions that will be scheduled, regardless of what thread the actions are scheduled on.

Internally, `EventLoopScheduler` holds an ordered-by-time queue of the action. Every scheduled action is enqueued and, when the scheduler finishes running an action, the next action is dequeued.

```
TestScheduler(new EventLoopScheduler());
```

The output is as follows (thread numbers could differ):

```
Calling thread: 1
Action1 - Thread:14
Action2 - Thread:14
```

The example shows that all scheduled actions are running on the same thread, but this thread is different from the one that EventLoopScheduler was created on.

In one of the projects I was consulting on, three observables emitted values at a high rate, and observers used and modified the state of a shared object. All the modifications of the shared object had to be synchronized, so the developers used locks and other synchronization primitives in many places inside the shared object, thus degrading the performance. A small but powerful tweak I made to improve the performance was to make all the observers run on the same EventLoopScheduler so that no locks were needed while the processing was still synchronized.

SCHEDULING ON THE SYNCHRONIZATIONCONTEXT

In the .NET Framework, SynchronizationContext is an object that handles the synchronization of work for a specific threading context, such as the UI thread in WPF and WinForms or an ASP.NET request. By using SynchronizationContext, you can dispatch work from a source thread to a target thread and let SynchronizationContext handle the details.

SynchronizationContextScheduler in Rx provides a bridge between the Rx schedulers' model and the .NET SynchronizationContext model so that each scheduled task is posted on SynchronizationContext. When creating the SynchronizationContextScheduler, you need to pass the SynchronizationContext you want to use. For example:

```
var syncContextScheduler = new SynchronizationContextScheduler(
                           SynchronizationContext.Current);
```

In both WinForms and XAML platforms, SynchronizationContext plays a big part because if you try to run code that interacts with the UI component from a thread different than the UI thread, an exception is thrown. So every operation related to the UI needs to go through the right SynchronizationContext. In WinForms, you can use the control itself to invoke the actions on the right thread:

```
control.BeginInvoke(() => {/* the action code */});
```

With XAML platforms (such as WPF or WinRT), you can use the Dispatcher class:

```
Dispatcher.CurrentDispatcher.BeginInvoke(() => {/* the action code */});
```

To ease the use of schedulers in those frameworks, Rx provides ControlScheduler and DispatcherScheduler, which wrap the right synchronization context for WinForms and XAML platforms. To access these schedulers, add a reference to the relevant platform package—System.Reactive.Windows.Threading for XAML platforms such as WPF or UAP (www.nuget.org/packages/System.Reactive.Windows.Threading) and `System.Reactive.Windows.Forms` for WinForms (www.nuget.org/packages/System.Reactive.Windows.Forms).

Fixing the primes observable from chapter 5

In chapter 5, I showed how to create observables from asynchronous code. For the sake of the example (and because schedulers were introduced only in this chapter), I introduced concurrency by explicitly creating a task inside the observable creation method of an observable that emits prime numbers. To make amends, I'll show here the correct way of introducing concurrency and parameterizing it. Note that the example can be optimized even more (by converting enumerables to observables, for example), but I want to show the simplest refactoring:

```
static IObservable<int> GeneratePrimes(int amount,          Uses the scheduler
Ischeduler scheduler = null)                                that was passed or
{                                                           a default one if
    scheduler = scheduler ?? DefaultScheduler.Instance;  ◁  none was provided
    return Observable.Create<int>(o =>
    {
        var cancellation = new CancellationDisposable();                    ◁
        var scheduledWork = scheduler.Schedule(() =>
        {                                          Allows canceling the
            try                                  concurrent work by disposing
            {                                          of the subscription
                var magicalPrimeGenerator = new MagicalPrimeGenerator();
                foreach (var prime in magicalPrimeGenerator
                .Generate(amount))
                {
                    cancellation.Token.ThrowIfCancellationRequested();  ◁
                    o.OnNext(prime);
                }                                           Exits with a
                o.OnCompleted();                   CancellationException when the
            }                                       subscription is disposed of.
            catch (Exception ex)
            {
                o.OnError(ex);
            }
        });
        return new CompositeDisposable(scheduledWork, cancellation);
    });
}
```

Schedules the prime generation and emissions with the scheduler. This allows the code to run concurrently.

10.2 Using time-based operators

The main difference between an observable sequence and traditional enumerables is the dimension of time. With observables, the time between two notifications is dynamic and can be predicated by the observer. This dimension of time can affect the way you want to react to notifications—ignoring them or delaying them if they're too fast.

In the previous chapters, you've already seen some of the operators that are time-based. In this section, I'm going to talk about them at a deeper level.

10.2.1 Adding a timestamp to a notification

Because the observable emits notifications at different times, it makes sense to ask what time each notification was emitted. Instead of manually adding the time information, Rx provides the `Timestamp` operator, which adds the UTC date and time details for each notification in the observable sequence. Figure 10.4 depicts the `Timestamp` operator.

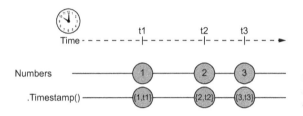

Figure 10.4 The `Timestamp` operator adds a timestamp of the emission time to every notification.

The `Timestamp` operator takes no parameters (except for an optional scheduler) and wraps the notification object with the `Timestamped<T>` type that holds the timestamp of the emission:

```
IObservable<Timestamped<TSource>> Timestamp<TSource>(
                                   this IObservable<TSource> source);
IObservable<Timestamped<TSource>> Timestamp<TSource>(
                                   this IObservable<TSource> source,
                                   IScheduler scheduler)
```

In the next example, you create an observable that emits a notification every 1 second, like a heartbeat notification received from a hardware product that your software monitors.[2] You add a timestamp by using the `Timestamp` operator so you can log the information for future analysis. Because you don't want the example to run forever, you're taking only three notifications:

```
IObservable<long> deviceHeartbeat =
    Observable.Interval(TimeSpan.FromSeconds(1));

deviceHeartbeat
    .Take(3)
    .Timestamp()
    .SubscribeConsole("Heartbeat");
Console.ReadLine();
```

---

[2] A heartbeat is a special notification used to monitor the availability of a resource; see https://en.wikipedia.org/wiki/Heartbeat_(computing).

Running this example on my machine shows this output:

```
Heartbeat - OnNext(0@25/12/2015 22:29:24 +00:00)
Heartbeat - OnNext(1@25/12/2015 22:29:25 +00:00)
Heartbeat - OnNext(2@25/12/2015 22:29:26 +00:00)
Heartbeat - OnCompleted()
```

The bolded text values were emitted by the observable. I got this formatted output because of the `Timestamped<T>` type. The `Timestamped<T>` type holds the notification object that was emitted by the timestamped observable and the timestamp of when the notification was emitted. It also implements a nice `ToString` method that helps when debugging.

The `Timestamp` operator can be useful when you need to investigate what's going on inside your observable and how the time dimension affects your handling.

10.2.2 Adding the time interval between notifications

Useful as the `Timestamp` operator can be, sometimes all you care about is the time interval between two emissions. Instead of calculating this interval by subtracting the two timestamps, you can use the `TimeInterval` operator, which records the time interval between consecutive elements in the observable. Figure 10.5 shows a marble diagram of the `TimeInterval` operator.

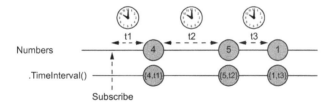

Figure 10.5 The `TimeInterval` operator computes the time interval between two notifications.

`TimeInterval` wraps every notification object with a `TimeInterval<T>` type:

```
IObservable<TimeInterval<TSource>> TimeInterval<TSource>
    (this IObservable<TSource> source);
IObservable<TimeInterval<TSource>> TimeInterval<TSource>
    (this IObservable<TSource> source, IScheduler scheduler);
```

In the next example, you simulate a hardware device that sends heartbeat signals that the application monitors. You create an observable that emits three notifications with the following intervals between them: 1 second, 2 seconds, and 4 seconds. You use the `TimeInterval` operator to record the interval between them. Obviously, when there's a long gap between heartbeats, it means that something is unhealthy with the device being monitored.

```
var deviceHeartbeat = Observable
    .Timer(TimeSpan.FromSeconds(1))
    .Concat(Observable.Timer(TimeSpan.FromSeconds(2)))
    .Concat(Observable.Timer(TimeSpan.FromSeconds(4)));
```

```
deviceHeartbeat
    .TimeInterval()
    .SubscribeConsole("time from last heartbeat");
Console.ReadLine();
```

This code prints the following output:

```
time from last heartbeat - OnNext(0@00:00:01.0120598)
time from last heartbeat - OnNext(0@00:00:02.0070871)
time from last heartbeat - OnNext(0@00:00:04.0029774)
time from last heartbeat - OnCompleted()
```

The bold text shows the time intervals that were recorded. Of course, the measured time isn't the same as what you've set. That's because many factors were involved in scheduling the notifications and in measuring the intervals: the preemptive OS, the time of the measurement itself, and so forth.

Even so, your application can now alert the user that something is wrong with the device simply by checking that the interval encapsulated in the `TimeInterval` type is within the normal time limits. The `TimeInterval` struct holds the `Interval` property (of type `TimeSpan`) and the `Value` property that contains the emitted notification, and implements a nice `ToString` method useful for debugging.

Using the `TimeInterval` operator lets you make decisions based on the distance between the emitted values. Sometimes the behavior you're trying to implement is that if the time distance is too long, you want to cancel the operation (or query). This is known as setting a time-out.

10.2.3 *Adding a time-out policy*

As discussed in previous chapters, observables can represent an asynchronous operation or can be a result of an observable pipeline that involves some kind of an asynchronous operation, such as a request from a remote service.

When doing things asynchronously, you must always ask how long it takes before you can say that the action was faulty. When you work with asynchronous service providers, it's common for some kind of error to happen that prevents you from receiving a response.

To make handling such cases easy, Rx provides the `Timeout` operator that, as its name indicates, handles the time-out cases for you. It monitors the notifications emitted by the observable and, if a notification hasn't been emitted (since the previous one) in the period of time that you configured, it raises an exception that will be passed to the observer by its `OnError` method. Figure 10.6 illustrates `Timeout`.

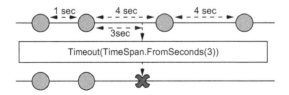

Figure 10.6 The `Timeout` operator emits an error notification when the time-out duration has passed without emitting.

The next example simulates a case in which four remote requests are sent, one after the other, and you're waiting for their responses. You set the time-out to 3 seconds, meaning that when a response takes more than 3 seconds to return, you can unsubscribe from the observable. To simulate this, you create an observable that emits two notifications with a 1-second gap between them, and two more notifications with a 4-second gap. You add the `Timeout` operator to your pipeline and configure it to 3 seconds:

```
var observable = Observable
    .Timer(TimeSpan.FromSeconds(1))
    .Concat(Observable.Timer(TimeSpan.FromSeconds(1)))
    .Concat(Observable.Timer(TimeSpan.FromSeconds(4)))
    .Concat(Observable.Timer(TimeSpan.FromSeconds(4)));

observable
    .Timeout(TimeSpan.FromSeconds(3))
    .SubscribeConsole("Timeout");
Console.ReadLine();
```

Running the example shows this output:

```
Timeout - OnNext(0)
Timeout - OnNext(0)
Timeout - OnError:
    System.TimeoutException: The operation has timed out.
```

You can see that because you define the time-out to be 3 seconds, and no notification was sent, you get a `TimeoutException`.

10.2.4 Delaying the notifications

The notifications emitted by the observable can come at any rate. In most cases, you'll want to react to them as soon as they arrive. But in some cases delaying the handling of a notification is preferred; for example, when you get requests that have different priorities (based on customer service-level agreement, or SLA), and you want to delay the processing of the lower-priority requests and give precedence to requests of a higher priority.

The `Delay` operator lets you add the delay you want, either constantly to all notifications or independently per notification. Figure 10.7 shows how the `Delay` operator affects the notification when passing it a relative time span. (Overloads that accept an absolute time exists as well.)

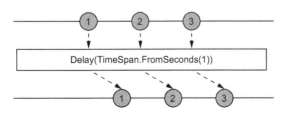

Figure 10.7 The `Delay` operator shifts the observable notifications by a time duration.

If you want to add a fixed time period for each notification delay, you can accomplish it using the `Delay` operator.

Listing 10.3   Delaying notifications with the `Delay` operator

```
var observable = Observable
    .Timer(TimeSpan.FromSeconds(1))                        ┐  Creates an observable that emits
    .Concat(Observable.Timer(TimeSpan.FromSeconds(1)))     │  four notifications with a different
    .Concat(Observable.Timer(TimeSpan.FromSeconds(4)))     │  duration between each
    .Concat(Observable.Timer(TimeSpan.FromSeconds(4)));    ┘

observable                        ┌  Captures the time the notification was
    .Timestamp()              ◄───┘  emitted by the source observable
    .Delay(TimeSpan.FromSeconds(2))                                    ◄──┐
    .Timestamp()                              ◄──┐                         │ Adds a 2-second delay
    .Take(5)                                      │ Captures the time the  │ for each notification
    .SubscribeConsole("Delay");                   │ notification was emitted
Console.ReadLine();                               │ after the delay
```

Running this example on my machine shows this output:

```
Delay - OnNext(0@26/12/2015 14:47:41 +00:00@26/12/2015 14:47:43 +00:00)
Delay - OnNext(0@26/12/2015 14:47:42 +00:00@26/12/2015 14:47:44 +00:00)
Delay - OnNext(0@26/12/2015 14:47:46 +00:00@26/12/2015 14:47:48 +00:00)
Delay - OnNext(0@26/12/2015 14:47:50 +00:00@26/12/2015 14:47:52 +00:00)
Delay - OnCompleted()
```

The important pieces of data here are the two timestamps. The one on the right (bolded text) is the time the notification was emitted after the delay, and the one on the left is the time the notification was emitted by the source observable. You can easily see that there's a 2-second difference between the timestamps for each notification.

ADDING A VARIABLE DELAY

When a constant delay doesn't fit your needs, you can use the `Delay` operator overloads that let you specify the delay duration per notification:

```
IObservable<TSource> Delay<TSource, TDelay>(                  ┐ Determines the subscription delay.
    this IObservable<TSource> source,                         │ Upon its emission, a subscription
    IObservable<TDelay> subscriptionDelay,            ◄───────┘ to the source observable is made.
    Func<TSource, IObservable<TDelay>> delayDurationSelector);           ◄──┐
                                                                             │
                                            Returns an observable for each element,
                                            which determines the delay duration. Its
                                            notification marks the delay end.
```

Another overload also exists whereby you can omit the `subscriptionDelay`, which is used to delay the subscription to the source observable.[3]

---

[3] The `subscriptionDelay` parameter gives a similar effect as the `DelaySubscription` operator I talked about in chapter 6.

In the next example, you create an observable of integers, and use each integer to determine the delay duration for each notification. These integers can be the request's priority in your application or the requested handling time of your application user:

```
var observable = new[] {4, 1, 2, 3}.ToObservable();

observable
    .Timestamp()
    .Delay(x => Observable.Timer(TimeSpan.FromSeconds(x.Value)))
    .Timestamp()
    .SubscribeConsole("Delay");
Console.ReadLine();
```

Captures the time the notification was emitted by the source observable

Delays the notification based on its value

Captures the time the notification was emitted after the delay

This is the output I got on my machine:

```
Delay - OnNext(1@26/12/2015 15:10:11 +00:00@26/12/2015 15:10:12 +00:00)
Delay - OnNext(2@26/12/2015 15:10:11 +00:00@26/12/2015 15:10:13 +00:00)
Delay - OnNext(3@26/12/2015 15:10:11 +00:00@26/12/2015 15:10:14 +00:00)
Delay - OnNext(4@26/12/2015 15:10:11 +00:00@26/12/2015 15:10:15 +00:00)
Delay - OnCompleted()
```

Because you create the observable from a collection of integers, all of them were emitted by the observable roughly at the same time. Each one was delayed independently, so even though number 4 was the first to be emitted by the source observable, it was the last to be received by the observer.

10.2.5 *Throttling the notifications*

In many cases, handling notifications emitted close to one another adds no real value. For example, if users update their details at a high rate (let's say three times per second), it might not be cost-effective to handle the first two updates because they're no longer relevant.

To add this kind of behavior to your observable pipeline, so notifications will be dropped unless a predefined period of time has passed without other notifications arriving, you can use the Throttle operator,[4] depicted in figure 10.8.

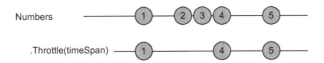

Figure 10.8 The Throttle operator emits an item from an observable only if a particular time span has passed without emitting another item.

---

[4] Some Rx implementations refer to this operator as Debounce.

In the next example, you simulate a case in which multiple updates are arriving, but only if 2 seconds have passed without another update coming will the update be allowed to proceed:

Emits five updates. The second, third, and fourth updates are close (in time) to one another.

```
var observable = Observable
  .Return("Update A")
  .Concat(Observable.Timer(TimeSpan.FromSeconds(2)).Select(_ => "Update B"))
  .Concat(Observable.Timer(TimeSpan.FromSeconds(1)).Select(_ => "Update C"))
  .Concat(Observable.Timer(TimeSpan.FromSeconds(1)).Select(_ => "Update D"))
 .Concat(Observable.Timer(TimeSpan.FromSeconds(3)).Select(_ => "Update E"));

observable.Throttle(TimeSpan.FromSeconds(2))
    .SubscribeConsole("Throttle");
Console.ReadLine();
```

Emits notifications that weren't followed by another notification for at least 2 seconds

Running the example displays this output:

```
Throttle - OnNext(Update A)
Throttle - OnNext(Update D)
Throttle - OnNext(Update E)
Throttle - OnCompleted()
```

You can see that updates B and C were dropped because both of them were followed by another notification that was emitted after less than 2 seconds.

VARIABLE THROTTLING

The `Throttle` operator lets you control the throttling duration for each element in an independent way. To achieve that, you can pass a function that returns an observable for each element that signals when the throttling period ends:

Returns an observable indicating the throttle duration for each given element

```
IObservable<TSource> Throttle<TSource, TThrottle>(
    this IObservable<TSource> source,
    Func<TSource, IObservable<TThrottle>> throttleDurationSelector)
```

Every emitted notification causes the `Throttle` operator to drop the previously returned observable and to start a new duration with the newly returned observable.

In listing 10.4, you extend your throttling example such that, in addition to the normal update messages, a new type of update message is created that triggers an immediate update. You use the `Throttle` operator to prevent handling of fast-rate messages, unless it's an Immediate Message, which is handled immediately. In your applications, an *Immediate Message* might be a notification of high importance or an item that comes from a source of high priority.

Listing 10.4   Throttling notifications

```
var observable = Observable
    .Return("Msg A")
    .Concat(Observable.Timer(TimeSpan.FromSeconds(2)).Select(_ => "Msg B"))
    .Concat(Observable.Timer(TimeSpan.FromSeconds(1))
    .Select(_ => "Immediate Update"))
```

```
         .Concat(Observable.Timer(TimeSpan.FromSeconds(1)).Select(_ => "Msg D"))
         .Concat(Observable.Timer(TimeSpan.FromSeconds(3)).Select(_ => "Msg E"));

observable
 .Throttle(x => x == "Immediate Update"
                    ? Observable.Empty<long>()
                    : Observable.Timer(TimeSpan.FromSeconds(2)))
    .SubscribeConsole("Variable Throttling");
```

Running the example creates this output:

```
Variable Throttling - OnNext(Msg A)
Variable Throttling - OnNext(Immediate Update)
Variable Throttling - OnNext(Msg D)
Variable Throttling - OnNext(Msg E)
Variable Throttling - OnCompleted()
```

In this example, you're checking each element. If it's an Immediate Update, you return an observable that emits a notification immediately (the OnCompleted notification). Otherwise, you create an observable that emits a notification after 2 seconds. That's why, even though notifications were emitted less than 2 seconds from when the Immediate Update was emitted, Immediate Update was emitted as well.

10.2.6 *Sampling the observable in intervals*

Another way of handling rapid observables is to slow the reaction rate to the notifications and to sample the emitted values in predefined intervals. The Sample operator lets you define the duration of the interval, so that when an interval ends, the last value emitted by the source observable is emitted by the resulting observable. Figure 10.9 provides a marble diagram of Sample.

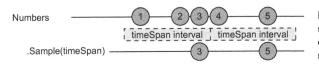

Figure 10.9 The Sample operator samples the observable sequence at each interval, emitting the last notification in the interval.

The next example shows how to take an observable that emits a notification every second and sample it every 3.5 seconds. (I limited the example to only three intervals.) In real-world scenarios, you might want to do that when the source of the notification is fast, but there isn't a lot of advantage to collecting all received values. For example, digital signal processing (DSP) applications usually sample the audio of video signals at a rate that's high enough to reconstruct the signal in a way that makes it understandable, even if some data is lost. (Displaying 24 frames per second is enough to fool our brains into seeing a moving picture.)

```
Observable.Interval(TimeSpan.FromSeconds(1))
       .Sample(TimeSpan.FromSeconds(3.5))
       .Take(3)
       .SubscribeConsole("Sample");
Console.ReadLine();
```

The example yields this output:

```
Sample - OnNext(2)
Sample - OnNext(5)
Sample - OnNext(9)
Sample - OnCompleted()
```

The duration of the interval doesn't have to be constant. The next `Sample` overload lets you control the duration of each interval by passing an observable that emits when the interval ends:

```
IObservable<TSource> Sample<TSource, TSample>(
    this IObservable<TSource> source,
    IObservable<TSample> sampler)
```

Upon each emission done by the `sampler` (sampling tick), the latest element (if any) in the source observable during the last sampling interval is sent to the resulting sequence. All the operators you've learned about in this chapter (and others covered in other chapters) can receive the `IScheduler` you want them to use for introducing concurrency. But, for the operators that don't introduce concurrency, you can't pass the scheduler. So what do you do if you want to change the execution context in the middle of your observable pipeline? You use the Rx-provided operators that add synchronization.

10.3   *Synchronizing the observable emissions*

From the observer's standpoint, the emissions done by the observables can happen on any thread and, therefore, the observer's reaction can happen on any thread as well. In many cases, this has no real importance, but when dealing with certain frameworks or libraries you might need to perform certain operations on a specific execution context (for example, the UI thread). Furthermore, at times you need to synchronize the processing between different observers from different observables, either by making them all happen on the same thread or by using concurrency primitives (for example, mutex, semaphor, and so on). Luckily, you don't need to write all that low-level code yourself; you can use the Rx synchronization operators.

10.3.1   *Changing the observation's execution context*

If you need to control the execution context (the observations of elements done by the observer), Rx provides the `ObserveOn` operator that lets you pass the scheduler that the emissions will be scheduled on. You have the ability (to some extent) to specify on which thread you want the `OnNext/OnError/OnCompleted` functions to run. Figure 10.10 is a marble diagram of `ObserveOn`.

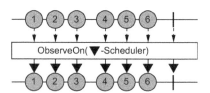

Figure 10.10   The `ObserveOn` **operator runs the observer functions on the specified scheduler.**

A classic use of `ObserveOn` occurs when you need your observer to modify a UI control (for example, changing the width of a button), and you need to make sure the observer runs in the UI thread. The UI thread is managed either by `Dispatcher-Scheduler` for XAML platforms or by `ControlScheduler` in WinForms.

The next example creates an observable from the `TextBox.TextChanged` event and throttles it. The text values that survive the throttling are then added to a `ListBox`. Because the `Throttle` operator uses a default scheduler (usually `ThreadPool`), you use the `ObserveOn` operator to make sure the `ListBox` is changed on the UI thread.

```
Observable.FromEventPattern(TextBox, "TextChanged")
    .Select(_ => TextBox.Text)
    .Throttle(TimeSpan.FromMilliseconds(400))
    .ObserveOn(DispatcherScheduler.Current)
    .Subscribe(t => ThrottledResults.Items.Add(t));
```

Because the observation on the `Dispatcher` is something that happens frequently, you can use the shortened operator `ObserveOnDispatcher`, which does the same thing. The `ObserveOn` operator also has overloads that let you pass the `SynchronizationContext` or the WinForms `Control` with which you want to make the observation. Under the hood, the `ObserveOn` operator creates an interceptor in the observable pipeline that intercepts each call done on the observer and executes it on the specified scheduler.

10.3.2 Changing the subscription/unsubscription execution context

In addition to controlling the execution context of the observation, you can control the execution context that runs the subscription and unsubscription, meaning the thread in which the `Subscribe` method of the observable and the `Dispose` method of the subscription is called.

This is something that you'd typically want to do if the observable's work must happen on a specific thread (as in Silverlight, where the registration to a control's events has to happen on the UI thread, but the processing of the notifications can happen anywhere).

Consider the code for an observable that does heavy processing before emitting its values, such as connecting to a hardware device that is slow, as shown here:

```
var observable =
    Observable.Create<int>(o =>
    {
        Thread.Sleep(TimeSpan.FromSeconds(5));      ◁────  Simulating a long
        o.OnNext(1);                                       operation done in the
        o.OnCompleted();                                   subscription time
        return Disposable.Empty;
    });

observable.SubscribeConsole("LongOperation");
```

When running this example, the calling thread will be blocked for 5 seconds, and only afterward do the messages appear. Adding `ObserveOn` to this example won't help because the long operation happens as part of the subscription. What you want is to make the subscription itself on another thread.

The `SubscribeOn` operator lets you pass the scheduler that'll be used to schedule the subscription and unsubscription. It creates interceptors in the observable pipeline that'll intercept the call to the observable `Subscribe` method and make these calls run on the specified `Scheduler`. Then, the interceptor wraps the disposable returned by the `Subscribe` method so that its `Dispose` method will also run under the specified scheduler. Figure 10.11 depicts the `SubscribeOn` operator.

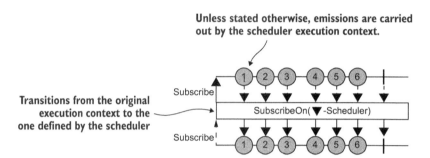

Figure 10.11   The `SubscribeOn` operator runs the observer subscription and unsubscription on the specified scheduler.

This interception over the unsubscription can cause confusion because the moment you call the `Dispose` method, it might go into effect only at a later time, based on the scheduler used. In the next example, you create an observable that emits every 1 second and uses the `EventLoopScheduler` for making the subscription. Then you schedule work items that take a long time to complete and dispose of the subscription. The unsubscription will take some time until it's complete and, in the meantime, notifications will still be processed inside the pipeline.

Listing 10.5   Confusion from using `SubscribeOn` when unsubscribing

```
var eventLoopScheduler = new EventLoopScheduler();
var subscription =
  Observable.Interval(TimeSpan.FromSeconds(1))
        .Do(x => Console.WriteLine("Inside Do"))         ◁────  Calls to Do will stop only when
        .SubscribeOn(eventLoopScheduler)      ◁──              the subscription is disposed of
        .SubscribeConsole();                            Sets the subscription and unsubscription
                                                        to run on the event loop
eventLoopScheduler.Schedule(1,
    (s, state) =>
    {
                                                        Simulates a long
        Console.WriteLine("Before sleep");              processing-time
        Thread.Sleep(TimeSpan.FromSeconds(3));          operation that's
        Console.WriteLine("After sleep");               happening in the
        return Disposable.Empty;                        event loop
    });
```

```
subscription.Dispose();
Console.WriteLine("Subscription disposed");
```

<- **Triggers the disposal of the underlying subscription on the event loop**

Running the example shows this output:

```
Subscription disposed
Before sleep
Inside Do
Inside Do
After sleep
Inside Do
```

Note that the call to `Dispose` happens almost immediately; but, because the real subscription will be disposed of on the event loop, it needs to wait until the long operation completes, and so you see the messages from the `Do` operator.

10.3.3 *Using SubscribeOn and ObserveOn together*

Depending on the observable you subscribe to, the thread on which you subscribe might also be the thread on which the emissions happens, or they might be totally different threads. You can combine the `SubscribeOn` and `ObserveOn` operators to gain better control over which thread will run in each step of your observable pipeline. And it's important to understand the order in which these operators happen and where their effect is coming into play.

To help with that, I created this simple `LogWithThread` operator to provide insight on the threads on which the subscriptions and emissions happen.

Listing 10.6 The `LogWithThread` operator logs both events and threads.

```
public static IObservable<T> LogWithThread<T>(
    this IObservable<T> observable,
    string msg = "")
{
    return Observable.Defer(() =>
    {
        Console.WriteLine("{0} Subscription happened on Thread: {1}", msg,
                          Thread.CurrentThread.ManagedThreadId);

        return observable.Do(
            x => Console.WriteLine("{0} - OnNext({1}) Thread: {2}", msg, x,
                                   Thread.CurrentThread.ManagedThreadId),
            ex =>
            {
                Console.WriteLine("{0} - OnError Thread:{1}", msg,
                                  Thread.CurrentThread.ManagedThreadId);
                Console.WriteLine("\t {0}", ex);
            },
            () => Console.WriteLine("{0} - OnCompleted() Thread {1}", msg,
                                    Thread.CurrentThread.ManagedThreadId));
    });
}
```

The LogWithThread operator prints messages to the console when the observer sub-scribes and for every notification done by the source observable. With each log mes-sage, the thread on which the event happens is also written.

Now let's see what happens when you use SubscribeOn and ObserveOn with LogWithThread to log the details for you. In the next example, you create a simple observable that emits three notifications (one every second), and you use the Sub-scribeOn and ObserveOn operators to control the execution context. The example creates an observable that emits five numbers and adds a few operators on it.

Listing 10.7   Testing the order of execution and effects of SubscribeOn and ObserveOn

```
new[] {0,1,2,3,4,5}.ToObservable()
    .Take(3).LogWithThread("A")
    .Where(x => x%2 == 0).LogWithThread("B")
    .SubscribeOn(NewThreadScheduler.Default).LogWithThread("C")
    .Select(x => x*x).LogWithThread("D")
    .ObserveOn(TaskPoolScheduler.Default).LogWithThread("E")
    .SubscribeConsole("squares by time");
Console.ReadLine();
```

Running the example on my machine shows this output:

```
E Subscription happened on Thread: 1
D Subscription happened on Thread: 1
C Subscription happened on Thread: 1
B Subscription happened on Thread: 3
A Subscription happened on Thread: 3
A - OnNext(0) Thread: 3
B - OnNext(0) Thread: 3
C - OnNext(0) Thread: 3
D - OnNext(0) Thread: 3
E - OnNext(0) Thread: 4
A - OnNext(1) Thread: 3
A - OnNext(2) Thread: 3
squares by time - OnNext(0)
B - OnNext(2) Thread: 3
C - OnNext(2) Thread: 3
D - OnNext(4) Thread: 3
E - OnNext(4) Thread: 4
squares by time - OnNext(4)
A - OnCompleted() Thread 3
B - OnCompleted() Thread 3
C - OnCompleted() Thread 3
D - OnCompleted() Thread 3
E - OnCompleted() Thread 4
squares by time - OnCompleted()
```

Figure 10.12 shows the marble diagram that displays what you see in the output.

Here are the key points in the example output:

- The order of the subscriptions is from the bottom to the top (the subscription is first executed at stage E, and only at the end at stage A). This is because the observable returned by the last `LogWithThread` operator is the one the observer is subscribing to.
- The subscriptions are executed on thread 1 until `SubscribeOn` is called, and then the subscriptions are made with thread 3 (step B).
- The notifications are done from top to bottom (A is first, and E is last).
- The notifications are emitted on thread 3 (where the subscriptions occur) until `ObserveOn` is called (right before E), and then the notifications are emitted on thread 4.

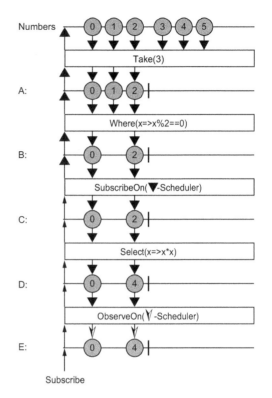

Figure 10.12 The effects of `SubscribeOn` and `ObserveOn` on the observable pipeline

- While the notification is observed on thread 4, thread 3 is free to observe the next notification. That's why you see the observation of 0 together with the emission of 2 (the bolded lines).

Next, I'll talk about how to synchronize processing of the notifications in the observable pipeline and between observables.

10.3.4 Synchronizing notifications

The notifications observed by the observer are assumed to arrive in a serialized fashion. The Rx Design Guidelines (see paragraphs 4.2 and 6.7) state that all Rx operators should safely assume that their inputs are serialized.[5] They won't receive notifications concurrently, but only one after the other. If this assumption isn't made, almost every operator and every observer should be written in a thread-safe way and use various kinds of locks to ensure the validity of their operations. This imposes a significant performance hit that isn't necessary.

---

[5] To read paragraphs 4.2 and 6.7 and for more details on the guidelines, see http://mng.bz/6bVR.

But you can't control every observable subscribed to. Some observables might be from a third party or might be constructed on top of a source that doesn't act in a serialized way. For these types of observables, you should synchronize their emissions in the observable pipeline.

Suppose you create an observable from an event exposed by a third-party component:

```
class Messenger
{
    public event EventHandler<string> MessageReceived;

    //Rest of the Messenger code
}
```

This is how to create the observable:

```
var messenger = new Messenger();
var messages =
    Observable.FromEventPattern<string>(
        h => messenger.MessageReceived += h,
        h => messenger.MessageReceived -= h);
```

And this is how to subscribe to it:

```
messages
    .Select(evt => evt.EventArgs)              ← Takes only the message itself (without the sender)
    .Subscribe(msg =>
    {
        Console.WriteLine("Message {0} arrived", msg);    Simulates processing
        Thread.Sleep(1000);                               done with the message
        Console.WriteLine("Message {0} exit", msg);
    });
```

When I ran this example and received three messages from multiple threads, this is what I got:

```
Message msg2 arrived
Message msg1 arrived
Message msg0 arrived
Message msg1 exit
Message msg0 exit
Message msg2 exit
```

It's obvious that the messages are received in an unserialized way. To serialize the notifications received in the observer (or in any operator), you need to use the Synchronize operator:

```
messages
    .Select(evt => evt.EventArgs)
    .Synchronize()              ← Synchronizes the notifications so they will be received in a serialized way
    .Subscribe(msg =>
    {
        Console.WriteLine("Message {0} arrived", msg);
        Thread.Sleep(1000);
```

```
        Console.WriteLine("Message {0} exit", msg);
    });
```

Now the messages are received in a serialized way, no matter from what thread the emission was made. Internally, the `Synchronize` operator creates a lock around every notification it makes to the observer. The lock is done on an inner object called the *gate*.

SYNCHRONIZING MULTIPLE OBSERVABLES

The `Synchronize` operator has an overload that lets you send the `gate` object that will be used to make the locks:

```
IObservable<TSource> Synchronize<TSource>(
    IObservable<TSource> source,
    object gate);
```

This overload can be useful when you need to share the lock between multiple subscribed observables. Suppose the `Messenger` class exposes another event, `FriendRequestReceived`, of all the friend requests you receive. After you create an observable, you want to synchronize the processing of the two types of notifications (friend requests and text messages). This how to do that:

```
var gate = new object();          ⟵┐ An object used as a lock
                                    │ between two observables
messages
    .Select(evt => evt.EventArgs)
    .Synchronize(gate)
    .Subscribe(msg => { /* processing the text message */  });

friendRequests
    .Select(evt => evt.EventArgs)
    .Synchronize(gate)
    .Subscribe(request => { /* processing the friend request */ });
```

Now the friend requests and the messages will be received in a serialized fashion.

This chapter dealt with many advanced topics of the Rx world. Let's summarize what you've learned.

10.4 Summary

In this chapter, you've learned about the way Rx models time and concurrency, and the techniques you can use to control the timing and execution context of the observable pipeline.

- In Rx, a scheduler is a unit that represents a clock and an execution context.
- With a scheduler, you can schedule work to be posted to an execution context at a specific time.
- All Rx schedulers implement the `IScheduler` interface.
- Some schedulers also implement the `ISchedulerPeriodic` or the `ISchedulerLongRunning` interfaces.

- Rx operators that introduce concurrency can receive a parameter of type `IScheduler`, allowing you to control the way concurrency is introduced.
- Out-of-the-box Rx comes with a handful of schedulers: `NewThreadScheduler`, `ThreadPoolScheduler`, `TaskPoolScheduler`, `CurrentThreadScheduler`, `ImmediateScheduler`, and `EventLoopScheduler`.
- Depending on the framework you use, other schedulers that are bound to the synchronization context will also be included (for example, `Control-Scheduler` or `DispatcherScheduler`).
- You use the `Timestamp` operator to add a timestamp of the emission time to every notification.
- You use the `TimeInterval` operator to add a time interval between two notifications.
- You use the `Timeout` operator to emit an error notification in case the time-out duration has passed without the source observable emitting.
- You use the `Delay` operator to shift the observable notifications by a time duration.
- You use the `Throttle` operator to emit an item from an observable if a particular time span has passed without the source observable emitting another item.
- You use the `Sample` operator to sample the observable sequence every time interval, emitting the last notification in each interval.
- You use the `ObserveOn` operator to enforce the observer functions to run on a specified scheduler.
- You use the `SubscribeOn` operator to enforce observer subscription and unsubscription to run on a specified scheduler.
- You use the `Synchronize` operator to create a lock so that the notifications are received in a serialized way.

The topics in this chapter are considered advanced and complex, but they're inherent in many of the operators you've seen throughout the book. Controlling them will help you achieve the goals of your observable pipelines. The next chapter covers something we all dislike but must take care of: errors. Because they're inevitable, I'll show you how to add error handling and recovery to your observable queries.

Error handling and recovery

This chapter covers

- Reacting to errors
- Properly freeing resources
- Dealing with backpressure

Errors happen; that's a fact of programming life. To provide high-quality service to the users of your applications, you must make sure your code handles errors and gracefully recovers when they happen. Otherwise, users experience application crashes or incorrect behavior (such as wrong computations or unexpected alerts) that can eventually turn them away from your product. In the case of an error, you might want to swallow it and continue, or add specific handling for a specific error. If an observable periodically emits updates from a central server, and one of the updates causes an unexpected error (for example, a network disconnection), handling the error by resubscribing observers to get the next set of updates might be the best solution. This chapter teaches you about the kinds of error-handling operators you can use to ensure that your observable pipeline is protected.

In addition to handling errors, you can prevent certain errors in advance, such as improper resource handling that can cause memory leaks, and unclosed server connections. An observable emitting at a rate faster than the rate the observer can consume is known as *backpressure*, which can result in errors and a high consumption of resources. This chapter shows you how to control the lifetime of your resources properly, even in the case of unexpected errors, and gives you solutions to backpressure.

11.1   Reacting to errors

In the .NET world, *error* means an exception, and an exception can be thrown for many reasons. Some (OutOfMemoryException, for example) aren't even under your control. It's important to differentiate the various places (or phases) an exception can be thrown from inside the observable pipeline because for different places you'll need different types of handling.

In the reactive pipeline, errors can happen in these four places:

- In the observable Subscribe method call during subscription
- In the observable code as it prepares the values to emit after subscription (for example, the observable tries to pull data from an external source that's disconnected)
- In operator code (for example, the selector function you provided for the Select operator throws an exception)
- In the observer's OnNext, OnCompleted, and OnError functions

For the first three cases, the Rx guidelines state that the observer should be notified of the error via its OnError function and the observer *subscription will terminate,* meaning no more notifications from the observable will be observed by the observer.

In the last case, where the *observer* is the one responsible for the error, it's the responsibility of the observer (and the developer) to handle the error. Rx provides no guarantee of what will happen in this case.

> **NOTE** I'd like to stress the last point again. If the code inside the observer function throws an exception, there's nothing in the Rx package to save you. So if you didn't provide an error-handling routine using a try-catch block around the "risky" code, the caller thread will have an unhandled exception. This will cause your process to terminate. This isn't different from any other code in your application that throws an exception that nobody handled. Your only option here is to make sure your code doesn't throw unwanted exceptions.

11.1.1   Errors from the observable side

Now that you understand that you must take care of exceptions that happen in the observer code explicitly, let's talk about the other three cases in the preceding list, where the exception is thrown by the observable or one of the operators in the pipeline.

The Rx Design Guidelines guarantee that errors from those places are propagated to the observer's OnError function. This makes error handling easy for you, because you now have a single place where you can react to them—the OnError function, depicted in figure 11.1. The OnError function receives a single argument (the Exception that was thrown) so your code can investigate what exactly that exception is and react to it.

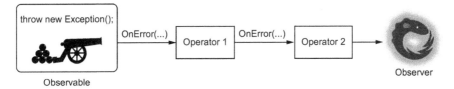

Figure 11.1 When an exception is thrown in the pipeline by the observable or one of the operators, it's propagated to the OnError function of the observer.

Listing 11.1 creates an observable that produces an error of type `OutOfMemory-Exception`. The weather simulation application implements a weather prediction observable that runs a data-intensive computation and then emits its results. Because the computation also creates a lot of data stored in memory, there's a risk of running out of memory. If this exception occurs, as a last resort the observer can run garbage collection (GC) together with Large Object Heap (LOH) compaction[1] to try to free memory.

Listing 11.1 Typical implementation of the observer's `OnError` function

```
IObservable<WeatherSimulation> weatherSimulationResults =
    Observable.Throw<WeatherSimulation>(new OutOfMemoryException());

weatherSimulationResults
    .Subscribe(
        _ => { /* OnNext code */ },
        e =>
        {
            if (e is OutOfMemoryException)
            {
                GCSettings.LargeObjectHeapCompactionMode =
                    GCLargeObjectHeapCompactionMode.CompactOnce;
                GC.Collect();
                GC.WaitForPendingFinalizers();
            }
        });
```

Creates an observable that emits an error

Focuses on the OnError function

Frees memory as a last attempt by calling for GC

One thing that you might think when looking at this example from the developer's standpoint is that reacting to errors isn't code friendly. You're absolutely right. You have to do type checking to see what the exception type is and, for each type of exception, the error handling requires your manual intervention, even if all you want to do is to dismiss it.

The Rx team realizes that developers tend to have common responses to errors happening in the observable pipeline. Those responses include catching a specific exception type and doing something accordingly, or dismissing the error and resuming the execution with the original observable or another observable.

---

[1] This is available for .NET version 4.5.1 and up, http://mng.bz/NVW5.

The Rx team, making sure the observable pipeline code will continue to be declarative and concise, created specific operators to make the developer's life easier.

11.1.2 *Catching errors*

In the traditional imperative programming model, you use a `try-catch` block around the potentially erroneous code and, in each `catch` block, specify the type of the exception you want to handle or leave it empty to say it should handle all exception types. After the catch code finishes, the application continues its work.

Semantically, the Rx `Catch` operator does the same thing, handling a specific exception type, but the way to specify the continuation of execution is by stipulating a fallback observable. In the case of an error, the observer is subscribed to the fallback observable (figure 11.2).

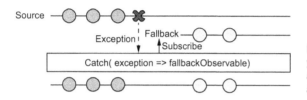

Figure 11.2   The `Catch` **operator lets you handle a specific exception type and set a fallback observable in case an exception is thrown.**

In the next example, you improve the error handling for the weather simulation observable shown in listing 11.1. Now, you add the `Catch` operator to handle the `OutOfMemoryException` and gracefully close the observable pipeline:

```
IObservable<WeatherSimulation> weatherSimulationResults =
    Observable.Throw<WeatherSimulation>(new OutOfMemoryException());
```

```
weatherSimulationResults
    .Catch((OutOfMemoryException ex) =>
    {
        Console.WriteLine("handling OOM exception");
        return Observable.Empty<WeatherSimulation>();
    })
    .SubscribeConsole("Catch (source throws)");
```

> **Returning an empty observable so that the observer will receive a completion notification instead of the error**

The output is as follows:

```
handling OOM exception
Catch (source throws) - OnCompleted()
```

`Catch` receives a function that handles a specific exception type; the function returns the observable that will be used for continuing execution of the observable pipeline. In this example, you return an empty observable so that the observable pipeline will complete, but in your code, this can be a fallback observable that will emit values instead of the original observable.

```
IObservable<TSource> Catch<TSource, TException>(
    IObservable<TSource> source,
    Func<TException, IObservable<TSource>> handler) where TException :
    Exception
```

If you want to return the same observable for any type of exception that might be thrown in the observable pipeline, you can use the `Catch` overload that receives only the observable that will be used in case of an error.

The next error gracefully finishes, in case the weather simulation observable signals an error:

```
weatherSimulationResults
    .Catch(Observable.Empty<WeatherSimulation>())
    .SubscribeConsole("Catch (handling all exception types)");
```

ONERRORRESUMENEXT—A VARIANT OF CATCH

The `Catch` operator concatenates observables if an error occurs. In chapter 10, you learned about the `Concat` operator. It also concatenates an observable, so when the first observable successfully completes, the second observable is being subscribed to and the observer receives its notifications. It makes sense to extend the `Concat` operator so concatenation happens not only when the observable completes, but also when it fails. This is the responsibility of the `OnErrorResumeNext` operator, illustrated in figure 11.3.

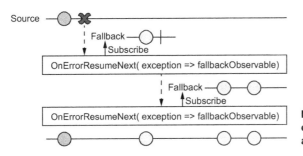

Figure 11.3 The `OnErrorResumeNext` operator is a hybrid of the `Catch` operator and the `Concat` operator.

The next example shows how to concatenate weather reports coming from two weather stations. The example shows that even if the first weather station observable (Station A) is terminated with an error, the second observable (Station B) is concatenated:

```
IObservable<WeatherReport> weatherStationA =
  Observable.Throw<WeatherReport>(new OutOfMemoryException());

IObservable<WeatherReport> weatherStationB =
  Observable.Return<WeatherReport>(new WeatherReport() { Station = "B",
    Temperature = 20.0 });

weatherStationA
    .OnErrorResumeNext(weatherStationB)
    .SubscribeConsole("OnErrorResumeNext(source throws)");
```

```
weatherStationB
    .OnErrorResumeNext(weatherStationB)
    .SubscribeConsole("OnErrorResumeNext(source completed)");
```

Running the example shows this output, where only Station B reports are received:

```
OnErrorResumeNext(source throws) - OnNext(Station: B, Temperature: 20)
OnErrorResumeNext(source throws) - OnCompleted()
OnErrorResumeNext(source completed) - OnNext(Station: B, Temperature: 20)
OnErrorResumeNext(source completed) - OnNext(Station: B, Temperature: 20)
OnErrorResumeNext(source completed) - OnCompleted()
```

With both `Catch` and `OnErrorResumeNext` operators, it's possible the concatenated observable is the original observable that throws the exception. In the case of an error, this resubscribes the observer to the observable. Conceptually, this means you want to *retry* the operation; however, you may want to limit the number of retries or explicitly set the number of retries to infinity. To make it easier for you to set the number of retries, use the `Retry` operator.

11.1.3 *Retrying to subscribe in case of an error*

The `Retry` operator, illustrated in figure 11.4, resubscribes an observer to the observable if an error occurs. Remember, the Rx guidelines state that if an error occurs, the subscription between the observer and observable is disconnected. If the observable is *cold* (which means the set of notifications isn't shared between the observers, such as an observable that reads lines from a file), the `Retry` operator will cause the observer to resubscribe, and the observable sequence will regenerate and possibly fail again. If the observable is hot, the new subscription will allow the observer to receive the ensuing emitted notifications.

NOTE   Observable temperature is explained in chapter 7.

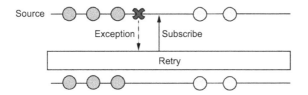

Figure 11.4   The `Retry` **operator resubscribes the observer to the observable when an error is emitted. In the case of a hot observable, as shown in the figure, the observer receives the rest of the emitted notifications.**

In the next example, the observable simulates weather reports received from a weather station. It's possible that the connection to the station fails due to a transient[2] error (such as a low network reception) and retrying is the best possible option. Of course, it's possible that the error isn't transient, so you'll want to limit the number of retries (in this case to three attempts), as shown in figure 11.5.

---

[2]   A transient is a property of any element in the system that is temporary. See https://en.wikipedia.org/wiki/Transient_(computer_programming).

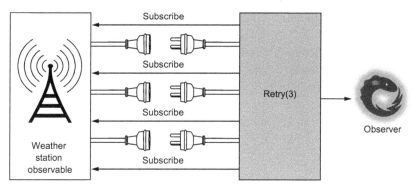

Figure 11.5 The `Retry` **operator automatically resubscribes to the weather station observable in the case of an error.**

```
IObservable<WeatherReport> weatherStationA =
  Observable.Throw<WeatherReport>(new OutOfMemoryException());

weatherStationA
    .Log()                                                          Adds a log message for every
    .Retry(3)                            Limits the number          notification received in this
    .SubscribeConsole("Retry");          of retries to three        part of the pipeline
```

Running the example shows this output (I removed some of the output for readability):

```
- OnError:
        System.OutOfMemoryException: Insufficient memory to continue ...
- OnError:
        System.OutOfMemoryException: Insufficient memory to continue ...
- OnError:
        System.OutOfMemoryException: Insufficient memory to continue ...
Retry - OnError:
        System.OutOfMemoryException: Insufficient memory to continue ...
```

You can see that the error is thrown four times. The first three messages are printed because of the original error and the first two retries, and the last message is from the last attempt to retry, which in this case causes the error again, and is received by the observer `OnNext` function.

> **NOTE** If you leave the `Retry` operator empty (without passing a number), the retries occur infinite times.

Next, I'll show you how to control the lifetime of the resources you use as part of your observable pipeline so that you can properly discard them.

11.2 Controlling the lifetime of resources

As part of the observable pipeline construction, different resources are allocated and used. This includes primitives and simple objects that occupy memory and resources that aren't managed (such as handles to files or connections to external services).

When the observable pipeline completes, either because the observable finishes its emissions or because the subscription is disposed of, it's important to free the resources that were allocated. It's twice as important to handle the deallocation of those resources when an error occurs; otherwise, your attempts to recover from the error might be doomed in advance (for example, a file might be locked because its handle wasn't freed).

The good news is that Rx operators take care of themselves and clean whatever they use. So you need to take care of only the things that you create and work with in the observable pipeline.

11.2.1 *Disposing in a deterministic way*

In .NET, the GC deallocates managed objects in a nondeterministic way. Even if an object is no longer in use (there are no root references to it), the object can stay in memory for a long time until the GC runs. Some managed objects might use unmanaged resources, such as connections or file handles and, in this case, it's important to dispose of them as soon as possible when they're no longer needed. This makes the disposal deterministic.

In .NET, you can achieve a deterministic disposal of resources by implementing the `IDisposable` interface on the class that holds the resource and by implementing the `Dispose` method with the code that frees the resource. During runtime, when you're finished using the resource (and the object that wraps it), you can invoke the `Dispose` method to free the resource. Of course, the managed memory of the wrapping object or any other objects used by the resource is reclaimed by the GC (garbage collection is nondeterministic in nature).

In C#, the easiest and safest way of working with an object of a type that implements the `IDisposable` interface is with the `using` statement:

```
class DisposableType : IDisposable
{
    public void Dispose() { /*Freeing the resource*/ }
}

private static void TraditionalUsingStatement()
{
    using (var disposable = new DisposableType())
    {
        //Rest of code
    }
}
```

When the execution reaches the end of the block, the `Dispose` method is automatically called, even if it's due to an exception thrown inside the block.

Alternatively, you can call the `Dispose` method and not use the `using` statement. This is usually done when the location of the creation of the disposable object is different from the location of where you need to dispose of it.

Because you'd like to use the same semantics of deterministic disposal inside your observable pipeline, Rx provides the Using operator, which works similarly to the using statement.

In our sample application, suppose you need to work with an observable that emits notifications coming from a heat sensor, and you're trying to trace a problem that's happening in your code. You want to write the notifications to a log file so you can analyze it later. When working with files, it's important to close the file when you're finished; otherwise, no one else can work with it, and the data that wasn't flushed to it disappears. Here's how to make sure the file handle will be disposed of:

```
string logFilePath = . . .
IObservable<SensorData> sensorData =. . .

var sensorDataWithLogging =
    Observable.Using(() => new StreamWriter(logFilePath),
        writer =>
        {
            return sensorData.Do(x => writer.WriteLine(x.Data));
        });

sensorDataWithLogging.SubscribeConsole("sensor");
```

A factory function that produces the resource

A factory function that creates the observable that uses the resource you created

The use of the Using operator looks similar to the using statement in that you create the resource and then use the created resource inside the block. The main difference is that the inner block (the second parameter) needs to return the observable that uses the resource, as shown in figure 11.6.

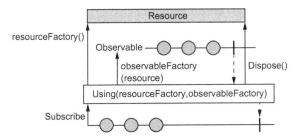

Figure 11.6 The Using operator creates a disposable resource that has the same lifespan as the observable.

The Using operator receives two parameters: the first is the *resource factory* (a function that creates the disposable object), and the second is the *observable factory* (a function that receives the disposable object and returns an observable that uses it).

The Using operator returns an observable that wraps the process of invoking the resource factory and then the observable factory every time an observer subscribes. The Using operator disposes of the resource when the observable terminates, no matter for what reason.

Here's an example that proves it:

```
Subject<int> subject = new Subject<int>();
var observable =
    Observable.Using(
        () => Disposable.Create(()=>{ Console.WriteLine("DISPOSED"); }),
        _ => subject);

Console.WriteLine("Disposed when completed");
observable.SubscribeConsole();
subject.OnCompleted();

Console.WriteLine("Disposed when error occurs");
subject = new Subject<int>();
observable.SubscribeConsole();
subject.OnError(new Exception("error"));

Console.WriteLine("Disposed when subscription disposed");
subject = new Subject<int>();
var subscription =
    observable.SubscribeConsole();
subscription.Dispose();
```

Creates an object that when disposed of by a call to the Dispose method prints the message "DISPOSED"

Returns the Subject currently referenced by the variable subject

In the resource factory, you create a disposable object that prints a message when it's disposed of. You use a `Subject` as the observable that you return from the observable factory. You then test what happens when the subject emits the notifications of `OnCompleted` and `OnError`, and also what happens when the subscription object itself is disposed of.

In all of these tests, the resource is disposed of. Note that between each test case, you create a new `Subject` because a completed `Subject` is no longer usable and will automatically notify its completeness to any a new observer that subscribes to it.

If you run this program, this is the output you'll see:

```
Disposed when completed
 - OnCompleted()
DISPOSED

Disposed when error occurs
 - OnError:
        System.Exception: error
DISPOSED

Disposed when subscription disposed
DISPOSED
```

This proves that for any termination of the observable, or the subscription, the resource will be gracefully disposed of.

The `Using` operator also includes an asynchronous version, in which the *resource factory* and the *observable factory* return `Tasks`:

```
IObservable<TResult> Using<TResult, TResource>(
    Func<CancellationToken, Task<TResource>> resourceFactoryAsync,
    Func<TResource, CancellationToken, Task<IObservable<TResult>>>
    observableFactoryAsync)
```

Because the factories are asynchronous, they both receive a cancellation token that will report cancellation in case the subscription was disposed of while the factories are still running. Other than that, the asynchronous version works the same as what you saw in the preceding synchronous version.

The `Using` operator works amazingly well when you need to dispose of resources. Nonetheless, in some cases cleanup operations aren't exposed through a disposable object. In C#, when you have a piece of code that needs to run at the end of an operation, no matter whether the operation succeeded or failed, you use the `try-finally` statement. Rx provides similar semantics.

11.2.2 Deterministic finalization

The `Finally` operator, illustrated in figure 11.7, works similarly to the `finally` block in C#. At the end of an operation, no matter whether it succeeded or failed, a piece of code is executed.

The code in the `finally` block usually handles cleanup of things that aren't necessarily disposable, and it runs the code related to the closure of a logical transaction. The `Finally` operator does the same thing for the observable: it runs the code you need to execute when the observable terminates—successfully or with an error.

Suppose you have a window that shows the progress of an operation (for example, loading a file or running a lengthy or complicated computation), and you want to close the window programmatically, no matter whether the operation succeeds or fails. This is how you can write code for that:

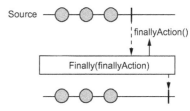

Figure 11.7 The `Finally` operator registers an action to take on the observable or subscription termination.

```
IObservable<int> progress =...

progress
    .Finally(() =>{/*close the window*/})
    .Subscribe(x =>{/*Update the UI /});
```

The piece of code that closes the window is called for in any case in which the observable terminates.

The next code example demonstrates the different cases when the action in the `Finally` clause is executed:

```
Console.WriteLine("Successful complete");
Observable.Interval(TimeSpan.FromSeconds(1))
    .Take(3)
    .Finally(() => Console.WriteLine("Finally Code"))
    .SubscribeConsole();
```
The final action is called when the observable completes.

```
Console.WriteLine("Error termination");
Observable.Throw<Exception>(new Exception("error"))
    .Finally(() => Console.WriteLine("Finally Code"))
    .SubscribeConsole();
```
The final action is called when the observable ends with an error.

```
Console.WriteLine("Unsubscribing");
Subject<int> subject = new Subject<int>();
var subscription =
    subject.AsObservable()
        .Finally(() => Console.WriteLine("Finally Code"))
        .SubscribeConsole();
subscription.Dispose();
```

> The final action is called when the subscription is disposed of.

Running this example produces the following output:

```
Successful complete
 - OnCompleted()
Finally Code

Error termination
 - OnError:
        System.Exception: error
Finally Code

Unsubscribing
Finally Code
```

The Finally operator can be helpful when you want to do the last step in the ongoing work of the observable and can't express it with a disposable object (for example, closing a connection or sending a message to an external service).

Next, I'll show you how to reduce the risk of having observers that are no longer necessary, yet never removed from memory—a situation called dangling observers.

11.2.3 Dangling observers

A *dangling observer* is the result of an observer being held (referenced) by nothing else but an observable, even though the logical lifetime of the observer has already finished. If the observer is the window that shows chat messages coming from the chat observable, it's possible that the window object will still be referenced by the observable, even though the user has closed the window.

Dangling observers appear when an observer subscribes to an observable but never unsubscribes from it by disposing of the subscription object. I define the object that subscribes the observer and that's in charge for its lifetime as the *observer's owner*.

Dangling observers result in memory leaks because observers are objects that occupy memory. Dangling observers also result in unwanted (and unexpected) behavior because the observer still reacts to notifications although it shouldn't. For example, the chat window mentioned previously still reacts to the chat messages and adds them to its inner collections even though it's closed. Figure 11.8 depicts a dangling observer.

As a reminder, when an observer is subscribed to an observable, you get in return a disposable object that holds the subscription. For example:

```
IObservable<int> observable = ...
IDisposable subscription = observable.Subscribe(x =>{/*the observer code*/});
```

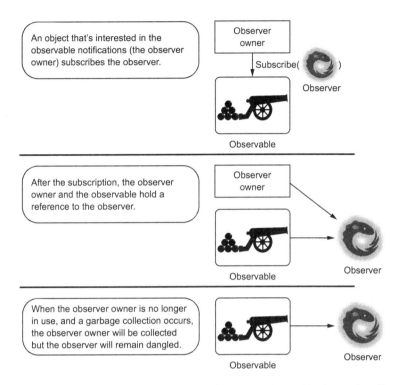

Figure 11.8 **When an observer is subscribed to an observable, it remains alive, regardless of its creator.**

Unfortunately, many developers throw away the subscription object and don't maintain it. Developers also forget to dispose of the subscription properly even if they do save it, which also results in a dangling observer.

If the observer holds references to other objects, this creates a chain of objects that aren't collected. A special case of such a reference occurs when you implicitly create an observer via the Subscribe operator to which you send the OnNext, OnError, and OnCompleted functions. This implicitly creates a reference from the observer to the object that created the subscription if the functions use the object's properties or methods.

Just to make it clear, if your application does need the observer to be kept alive for the lifetime of the observable it's subscribed to, then leaving the observer dangled is the expected behavior. But, in many cases, the observer should be kept alive for the duration of its owner (or creator) and, in those cases, it's crucial that you save the subscription and dispose of it when needed.

> **NOTE** One of the misunderstandings about the subscription object is the false assumption that when the GC collects the subscription, its Dispose method is called. Rx disposables don't implement a finalizer and, if the GC

collects it, the memory is reclaimed but the subscription isn't. You can't rely on the GC to unsubscribe observers for you.

In some cases, you can't determine when the life of the subscription should end and you'd like to keep it dynamic so that when there are no more references to the observer (except from the observable), it should be disposed of. An example of such a case is when working with platforms such as Windows Phone, where the application pages are kept inside a backstack. (The *backstack* is what allows the user to press the Back key on the machine and navigate to the previous page.) The Windows Phone application can also clear the backstack when it wants to prevent user navigation (for example, when the user logs out and returns to the login page, all the previous pages visited are no longer relevant).

Suppose a page (or its `ViewModel`) subscribes to an observable. Because of the nondeterministic nature of the page's lifetime, the page doesn't know whether it's still in the backstack. You have no way of knowing exactly when to dispose of the subscription. For those cases, you need a weak observer.

CREATING A WEAK OBSERVER

The problem of dangling observers is similar to the problem of dangling event handlers. In traditional .NET events, the registration of the event handler to the event creates a reference from the event source to the object that contains the event handler (unless the event handler is static). So unless you unregister from the event with the `-=` operator, the object that contains the event handler will be kept alive as long as the event source is alive.

To remove this risk, a common pattern is to change the references held by the event to weak references.[3] The `WeakReference` class represents a reference that still allows the referenced object to be reclaimed by the GC. The code that uses the `Weak-Reference` object can query it to check whether the object is still alive.

The next example demonstrates that as long as a strong reference to an object exists, the `WeakReference` shows that the object is alive. When there are no more strong references, the `WeakReference` shows that it's no longer alive.

```
object obj = new object();
WeakReference weak = new WeakReference(obj);

GC.Collect();
Console.WriteLine("IsAlive: {0} obj!=null is {1}", weak.IsAlive,obj!=null);

obj = null;
GC.Collect();
Console.WriteLine("IsAlive: {0}", weak.IsAlive);
```

This is the output you'll see when running the example:

```
IsAlive: True obj!=null is True
IsAlive: False
```

---

[3] A weak reference is a reference that doesn't prevent the GC from collecting the object, http://mng.bz/73ux.

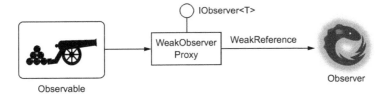

Observable   IObserver<T>   WeakObserver Proxy   WeakReference   Observer

Figure 11.9 Disconnecting the observable and its observer with a mediator observer that weakly references the real observer

You can use `WeakReference` to make the subscription of the observer weak as well, so if the only thing that keeps the observer alive is observable, it won't prevent the GC from reclaiming it. I call this pattern the *weak observer*.

Figure 11.9 illustrates what you're trying to achieve. The idea here is to create a proxy object that holds a weak reference to the observer and delegates the calls from the source observable to the observer. In order for the proxy to receive the notifications from the observable, it must implement the `IObserver<T>` interface.

For each notification the `WeakObserverProxy` receives from the observable, it checks whether the object is still alive and isn't reclaimed by the GC. If so, it will pass the notification to it. If the observer has already been reclaimed, `WeakObserver-Proxy` disposes of the subscription to the source observable.

Here's an example of how this looks for the `OnNext` method:

```
IObserver<T> observer;
if (_weakObserver.TryGetTarget(out observer))
{
    observer.OnNext(value);
}
else
{
    _subscriptionToSource.Dispose();
}
```

The `OnError` and `OnCompleted` methods will do the same thing, so I refactored my code into this:

```
void NotifyObserver(Action<IObserver<T>> action)
{
    IObserver<T> observer;
    if (_weakObserver.TryGetTarget(out observer))
    {
        action(observer);
    }
    else
    {
        _subscriptionToSource.Dispose();
    }
}
```

```
public void OnNext(T value)
{
    NotifyObserver(observer=>observer.OnNext(value));
}
```

Besides the fact that the inner observer might get collected, the user can dispose of the subscription at any time. The `WeakObserverProxy` object holds the subscription object to the source observable and exposes it through the `AsDisposable` method. The exposed disposable is then returned to the client code that subscribes to the observable.

This is the complete code for the `WeakObserverProxy`.

Listing 11.2 The `WeakObserverProxy`

```
class WeakObserverProxy<T>:IObserver<T>
{
    private IDisposable _subscriptionToSource;
    private WeakReference<IObserver<T>> _weakObserver;

    public WeakObserverProxy(IObserver<T> observer)
    {
        _weakObserver = new WeakReference<IObserver<T>>(observer);
    }

    internal void SetSubscription(IDisposable subscriptionToSource)
    {
        _subscriptionToSource = subscriptionToSource;
    }

    void NotifyObserver(Action<IObserver<T>> action)
    {
        IObserver<T> observer;
        if (_weakObserver.TryGetTarget(out observer))
        {
            action(observer);
        }
        else
        {
            _subscriptionToSource.Dispose();
        }
    }
    public void OnNext(T value)
    {
        NotifyObserver(observer=>observer.OnNext(value));
    }

    public void OnError(Exception error)
    {
        NotifyObserver(observer => observer.OnError(error));
    }

    public void OnCompleted()
    {
        NotifyObserver(observer => observer.OnCompleted());
    }
```

```
    public IDisposable AsDisposable()
    {
        return _subscriptionToSource;
    }
}
```

To make your life easier, I created the extension method `AsWeakObservable` that will wrap any observable that you want to subscribe to weakly.

Now, when the observer subscribes, a `WeakObserverProxy` is created, and the observer and the subscription to the source observable are passed to it. Finally, you return the inner subscription to the caller:

```
public static IObservable<T> AsWeakObservable<T>(this IObservable<T> source)
{
    return Observable.Create<T>(o =>
    {
        var weakObserverProxy = new WeakObserverProxy<T>(o);
        var subscription = source.Subscribe(weakObserverProxy);
        weakObserverProxy.SetSubscription(subscription);
        return weakObserverProxy.AsDisposable();;
    });
}
```

Here's an example to test that the weak observer works. In the following code, you create an observable that emits a notification each second (like a sensor that reports the measurement it takes), and weakly subscribes an observer to it. The program holds the subscription for 2 seconds in order to keep the observer alive. Then you remove the reference to the subscription object (setting it to `null`) and force a GC. Afterward, no more notifications are emitted even though you haven't called the `Dispose` method explicitly:

```
 var subscription =
    Observable.Interval(TimeSpan.FromSeconds(1))
        .AsWeakObservable()
        .SubscribeConsole("Interval");

Console.WriteLine("Collecting");
GC.Collect();
Thread.Sleep(2000); //2 seconds

GC.KeepAlive(subscription);
Console.WriteLine("Done sleeping");
Console.WriteLine("Collecting");

subscription = null;
GC.Collect();
Thread.Sleep(2000); //2 seconds
Console.WriteLine("Done sleeping");
```

This is my output after running the program:

```
Collecting
Interval - OnNext(0)
Interval - OnNext(1)
```

```
Done sleeping
Collecting
Done sleeping
```

From the output, you can see that while the subscription is held by a strong reference, notifications keep on coming. When there are no more strong references that are roots to the underlying observer, the notifications stop.

Using weak observers isn't something you should do on a regular basis (just as with weak events), because in most cases you want to be in control of the subscription. But if you find yourself unable to deterministically predict the lifespan of an observer (with the Windows Store application's backstack, for example), then a weak observer is a strong utility to make your life easier and level your application resource usage.

You need to remember that the `WeakObserverProxy` object might stay alive for a long time after the observer it references is collected. This is because when the observable emits a notification, the `WeakObserverProxy` can check whether it's still needed, and if not, it can unsubscribe itself from the observable.

Next, you'll dive into another situation where the consumption of resources in your application increases even though nothing is wrong with the code you write. This might occur when the number of notifications an observer receives per time frame is large. This is called *backpressure*.

11.3   Dealing with backpressure

The observable provides an abstraction over the source of the notifications that emits them, and nothing in the observable interface provides any clue about the rate at which those notifications are emitted.

11.3.1   Observables of different rates

There are three possible outcomes regarding the rate of processing done by the observer; these are illustrated in figure 11.10:

1   The observer processes the notifications at the same rate as the observable emits them.
2   The observable is faster than the observer. This is a case of overload.
3   The observer is faster than the observable. In this case, the observer can process more notifications per time frame than what is emitted by the observable.

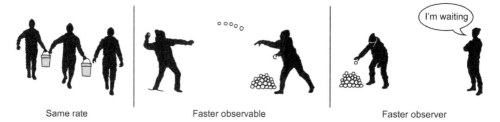

Same rate   Faster observable   Faster observer

Figure 11.10   The effect of different rates between an observable and an observer

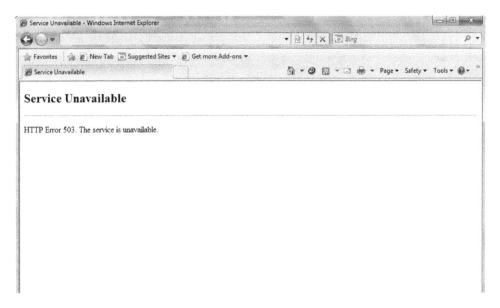

Figure 11.11   A Service Unavailable error page that you might get when the website is overloaded

You can compare those situations to a website that gets requests from clients. The web server that hosts the website can handle a limited number of requests. When the number of requests is too high, you might get an error that says the website isn't available, as shown in figure 11.11.

For cases 1 and 3, where the observer is just as fast as or faster than the observable, no problems will arise and the system will work great. But when the rate of the observable becomes greater than the ability of the observer to consume the notifications, you're on the road to an overload that will eventually crash your system, unless you slow things down in some way.

As stated previously, we call this kind of overload backpressure, and it's something that's easy to get into, as the next example shows.

> **NOTE**   Backpressure is also defined as the ability to tell a source to slow down in order to prevent flooding.

In the following example, you use the `Zip` operator to combine an observable that emits a notification each second with another observable that emits a notification every 2 seconds. These observables might emit notifications from two sensors or from two remote servers, but in any case, the result will be that the slow observable notifications will be buffered by the `Zip` operator:

```
var fast = Observable.Interval(TimeSpan.FromSeconds(1));
var slow = Observable.Interval(TimeSpan.FromSeconds(2));

var zipped = slow.Zip(fast, (x, y) => x + y);
```

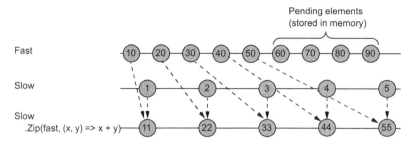

Figure 11.12   Zipping a *fast* observable with a *slow* observable leads to pending elements stored in memory.

The `Zip` operator combines the elements based on their ordinal position, so it must store the elements from the fast observable until the corresponding items are emitted by the slow observable. After 10 seconds, the fast observable emits 10 elements, and the slow observable emits only 5, so the `Zip` operator currently contains only 5 elements in memory. If you run this example for a full day (total time of 86,400 seconds), you'll have 43,200 elements in memory. An illustration of the problem is shown in figure 11.12.

Now that we've established what backpressure is, we can discuss ways to deal with it.

11.3.2 *Mitigating backpressure*

Imagine someone is throwing balls at you at a high rate of speed, and you need to catch them and organize them on a shelf. You have three possible ways to handle this:

1 Ignore some of the balls and let them drop (the lossy approach).
2 Temporarily put some of the balls in a box and get them later (the lossless approach).
3 Signal the thrower to slow down until you're free to catch the balls (the controlled lossless approach).

Some Rx operators take the lossy approach and some take the lossless, but none of them take the controlled lossless approach.

> **TIP** *Reactive* Streams (www.reactive-streams.org/) tries to provide a controlled lossless approach to observables. As stated on the Reactive Streams website, this initiative provides a standard for asynchronous stream processing with nonblocking backpressure (controlled lossless). This standard extends the Rx model to allow the observer to notify the observable about the load it can take. Reactive Streams is not supported by Rx.NET at the time of this writing.

LOSSY APPROACH

Say you have two sensors that emit notifications. One emits twice as fast as the second, and you need to combine the notifications. You need to consider whether the notification emitted by the slower sensor is still relevant. If the sensor emits heart rate, ask yourself whether the heart that was measured an hour ago is still relevant. Is it better to drop it and use only the latest one? In cases like these, where dropping a message is reasonable, here's a list of the options you can take:

- If you're combining observables, but it's sufficient to combine only the latest emitted notification from each of them, use the `CombineLatest` operator (chapter 9).
- If the rate of the observable is high at times, and a notification is irrelevant if another one comes in a short while, use the `Throttle` operator (chapter 10).
- If you need to consume the notifications at a steady pace, no matter how many notifications are emitted in each fragment of time, use the `Scan` operator (chapter 10).

If you need to combine notifications coming from a heart-rate monitor with notifications coming from a speedometer, and there's a chance that the heart-rate monitor produces values faster than the speedometer, this is how you'll overcome backpressure with the `CombineLatest` operator:

```
heartRates.CombineLatest(speeds, (h, s) => String.Format("Heart:{0}
    Speed:{1}", h, s))
```

In all of the lossy approach options, you'll lose some notifications in favor of lower resource consumption, and this is ideal if being responsive and available is your highest priority. When your priority is in consuming each of the notifications emitted, you need to take the lossless approach.

LOSSLESS APPROACH

Say an observable is emitting text messages that you need to display onscreen. Every time a change is made to the screen, it needs to refresh itself, which takes time. When the rate of messages is high, the screen refreshes can cause the UI to be unresponsive and make the user unhappy. A better solution would be to refresh the screen with bulk messages instead of doing it one a time. In such scenarios, you can't drop messages just because they come in at a high rate. Therefore, you need a lossless approach to handle the backpressure. The lossless approach that Rx supports is through buffering, whereby items are stored and then processed as a bulk operation.

The `Buffer` operator you learned about in chapter 9 lets you specify the buffer period by time or amount. This should be handled with care; otherwise, the memory consumption of your application will increase and possibly crash your application.

11.4 Summary

In this final chapter, you looked at methods for optimizing your Rx code. You saw how to react to errors in a graceful manner and how to control the resources your code uses.

- The `Catch` operator lets you react to a specific type of exception that's thrown in the observable pipeline. It sets a fallback observable that the observer will be subscribed to in case an exception is thrown.

- The `OnErrorResumeNext` operator concatenates the observable to another for both successful completion and error termination.
- The `Retry` operator resubscribes the observer to the observable in the case of error.
- The `Using` operator deterministically disposes of an object in case the observable terminates. This way, resources used inside the observable pipeline can be properly cleaned.
- The `Finally` operator runs specific code (like cleanup or logging) in case the observable terminates. This way, you can run cleanup code at the end of the observable processing.
- The observable holds a strong reference to the observers, which can cause the observers to stay alive longer than they should (dangling observers).
- `WeakObservers` change the reference that's used to hold the observer into a `WeakReference`, eliminating cases in which an observer isn't collected because an observable holds it.
- Backpressure occurs when a consumer is slower than the producer.
- Backpressure can cause system performance to degrade, both in memory and throughput.
- The `CombineLatest`, `Throttle`, and `Scan` operators handle backpressure with a lossy approach; some notifications are dropped in favor of lower resource consumption.
- The `Buffer` operator handles backpressure by saving the notifications into a bulk operation that can then be processed as a whole.

appendix A
Writing asynchronous code in .NET

For modern applications to be responsive, writing asynchronous code is crucial, and it's a key trait for being reactive. This appendix summarizes what asynchronous code is, what it's good for, how you can write asynchronous code in .NET, and the best practices for doing so.

A.1 Writing asynchronous code

Imagine you want to ask your friend to send you important information from a document (such as the content of the ReactiveX.io portal). You have two options: you can use the phone to ask your friend to read the information to you, or you can send an email with your request so you both can work on getting the information later. Figure A.1 shows the two options.

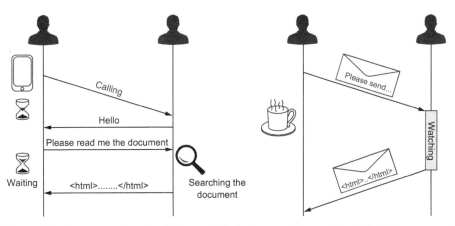

Figure A.1 Two approaches to get the content of a document from a friend. The left sequence shows the synchronous way via phone call. The right sequence shows the asynchronous way via email.

When you make a phone call to retrieve information (the left sequence in the figure), you're using the *synchronous* approach. With this method, you have to wait until the call is answered and then you need to wait for the other side to complete the requested task (such as retrieving the document).

When you choose to send an email (the right sequence in the figure), you're using the *asynchronous* approach. The benefit of the asynchronous operation is obvious: while your message is being sent to the other participant and while it's being handled, you can continue doing other things.

Running code in an asynchronous way is crucial for the modern application for two main reasons:

- *Responsiveness*—Imagine your client application copies a big file. It'd be awful if the UI is blocked the entire time. The user might think the application is stuck. It'd be much better if the long copy operation were asynchronous, with the UI showing progress until the operation finishes.
- *Scalability*—Nowadays almost every computer has more than one core, so running tasks or jobs in real-time parallelism lets your application handle multiple tasks at the same time. Suppose your application needs to handle multiple user requests. Each request that arrives can run asynchronously, and your application can scale accordingly.

A.2 *Asynchronous code in .NET*

Writing asynchronous code isn't hard; all it takes is to delegate the work to another thread, process, or machine, and then not to wait for it to complete. Sounds simple, doesn't it? Unfortunately, writing asynchronous code tends to be much more difficult than that.

For starters, you need to decide how to create a thread, a process, or a task. Or you need to decide how to communicate with another machine to run your code. Then, after you decide how to run your asynchronous code, you need to determine whether it has finished successfully or failed. If it finishes, you'll want to capture the result (or the error).

Not every asynchronous operation (such as reading a file from the hard drive or running a query against a database) is CPU bound, which is great because the CPU is free to process other threads.

.NET has always had ways to run code in an asynchronous fashion, and that has evolved throughout the years.

Here's a simple application that runs a lengthy task in an asynchronous way:

```
class Program
{
    static void Main(string[] args)
    {
        var thread = new Thread(() =>
        {
            //Performing a very long task
```

```
        Console.WriteLine("Long work is done, the result is ...");
    });

    thread.Start();
    Console.ReadLine();
    }
}
```

In this simple program, you create a thread that runs the long-running job. After starting the thread, the main thread is free to proceed with another task. In this case, you wait for user input. When the long-running job is done, the result is written to the console. Figure A.2 shows how the two threads work concurrently.

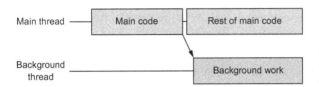

Figure A.2 Creating a background thread. After the thread is created, the main thread continues its execution concurrently to the background thread.

This sample works, but it's far from ideal. Creating a thread is a relatively expensive operation because the OS needs to allocate the thread. For this example, together with all data structures involved, it's approximately 1 MB of memory. Not only is the creation of the thread expensive, when the thread is destroyed and given back to the OS, your application suffers again. For every thread you create, you lose precious resources (time and memory) that the application could've used for additional work. Inside .NET, you have ways to improve the sample code. The `System.Threading` `.ThreadPool` class, for example, handles the creation and destruction of threads, and it does so in a way that reuses threads and adapts to the workload of your application. Thus, the long-running job could've been written like this:

```
ThreadPool.QueueUserWorkItem((_) =>
{
    //Performing a very long task

    Console.WriteLine("Long work is done, the result is ...");
});
```

In this code, you assign the work that needs to be done asynchronously to the `ThreadPool` that adds it to an internal queue. Then, a worker thread that's managed by the `ThreadPool` will pick the work item and execute it.

But creating threads to run every code you want to run asynchronously can work against you. For example, in the previous code, you call to the `Console.WriteLine` method to keep the output from displaying characters that arrive from simultaneous calls. The `Console` class holds a lock to prevent multiple threads from executing at the same time. If you have many threads to write to the console, they'll be blocked until the current write is finished. If you take into consideration the overhead of managing the threads and the code that runs them, you might find that the performance of your application decreases, which is counterproductive to what you want to achieve.

Beside the performance issues, there's another downside to using the thread approach: There's no standard and easy way to know whether the thread completes and no way to receive the response. This makes this approach unfriendly in many situations. In many cases, you'll want to delegate calculations to other threads, and when the calculation is done, you'll want to take the results and combine them. Sometimes this is also done in another thread (or threads).

.NET provides a few patterns to achieve this behavior. The following list describes two that are now considered obsolete, but there's still a chance you'll run into them:

- *The Asynchronous Programming Model (APM) pattern*: In this pattern, two methods (`Begin[OperationName]` and `End[OperationName]`) begin and end the operation. After calling `Begin`, an object of a type that implements `IAsync-Result` is returned immediately. The calling thread isn't blocked and can continue processing the next line. The application can be notified that the operation completed, either by checking the `IsCompleted` property of the `IAsyncResult` object or by a callback that's supplied to the `Begin[Operation Name]` method. When the operation completes, the application calls the `End[OperationName]` method and provides the `IAsyncResult` as an argument; that is, `End[OperationName]` returns the operation's result.
- *The Event-Based Asynchronous Pattern (EAP)*: In this pattern, you call the method that's making the time-consuming work, `[MethodName]Async`. The containing class will have a corresponding event called `[MethodName]Completed`, which will be raised when the operation completes.

Beginning with .NET Framework 4, the recommended pattern for creating asynchronous code is the Task-Based Asynchronous Pattern (TAP), which is based on the Task Parallel Library (TPL). And, because all the other patterns can be converted to the TPL, I use it in the rest of the appendix.

> **TIP** If you do bump into the older asynchronous patterns, the easiest (also recommended) way to work with them is to create a task that abstracts them. For the APM pattern, you can use the `Task.FromAsync` static method, but for EAP you need to work a bit and use the type `TaskCompletion-Source<TResult>`. You can find more information in an MSDN article at http://mng.bz/dJ6K.

A.3 *Task-Based Asynchronous Pattern*

TAP is based on two important types that exist in the .NET Framework: `System .Threading.Tasks.Task` and `System.Threading.Tasks.Task<TResult>`. Tasks are the .NET implementation of futures. A *future* is a stand-in for a computational

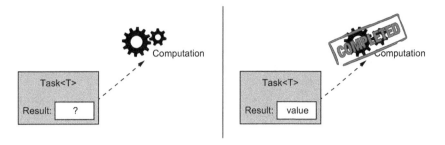

Figure A.3 The task is a .NET implementation of a future: a stand-in for a computational result that's initially unknown but becomes available at a later time.

result that's initially unknown but becomes available at a later time (hence the name future), as shown in figure A.3.

With TAP, methods that perform an asynchronous computation return tasks, and the task is the contact point from which you can know the state of the computation and the final result.

The process of calculating the result can occur in parallel with other computations. `Task` represents a computation that yields no value, while `Task<TResult>` yields a value of type `TResult`. After the computation completes, you can get the result from the task's property `Result`. Here's a small example that asynchronously gets the headers of the ReactiveX portal home page. For brevity, error handling wasn't added to this example:

```
var httpClient = new HttpClient();
Task<HttpResponseMessage> requestTask =
httpClient.GetAsync("http://ReactiveX.io");
```
> Initiates an asynchronous call. The calling thread isn't blocked, and the task is returned immediately.

```
Console.WriteLine("the request was sent, status:{0}",requestTask.Status);
```

```
Console.WriteLine(requestTask.Result.Headers);
```
> The request hasn't finished, so the task status is either waiting or running.

> The call to Result blocks the thread until the request finishes; then the headers will print.

When I ran the sample on my machine, this is what I got:

```
the request was sent, status:WaitingForActivation
Access-Control-Allow-Origin: *
Accept-Ranges: bytes
Cache-Control: max-age=600
Date: Mon, 27 Jul 2015 19:17:26 GMT
Server: GitHub.com
```

A little explanation is in order. When a task is created and started, it's added to a queue that's managed by the `TaskScheduler`. At this point, the task state is `Waiting ForActivation`, which is why the first line that prints shows this status. The

`TaskScheduler` assigns the task into a thread, and this changes the task status to `Running`. When you try to get the `Result` from the task while it's still running, the calling thread is blocked until the task finishes, which causes its state to change to `RanToCompletion`. Upon completion, the calling thread resumes, and the task result is returned. This is when the headers are printed to the console.

Waiting for the task to finish by calling `Result` (or `Wait`) is a little counterproductive for what you want to achieve—getting the headers asynchronously without blocking the calling threads. You can achieve this thanks to the `Continuation` functionality, which tasks support. Here's what the previous example looks like when using the `Continuation` functionality:

```
var httpClient = new HttpClient();
httpClient.GetAsync("http://ReactiveX.io")
    .ContinueWith(requestTask =>
    {
        Console.WriteLine("the request was sent, status:{0}",
     requestTask.Status);
        Console.WriteLine(requestTask.Result.Headers);
    });
```

Adds a continuation to the task returned from the GetAsync method. The code inside starts when the task completes.

Running this version of the code produces this output:

```
the request was sent, status:RanToCompletion
Access-Control-Allow-Origin: *
Accept-Ranges: bytes
Cache-Control: max-age=600
Date: Tue, 28 Jul 2015 20:08:55 GMT
Server: GitHub.com
```

You use the `ContinueWith` method to attach code that'll be executed when the task completes (successfully or not), and the task you're attaching to is sent as an argument (the `requestTask` in the lambda expression). This is why the output you received shows that the status of the task is `RanToCompletion`. Now, in the time that it takes to get the headers and process them (writing to the console), your code works in an asynchronous way. The main thread isn't blocked, and everything runs in the background.

Continuation makes the creation of asynchronous code nice, but it can be lengthy. To demonstrate, let's see what happens when you want to print the content of the page as well as the headers:

```
var httpClient = new HttpClient();

httpClient.GetAsync("http://ReactiveX.io")
    .ContinueWith(requestTask =>
    {
        var httpContent = requestTask.Result.Content;
        httpContent.ReadAsStringAsync()
            .ContinueWith(contentTask =>
            {
```

To use the value of the httpContent object, it needs to be transformed to a meaningful format. This is done asynchronously.

```
            Console.WriteLine(contentTask.Result);
        });
    });
```

As you can see, the more asynchronous methods you use on the way to your target, the more continuations you'll need and the less readable your code becomes. To help with that, C# provides language-based support to hide the complexity of continuations by awaiting the tasks while maintaining regular control flow. This is also known as the `async-await` pattern.

A.4   *Simplifying asynchronous code with async-await*

Instead of repeating the pattern of continuing a task and getting the result when it finishes and then making another continuation on another task, the `async-await` pattern lets you write your asynchronous code as if it were simple and sequential. When calling the asynchronous method (which returns a task), you can instruct the compiler that you want to *await* it, meaning you want the rest of the code to execute when the `async-await` pattern finishes and its result is returned.

Let's look at an example of getting the reactivex.io page with `async-await`:

```
async void GetPageAsync()                          Adds the async modifier
{                                                  to the method definition
    var httpClient = new HttpClient();
    var response = await httpClient.GetAsync("http://ReactiveX.io");
    string page = await response.Content.ReadAsStringAsync();
    Console.WriteLine(page);                              After the response arrives,
}                                                        reads the content as a string
                                                          and awaits its completion
Sends a request to the server and awaits
its response without blocking
```

To use `async-await`, the method that contains `await` must be marked with the `async` modifier. Inside the method, you can now call the asynchronous methods that return either `Task` or `Task<TResult>` and await them (any type can be awaited as long as it provides an awaiter). When the task is complete, the rest of the code is executed and, if you awaited `Task<TResult>`, the `TResult` value is returned without the need to explicitly use the `Result` property on the task. If the task throws an exception, it will be caught in the calling code as if it were a synchronous call.

> **TIP** Any type can be awaited as long as it provides an awaiter by exposing a `GetAwaiter` method. An *awaiter* is any class that conforms to a particular pattern. You can find more details in the Async/Await FAQ: http://mng.bz/27mZ.

Suppose the method you wrote needs to return the downloaded string content. `async-await` is viral! Because you call async methods inside your code, this makes your code asynchronous by itself, which means that the value you want to return will be available when the async calls complete. To expose that information to the caller, and to allow it to await on the completeness of your code, you must also return a task (in this case, Task<string>). Methods marked with async can only return Task, Task<TResult>, or void. This is how the method signature looks now:

```
async Task<string> GetPageAsync()
```

When you need to return a value inside an async method that returns a task, you don't need to return the task explicitly. You can regularly return the value as if it were a simple synchronous method. The compiler makes the transformations behind the scenes:

```
private static async Task<string> GetPageAsync()
{
    var httpClient = new HttpClient();

    var response = await httpClient.GetAsync("http://ReactiveX.io");
    string page = await response.Content.ReadAsStringAsync();
    return page;                                          ⟵┐ Returns a string value,
}                                                          │ not a task object
```

The GetPageAsync method calls to other async methods and then returns the end result that's of type string. The method is asynchronous because it uses other asynchronous methods, but you have no real idea of what's going on inside and whether it's truly asynchronous. Because we haven't discussed how to write methods that run their code inside an asynchronous task, we'll look at that next.

A.5   *Creating tasks*

In the previous examples, I haven't talked about how to create tasks in the code that you write. All you saw is that when you add the async modifier to your methods, the compiler generates a returned task for you. This can be misleading, as the next example shows.

Look at the following code and predict what will be printed:

```
async void AsyncMethodCaller()
{
    bool isSame = await MyAsyncMethod(Thread.CurrentThread.ManagedThreadId);
    Console.WriteLine(isSame);
}

async Task<bool> MyAsyncMethod(int callingThreadId)
{
    return Thread.CurrentThread.ManagedThreadId == callingThreadId;
}
```

The method AsyncMethodCaller calls MyAsyncMethod and passes the thread ID. Because MyAsyncMethod returns a task, the call can be awaited. The MyAsync-Method checks whether the ID of the thread it's running on is the same as the thread ID it received as a parameter and returns the result, which is then printed by the caller method.

When you run this program, you'll see that the printed value will be true, which might surprise you. You see, marking a method as async and returning a task doesn't by itself make the code inside the method perform asynchronously. It's a way to instruct the compiler that the code inside might perform as an asynchronous operation and that you request its help to make a continuation when that happens.

In the previous method, you haven't done anything asynchronous, so that's why the calling thread is the same thread as the one running the method's code. The only thing you did is hurt the performance of your simple code because, behind the scenes, the compiler created a state machine[1] that has only one state, and the overhead of managing this state machine has a performance hit.

To make your method asynchronous, you need to span the work to another task, and this can be done by using `Task.Run`. Here's a real asynchronous version of `MyAsyncMethod`:

```
async void AsyncMethodCaller()
{
    Console.WriteLine();
    Console.WriteLine("----- Using Task.Run(...) to create async code ----");

    bool isSame = await MyAsyncMethod(Thread.CurrentThread.ManagedThreadId);
    Console.WriteLine("Caller thread is the same as executing thread: {0}",
isSame);
}
```

⟵ **After the call, this will print "false."**

The call to Task.Run will cause the code passed in the lambda expression to run in another thread.

```
async Task<bool> MyAsyncMethod(int callingThreadId)
{
    return await Task.Run(() =>
Thread.CurrentThread.ManagedThreadId == callingThreadId);
}
```
⟵

In this version, you create a new task and start it by passing the lambda expression to the `Task.Run` method. This causes the `TaskScheduler` to assign a thread that will run your code. The printed value you see now is `false`.

In this appendix, I've tried to show a few techniques that you can use to write asynchronous code. I haven't touched upon many other techniques that we could talk about for hours. But this book is about Rx and not about how to write multithreaded applications; many books have been written to explain that. Because this topic is interesting to me and, I'm sure, to you too, you can learn more about what .NET provides when dealing with multithreading by reading Jeffrey Richter's *CLR via C#* (Microsoft Press, 2012). I also recommend *Concurrency in C# Cookbook* by Stephen Cleary (O'Reilly, 2014).

A.6   *Summary*

This appendix provided a short recap about writing asynchronous code in .NET. Asynchronicity plays a major role in the Rx world, and the material in this book relies on the concepts explained here.

---

[1] To learn more about state machines, see https://en.wikipedia.org/wiki/Finite-state_machine.

Here's a summary of what you learned:

- Asynchronous code execution is crucial for the modern application to be both scalable and responsive.
- .NET provides a few ways to achieve asynchronicity, which rely on thread creation and I/O operations.
- The recommended approach is to use the Task Parallel Library (TPL), which allows spanning new tasks, and to create continuations on tasks (completed or failed).
- The `async-await` pattern lets you write asynchronous code in a way that makes it look sequential and natural.

appendix B
The Rx Disposables library

The `System.Reactive.Core` package includes an additional treat that can be helpful: the Rx Disposables library. It's a set of types that implement the `IDisposable` interface and provides generic implementations to recurring patterns to help you accomplish most of the things you'll need your disposable to do, without creating your own type! All the types listed in this appendix reside in the `System.Reactive.Disposables` namespace.

> **NOTE** The `System.Reactive.Core` package is the main Rx package. For details about other Rx packages, see chapter 2.

Table B.1 will help you remember what the disposable utilities and types do.

Table B.1   The tenets of the Rx Disposables library

Type/utility	Description
`Disposable.Create`	A static method used to create a disposable that executes a given code when disposed of.
`Disposable.Empty`	Creates an empty disposable.
`ContextDisposable`	Runs the disposal of its underlying disposable resource on a given `SynchronizationContext`.
`ScheduledDisposable`	Runs the disposal of its underlying disposable resource on a given `IScheduler`.
`SerialDisposable`	Holds a replaceable underlying disposable and disposes of the previous disposable when replaced.
`MultipleAssignmentDisposable`	Holds a replaceable underlying disposable but doesn't dispose of the previous disposable when replaced.
`RefCountDisposable`	Disposes of the underlying disposable when all the referencing disposables are disposed of.

Table B.1   The tenets of the Rx Disposables library *(continued)*

Type/utility	Description
CompositeDisposable	Combines multiple disposables into a single disposable object that will dispose of all the disposables together.
CancellationDisposable	Cancels a given CancellationTokenSource when disposed of.
BooleanDisposable	Sets a Boolean flag when disposed of. You can query whether the BooleanDisposable type was disposed of by using the IsDisposed property.

B.1   Disposable.Create

The most flexible way to create a disposable is with the Disposable.Create static factory method. All you need to do is pass the action you want the disposable to execute upon calling the Dispose method. The next example creates a disposable that changes the state of a screen (from busy to nonbusy). The screen shows news items after they're downloaded. While the screen is in the busy state, the UI can display a progress bar to show the user that something is happening in the background.

```
private async Task RefreshNewsAsync()
{
    IsBusy = true;
    NewsItems = Enumerable.Empty<string>();
    using (Disposable.Create(() => IsBusy = false))
    {
        NewsItems = await DownloadNewsItems();
    }
}
```

The IsBusy property is bound to a busy indicator on the screen, so when it's set to true, the busy indicator is shown, and when it's set to false, the busy indicator is invisible. The nice thing about working with disposables is that the using statement ensures that the Dispose method is executed even if the code throws an exception, so you can be assured that the screen won't get stuck in a busy state.

B.2   Disposable.Empty

The static property Disposable.Empty returns a disposable object that has an empty Dispose method. This can be handy for initializing an IDisposable variable or member so you won't have to write code to check for null and risk forgetting it. It can also serve to return a disposable object, such as when you create your own Rx operators that must return a disposable object from their Subscribe method, but you don't need any special disposing functionality. Here's a simplified version of the Observable.Return operator that uses Disposable.Empty:

```
public static IObservable<T> Return<T>(T value)
{
```

```
    return Observable.Create<T>(o =>
    {
        o.OnNext(value);
        o.OnCompleted();
        return Disposable.Empty;
    });
}
```

The value has already been emitted so the returned disposable has nothing it can do. You return an empty one.

B.3 ContextDisposable

The `ContextDisposable` class wraps a disposable object and executes its `Dispose` method on a specified `SynchronizationContext`. Executing the `Dispose` method on a `SynchronizationContext` is important when the operation is tied to a specific context (for example, when changing a UI element). This code creates a `StartBusy` method to create a disposable that turns off the busy indicator on the UI's `SynchronizationContext`:

```
public IDisposable StartBusy()
{
    IsBusy = true;
    return new ContextDisposable(
        SynchronizationContext.Current,
        Disposable.Create(() => IsBusy = false));
}
```

Wrap the disposable in a ContextDisposable to make sure the change to the IsBusy property will happen on the UI thread.

B.4 ScheduledDisposable

The `ScheduledDisposable` class works similarly to `ContextDisposable`, but instead of specifying a `SynchronizationContext`, you specify an `IScheduler` on which the disposal invocation is scheduled. For example, when you use the `SubscribeOn` operator on an observable, the returned disposable from your subscription is wrapped with a `ScheduledDisposable` that uses the `IScheduler` provided. See the next section for an example.

B.5 SerialDisposable

The `SerialDisposable` class lets you wrap a replaceable disposable object. Upon replacing the inner disposable, the previous one is automatically disposed of. Besides that, `SerialDisposable` remembers whether it's been disposed of, and if it was and the inner disposable is replaced, then the inner disposable will also be disposed of. An example is shown in a simplified version of the `SubscribeOn` operator. Because I can't predict exactly when the scheduler will execute work that I schedule, I'm creating a `SerialDisposable` and set its inner disposable inside the scheduled operation:

```
public static IObservable<TSource> MySubscribeOn<TSource>(
    this IObservable<TSource> source,
    IScheduler scheduler)
{
    return Observable.Create<TSource>(observer =>
    {
```

```
        var d = new SerialDisposable();

        d.Disposable = scheduler.Schedule(() =>
        {
            d.Disposable = new ScheduledDisposable(scheduler,
            source.SubscribeSafe(observer));
        });

        return d;
    });
}
```

After the scheduled task executes the subscription to the source observable, the underlying disposable of `SerialDisposable` is set to the subscription that's wrapped with a `ScheduledDisposable`, so its disposal takes place on the scheduler. If it's already disposed of, the assigned disposable will also be disposed of.

B.6   RefCountDisposable

The `RefCountDisposable` class wraps a disposable object and disposes of it only after all referencing disposables have been disposed of. A referencing disposable is created by calling the method `GetDisposable` on the `RefCountDisposable`.

Here's an example that shows that the inner disposable is disposed of only after the two referencing disposables are disposed of:

```
var inner = Disposable.Create(
    () => Console.WriteLine("Disposing inner-disposable"));
var refCountDisposable = new RefCountDisposable(inner);
var d1=refCountDisposable.GetDisposable();
var d2=refCountDisposable.GetDisposable();

refCountDisposable.Dispose();
Console.WriteLine("Disposing 1st");
d1.Dispose();
Console.WriteLine("Disposing 2nd");
d2.Dispose();
```

The output is as follows:

```
Disposing 1st
Disposing 2nd
Disposing inner-disposable
```

B.7   MultipleAssignmentDisposable

The `MultiAssignmentDisposable` class holds an underlying disposable object that can be replaced at any time, but unlike the `SerialDisposable`, replacing the underlying disposable doesn't automatically dispose of the previous one. But `MultiAssignmentDisposable` remembers whether the disposable has been disposed of. If so, and the underlying disposable is replaced, `MultiAssignmentDisposable` will automatically dispose of it.

B.8   *CompositeDisposable*

The `CompositeDisposable` class lets you group multiple disposable objects into one, so that when the `CompositeDisposable` is disposed of, all its inner disposables are disposed of as well.

```
var compositeDisposable = new CompositeDisposable(
    Disposable.Create(() => Console.WriteLine("1st disposed")),
    Disposable.Create(() => Console.WriteLine("2nd disposed")));

compositeDisposable.Dispose();
```

The same can also be written using the `Add` method:

```
var compositeDisposable = new CompositeDisposable();
compositeDisposable.Add(Disposable.Create(
    () => Console.WriteLine("1st disposed")));
compositeDisposable.Add(Disposable.Create(
    () => Console.WriteLine("2nd disposed")));

compositeDisposable.Dispose();
```

Often when I subscribe to multiple observables inside my class, I want to group all the subscriptions together so I can dispose of them at the same time. To keep my observable pipelines fluent, I created this handy extension method:

```
static CompositeDisposable AddToCompositeDisposable(this IDisposable @this,
    CompositeDisposable compositeDisposable)
{
    if (compositeDisposable==null)
        throw new ArgumentNullException(nameof(compositeDisposable));
    compositeDisposable.Add(@this);
    return compositeDisposable;
}
```

Then I can use it like this:

```
IObservable<string> observable = ...

observable.Where(x => x.Length%2 == 0)
    .Select(x => x.ToUpper())
    .Subscribe(x => Console.WriteLine(x))
    .AddToCompositeDisposable(compositeDisposable);

observable.Where(x => x.Length % 2 == 1)
    .Select(x => x.ToLower())
    .Subscribe(x => Console.WriteLine(x))
    .AddToCompositeDisposable(compositeDisposable);
```

B.9   *SingleAssignmentDisposable*

The `SingleAssignmentDisposable` class allows only a single assignment of its underlying disposable object. If there's an attempt to set the underlying disposable object when it's already set, an `InvalidOperationException` is thrown.

B.10   *CancellationDisposable*

The `CancellationDisposable` class is an adapter between the `IDisposable` world and the `CancellationTokenSource` world. When `CancellationDisposable` is disposed of, the underlying `CancellationTokenSource` is canceled. This is used, for example, in the Rx `TaskPoolScheduler` so the returned disposable from `Schedule` will be tied to the `CancellationToken` that's sent to the `TaskScheduler`. Here's a simplified version of how it looks:

```
IDisposable Schedule<TState>(TState state,
    Func<IScheduler, TState, IDisposable> action)
{
    var d = new SerialDisposable();
    var cancelable = new CancellationDisposable();
    d.Disposable = cancelable;
    Task.Run(() =>
    {
        d.Disposable = action(this, state);
    }, cancelable.Token);
    return d;
}
```

The `CancellationToken` created by the underlying `CancellationTokenSource` of the `CancellationDisposable` is sent to the `TaskScheduler` to prevent it from running the `Task` if the user disposed of the disposable that was returned from the method.

B.11   *BooleanDisposable*

The `BooleanDisposable` class holds a Boolean flag that lets you check whether it has already been disposed of. For example:

```
var booleanDisposable = new BooleanDisposable();
Console.WriteLine("Before dispose, booleanDisposable.IsDisposed = {0}",
    booleanDisposable.IsDisposed);
    booleanDisposable.Dispose();
Console.WriteLine("After dispose, booleanDisposable.IsDisposed = {0}",
    booleanDisposable.IsDisposed);
```

The output is as follows:

```
Before dispose, booleanDisposable.IsDisposed = False
After dispose, booleanDisposable.IsDisposed = True
```

B.12   *Summary*

The Rx package provides not only Rx-specific types and utilities, but also a rich library to ease your life when creating disposables.

- To create a disposable that executes a given code when disposed of, use the `Disposable.Create` static method.
- To create an empty disposable, use the `Disposable.Empty` static property.
- To make sure that a disposable will be disposed of in a specific `SynchronizationContext`, wrap it with an instance of `ContextDisposable`.

- To make sure that a disposable will be disposed of in a specific `IScheduler`, wrap it with an instance of `ScheduledDisposable`.
- Use the `SerialDisposable` class when you need a disposable that holds an underlying disposable resource that can be replaced, causing an automatic disposal of the previous underlying disposable resource.
- When you need a disposable whose underlying disposable resource can be replaced but without disposing the previous one, use the `MultipleAssignmentDisposable` class.
- To make sure that a disposable object will be disposed of only after all referencing disposables are disposed of, use the `RefCountDisposable` class.
- To combine multiple disposables into a single disposable object that will dispose of all the disposables together, use the `CompositeDisposable` class.
- Use the `SingleAssignmentDisposable` when you need to make sure that only a single underlying disposable will be set.
- Use the `CancellationDisposable` to cancel a `CancellationTokenSource` upon disposal.
- Use the `BooleanDisposable` when you need to query a disposable about whether it was disposed of.

appendix C
Testing Rx queries and operators

One of the things that differentiates an amateur programmer from a professional is the ability to test the code that was written and ensure that it does what it needs to do. Writing unit tests allows you, the programmer, to validate that you created the right solution, and be certain that your future development won't affect or ruin the code you previously wrote (known as regression). Rx queries and operators are no different, and you should invest the time to test them as well. I'll even go so far as to say that by testing, you'll get a better understanding of your craft and improve your design. In this appendix, you'll learn the utilities that the Rx library provides to facilitate your testing and strategies you can use to improve your Rx code testability.

C.1   Testing Rx code

As you progress with your Rx work, at times you'll find yourself writing the same pattern of code over and over. When this happens, you should follow the DRY principle and encapsulate the recurring pattern in a new operator. Of course, once you create a new operator, you need to test it and be certain you implement it correctly.

Imagine that you have a proximity sensor that emits notifications whenever a near object is sensed. The proximity sensor is sensitive, and every time an object gets closer, you get a burst of notifications, one after the other. Your application wants to react to the sensor notifications, but it's necessary to filter the bursts so only a single emission will take place. At the same time, another application you write needs to react to mouse moves, but you don't want to react to each and every one; you want to make the reaction smoother and react to a single emission from the burst. This type of filtering is known as *throttling*. Rx even provides the `Throttle` operator (discussed in chapter 10), but it emits only the *last* notification in a burst, whereas what you need here is emitting the *first* notification in the burst. Because you need this kind of logic in more than one place, you create a new Rx operator called `FilterBursts`. This operator receives the expected size of a burst, and emits back the first item of each burst:

```
public static class ObservableExtensions
{
    public static IObservable<T> FilterBursts<T>(
      this IObservable<T> src,
      int burstSize)
    {
        //The operator implementation
    }
}
```

> **NOTE** This appendix focuses on testing, not implementing the Rx code, so the operator implementation isn't shown here. It's available with the book source code, and I encourage you to check it out, or even better, try to implement it yourself as an exercise.

Now that you have the operator implementation, you want to test it. The examples in this chapter use xUnit (https://xunit.github.io/). Beside being a good testing framework, it's the one used by the Rx team and is also one of the few frameworks that supports .NET Core at the time of this writing. Feel free to use whatever testing framework you like; the concepts I'll show are applicable to all frameworks.

Before you can start writing the unit tests, you need to add the Rx testing library. To install it, you need to add the NuGet package `Microsoft.Reactive.Testing`.

Your first unit test, shown in the following listing, asserts that when applying the `FilterBursts` operator with a `burstSize` of 5 to a source observable of 10 values, the resulted observable will emit only the first and the sixth values.

Listing C.1   A basic unit test on an Rx operator

```
using Microsoft.Reactive.Testing;

public class FilterBurstsTests
{                                                     ┐ xUnit declaration
    [Fact]                                        ◄──┘ of a test method
    public static void FilterBursts_SourceOf10AndBurstSize5_TwoEmissions()
    {
        var sequenceSize = 10;
        var burstSize = 5;
        var expected = new[] { 0, 5 };
        var xs = Observable.Range(0, sequenceSize);   ◄──┐ Creates the source
                                                         │ observable that will
        xs.FilterBursts(burstSize)                       │ emit 10 values
            .AssertEqual(expected.ToObservable());
    }
}
```

`AssertEqual` is part of the Rx test library. It checks that the resulted observable emits the same value as the observable it receives as an argument.

> **NOTE** It's a common convention to name the source observables in unit tests as xs and ys.

The preceding unit test works as expected and is small and clear. So now you want to add more test cases to make sure that your operator behaves as it should. For this, you can use the *xUnit theory*[1] feature that allows you to specify multiple inputs to the same test method (also known as a *data-driven test*).

Listing C.2   A data-driven test of an Rx operator

```
[Theory]
[InlineData(1, 1, new[] { 0 })]
[InlineData(5, 1, new[] { 0 })]
[InlineData(1, 5, new[] { 0, 1, 2, 3, 4 })]
[InlineData(5, 5, new[] { 0 })]
[InlineData(5, 8, new[] { 0, 5 })]
public void FilterBursts(int burstSize, int sequenceSize, int[] expected)
{
    var xs = Observable.Range(0, sequenceSize);
    xs.FilterBursts(burstSize)
        .AssertEqual(expected.ToObservable());
}
```

← **Each InlineData attribute represents a single test case. Set each InlineData with a collection of values that will be the test method arguments for this test case.**

Running this test yields the results shown in figure C.1 in the Visual Studio Test Explorer.

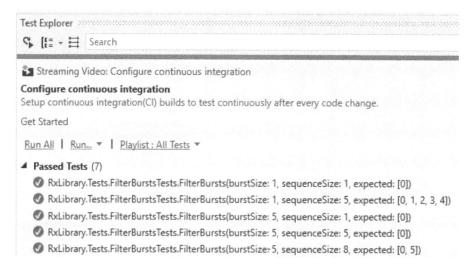

Figure C.1   The results of the xUnit data-driven test, as shown in Visual Studio Test Explorer

---

[1] For more details, see http://mng.bz/Pe5x.

So far you've managed to write simple tests the can validate the logical purpose of the Rx operator. Next I'll show you how to write tests that take the time dimension into consideration, and you can assert that emissions were indeed what happened *when* they should've happened.

C.1.1 *Writing reactive tests with the TestScheduler*

The tests you've written in the previous section work well, but they're limited because they don't take the time dimension into consideration. When developing Rx operators and queries, you want to ensure that they behave correctly even if there's a time difference in certain positions in the observer-observable relationship, for example:

- When there's a time pause between emissions
- When there's a time difference between the observer subscription and observable creation
- When the emission time the observer experiences is different from the time the source observable has emitted its value
- Any other time-related case that could influence the Rx code

Writing tests that involve timing is a complex thing to do by yourself, but luckily, Rx provides a way to virtualize time by using the TestScheduler and the ReactiveTest base class.

In chapter 10, I introduced schedulers and explained how they allow you to control and parameterize concurrency in the Rx pipeline. A *scheduler* is a unit that holds a clock and an execution location (such as a thread or a task) and enables scheduling the execution of work items to a specific time.

The TestScheduler (part of the Microsoft.Reactive.Testing namespace) is a special kind of scheduler that allows you to control its inner clock and configure when events will occur. The TestScheduler provides a clock of a virtual time counted by ticks, and ticks can be converted to (and from) DateTime and TimeSpan.

> **TIP** Both TimeSpan and DateTime implement a property called Ticks that returns the aforementioned value as ticks. You can convert ticks to TimeSpan by using the static method TimeSpan.FromTicks, and you can create a DateTime from ticks by using its dedicated constructor.

When you create the TestScheduler, it initializes its clock to the time 0. Until you explicitly start the clock, the time is frozen.

The following code shows an example of creating an observable that, after the observer subscription, will emit the values 1 and 2 with a gap of 20 ticks between them and then complete after another 20 ticks:

```
var testScheduler = new TestScheduler();

ITestableObservable<int> coldObservable =
    testScheduler.CreateColdObservable<int>(
    new Recorded<Notification<int>>(20, Notification.CreateOnNext<int>(1)),
    new Recorded<Notification<int>>(40, Notification.CreateOnNext<int>(2)),
```

```
new Recorded<Notification<int>>(60,Notification.CreateOnCompleted<int>())
);
```

NOTE What is shown here is the full, long, and detailed way to create Test-ableObservable. After you inherit from ReactiveTest, this task becomes shorter, as you'll see soon.

TestScheduler provides two methods for creating observables:

- CreateColdObservable—Creates an observable that emits its value relatively to when each observer subscribes
- CreateHotObservable—Creates an observable that emits its values regardless of the observer subscription time, and each emission is configured to the absolute scheduler clock

Both methods receive a collection of Recorded<Notification<T>> objects that specify the scheduling of the OnNext, OnError, and OnCompleted notifications you want the observable to emit, and return an observable of type ITestableObservable that lets you examine its messages and subscriptions so you can assert they're what you expect them to be.

It's important to remember that when you create a TestScheduler, its clock is frozen. Until you start it or advance its time explicitly, no emissions will be made. After you start the scheduler, it'll execute every work item that was scheduled to it. After each one, it'll increment its inner clock to the scheduled time of the next work item. After the last work item, the scheduler will increment its clock by one, and stop, so you'll have to start it again after you schedule another work item.

The Rx testing library Microsoft.Reactive.Testing includes the Reactive Test base class that I recommend using whenever you write unit tests for Rx code. The ReactiveTest base class includes a few factory methods that make the unit-test code more fluent and concise so the observable you just created can now be declared, as shown in the following listing.

Listing C.3   An example of a reactive unit test with the ReactiveTest base class

```
public class CreatColdObservableTests : ReactiveTest
{

    [Fact]
    public void CreatColdObservable()
    {
        var testScheduler = new TestScheduler();
        ITestableObservable<int> coldObservable =
            testScheduler.CreateColdObservable<int>(

                OnNext(20, 1),
                OnNext(40, 2),
                OnCompleted<int>(60)
            );
```

Creates the Recorded<Notification<T>> objects. They're provided by the ReactiveTest base class that makes the configuration of the observable emissions much shorter and more concise.

```
                    // rest of unit-test
            }
    }
}
```

C.1.2 Observing the TestableObservable

Now that you know how to create `TestableObservables`, you can continue to embed them in your tests so you can observe the Rx query they're part of and take the time dimension into consideration.

Continuing with the tests of the `FilterBursts` operator introduced earlier, you can now test how time issues might affect it. The next test, shown in listing C.4, asserts that when two bursts of three values happen one after the other with a gap of 100 ticks between them, `FilterBursts` will emit the first value from each burst (a visualization of this is shown in figure C.2).

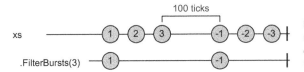

Figure C.2 **Visualization of the expected result of applying the** `FilterBursts` **operator on an observable that emits two bursts with a time gap between them**

Listing C.4 An example of a reactive unit test that embeds the time dimension

```
[Fact]
public void FilterBursts_TwoBurstWithAGap_FirstInEachBurstEmitted()
{
    var scheduler = new TestScheduler();

    var xs = scheduler.CreateHotObservable(
        OnNext(250, 1),
        OnNext(275, 2),                    Creates an observable that will
        OnNext(300, 3),                    emit two bursts, of values 1 to 3
                                           and of −1 to −3, at the absolute
        OnNext(400, -1),                   times specified by the ticks
        OnNext(401, -2),                   parameter (the first parameter)
        OnNext(405, -3),                   of each notification

        OnCompleted<int>(500)
        );

    var testableObserver = scheduler.CreateObserver<int>();    ◁── Creates a
                                                                   testableObserver
    xs.FilterBursts(3)            Code to test. Because the scheduler  capable of
        .Subscribe(testableObserver);    hasn't been started, its clock time is 0.  recording its
                                                                   observations
    scheduler.Start();                          ◁──            Starts the Scheduler so
                                                               the testableObservable
    testableObserver.Messages.AssertEqual(   Asserts that the   will start emitting
        OnNext(250, 1),                      notifications that
        OnNext(400, -1),                     testableObserver
        OnCompleted<int>(500));              observed are the same
```

```
xs.Subscriptions.AssertEqual(
    Subscribe(0, 500));
}
```

Asserts that only one observer was subscribed, starting at time 0 and ending at time 500, the time of the observable completion

In the preceding code, you use the `TestableObserver` class to assert that the expected emission indeed took effect.

`TestableObserver` is created by calling the `TestScheduler.CreateObserver` method. This special observer records the notifications it observes and then exposes them through its `Messages` property so you can later inspect them and assert they're correct.

As mentioned before, when created, the `TestScheduler` is in a stopped state, which means that the time is frozen. Calling the `Start` method causes the scheduler to begin executing all the work items that were scheduled to it. In the preceding unit test, you've created a hot observable with a set of scheduled emissions, so when the scheduler was started, those emissions were emitted and the observer that was subscribed observed them.

At the end of the unit test, you're asserting that (a) all the notifications were indeed observed, and (b) the subscription lifetime of the single observer is as expected.

TIP The `OnNext` factory method has another overload that accepts a predicate (of type `Func<T,bool>`) as a second parameter. This overload can be used in the `Assertion` phase to check that the emitted value is what was expected by using a logical condition.

Next, I want to take you through the fundamentals of testing operators that introduce concurrency and use *time* as part of their logic.

C.1.3 *Testing concurrent Rx code*

The `FilterBurst` operator used in the previous sections, as useful as it may be, tackled the problem of bursts from an items-amount perspective. This perspective ignores an important aspect of many Rx queries in which the time distance between items might be relatively large and might affect the resulted emissions. Therefore, another overload of this operator was created that deals with bursts of values over time (shown in figure C.3). According to the approach that this operator takes, the concept of a burst is defined as *a sequence of values that has a maximal time difference between two adjacent values.*

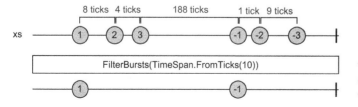

Figure C.3
The `FilterBursts` operator emits the first value from every burst of items

Here are the signatures of this overload:

```
public static class ObservableExtensions
{
    public static IObservable<T> FilterBursts<T>(
      this IObservable<T> src,
      TimeSpan maximalDistance)
    {
        //...
    }

    public static IObservable<T> FilterBursts<T>(
      this IObservable<T> src,
      TimeSpan maximalDistance,
      IScheduler scheduler)
    {
        //...
    }
}
```

As discussed in chapter 10, every operator that introduces concurrency as part of its logic should accept a scheduler that'll be used to control that concurrency. One of the benefits of this rule is that it allows you to test the operator under different scenarios.

Here's how to write the test for the scenario shown in figure C.3.

Listing C.5 An example of a reactive unit test on a time-based operator

```
[Fact]
public void FilterBurstsInColdObservable()
{
    var scheduler = new TestScheduler();

    var xs = scheduler.CreateColdObservable(
        OnNext(250, 1),
        OnNext(258, 2),
        OnNext(262, 3),

        OnNext(450, -1),
        OnNext(451, -2),
        OnNext(460, -3),

        OnCompleted<int>(500)
        );

    var res = scheduler.Start(
        () => xs.FilterBursts(TimeSpan.FromTicks(10), scheduler));

    res.Messages.AssertEqual(
        OnNext(450, 1),
        OnNext(650, -1),
        OnCompleted<int>(700));

    xs.Subscriptions.AssertEqual(
        Subscribe(ReactiveTest.Subscribed, 700));
}
```

Creates a cold observable that'll emit two bursts of values 1 to 3 and of –1 to –3 at the relative times to when the observer subscribed

Orders the TestScheduler to start its clock and monitor the given observable by creating a TestableObserver that'll be subscribed to it.

By default, the time in which the TestableObserver is subscribed to the observable you test is initialized to the value specified in the ReactiveTest.Subscribed constant.

Reactive tests tend to have a repetitive structure: you create a testable observable and a testable observer, subscribe the observer to the observable (not necessarily immediately), start the scheduler, and then assert the recorded notifications. Because this structure is repeated in many tests, the `TestScheduler.Start` method has overloads that encapsulate this structure.

In the preceding unit test, you use this kind of overload that has the following signature:

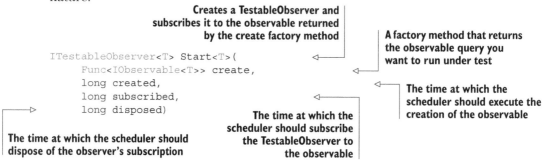

Creates a TestableObserver and subscribes it to the observable returned by the create factory method

A factory method that returns the observable query you want to run under test

```
ITestableObserver<T> Start<T>(
    Func<IObservable<T>> create,
    long created,
    long subscribed,
    long disposed)
```

The time at which the scheduler should execute the creation of the observable

The time at which the scheduler should subscribe the TestableObserver to the observable

The time at which the scheduler should dispose of the observer's subscription

By default, the time at which the observer is subscribed to the observable is 200 (configured by the `ReactiveTest.Subscribed` constant). That's why I assert that the first emitted value observed by the `TestableObserver` was observed at the time 450.

C.1.4 *Finer control on the TestScheduler*

Some tests require you to have finer control over the `TestScheduler` clock. Usually, in these cases, you need to break the test into two or more phases. Table C.1 lists the most used methods and members for controlling the scheduler.

Table C.1 The most used `TestScheduler` members (partial list)

Method/member	Description
`Start`	Starts the scheduler clock. Each work item that was scheduled will be executed, and the clock will increment its time after each one.
`AdvanceTo(long time)`	Advances the scheduler clock to the specified absolute time. Every work item that was scheduled to a point between the current time and given time will be executed.
`AdvanceBy(long time)`	Advances the scheduler clock by the specified relative time. Every work item that was scheduled to a point between the current time and given time will be executed.
`Sleep(long time)`	Advances the scheduler by the specified relative time *without* executing the queued work items that were scheduled to that time frame.
`Stop`	Stops the scheduler.
`Clock`	Gets the current clock time (as ticks).
`IsEnabled`	Gets whether the scheduler is enabled to run work.

C.2 Testing Rx queries

Everything you've learned in the previous sections about testing Rx operators is applicable to testing other Rx constructs and queries. The only difference is the lack of accessibility you might have to the Rx code when you write the test for the class that contains it. This lack of accessibility is usually a good thing (because you don't want the test to rely on implementation details), but when you use time-based operators, this can cause the testing to be hard or even impossible.

C.2.1 Injecting schedulers

Consider this example: you've created a class named `MachineMonitor` that monitors a manufacturing machine that produces a lot of heat during its work. The monitor uses a proximity sensor and temperature sensor, so that if someone is getting near the machine while it's hot, an alert is produced.

The rate of notifications produced by the proximity sensor and the temperature sensor is high, and therefore the `MachineMonitor` class emits many alerts. To slow the number of alerts produced, you add the `FilterBursts` operator that was discussed earlier in this chapter. This time, `FilterBursts` was extended so that it won't filter emissions from the burst forever. Instead, a maximum burst duration is provided to the operator, such that if a burst is longer than the maximum burst duration, the burst is considered closed and the emission isn't filtered.

The initial monitor class basic structure is shown here.

Listing C.6 Initial implementation of the `MachineMonitor` class

```
public class MachineMonitor
{

    public MachineMonitor(
        ITemperatureSensor temperatureSensor,
        IProximitySensor proximitySensor)
    {
        _temperatureSensor = temperatureSensor;
        _proximitySensor = proximitySensor;
    }

    public TimeSpan MinAlertPause { get; set; }        ◁─── Maximal amount of time you
    public TimeSpan MaxAlertBurstTime { get; set; }    ◁───  consider a sequence of
                                                             notifications as a burst. After
                                                             this time, emissions are
                                                             considered as a new burst.

    public IObservable<Alert> ObserveAlerts()          Amount of time you
    {                                                  allow between two
        return Observable.Defer(() =>                  consecutive alerts
        {
            IObservable<Alert> alerts = //Rx query that emits alerts

            return alerts.FilterBursts(MinAlertPause, MaxAlertBurstTime);
        });
    }
}
```

Slows down the alerts that are emitted when someone is close to a hot machine

NOTE   The focus of this appendix is about *testing* and *not* the implementation of the Rx code, so the full implementation isn't shown here. It's available with the book source code, and I encourage you to check it out, or even better, implement it yourself as an exercise.

Looking at this code might make you wonder how you can test it for various scenarios. How can you make sure that if notifications are produced over a long period of time, they won't be filtered?

The answer is, you can't, at least not the way it's written now. `MachineMonitor` isn't testable. To make this class testable, you need a way to control the time from the outside and provide `MachineMonitor` the scheduler you want it to use in its queries.

The pattern often used to inject schedulers wraps them inside a class that provides the schedulers you need to use in your system. Then, you register this class in your IoC container.[2] This is the interface that I usually use in my projects:

```
public interface IConcurrencyProvider
{
    IScheduler TimeBasedOperations { get; }
    IScheduler Task { get; }
    IScheduler Thread { get; }
    IScheduler Dispatcher { get; }
}
```

Note that the members of this interface might be different based on the platform or type of application you write (for example, `Dispatcher` isn't relevant to platforms that don't support it). The implementation for this interface is also easy:

```
class ConcurrencyProvider : IConcurrencyProvider
{
    public ConcurrencyProvider()
    {
        TimeBasedOperations = DefaultScheduler.Instance;
        Task = TaskPoolScheduler.Default;
        Thread = NewThreadScheduler.Default;
        Dispatcher = DispatcherScheduler.Current;
    }

    public IScheduler TimeBasedOperations { get; }
    public IScheduler Task { get; }
    public IScheduler Thread { get; }
    public IScheduler Dispatcher { get;  }
}
```

Now that you have the `IConcurrencyProvider` in place, you can change the `MachineMonitor` implementation to make it testable by injecting the `IConcurrency-Provider` through its constructor:

---

[2] An inversion of control container (also called a dependency injection, or DI container) is a class that's in charge of creating other objects based on the configuration you specify, such as the implementation that's registered for an interface. Read more at http://martinfowler.com/articles/injection.html.

```
public MachineMonitor(
    IConcurrencyProvider concurrencyProvider,
    ITemperatureSensor temperatureSensor,
    IProximitySensor proximitySensor)
{
    _concurrencyProvider = concurrencyProvider;
    _temperatureSensor = temperatureSensor;
    _proximitySensor = proximitySensor;
}
```

C.2.2 Injecting the TestScheduler

In this implementation of the MachineMonitor class, you set the value of the Max-AlertBurstTime property to 5 seconds and the value of the MinAlertPause property to 1 second. If two notifications are produced in less than a second from one another, you discard the latter one, but if more notifications are produced close to each other and 5 seconds has passed, then another notification will be emitted.

Listing C.7 shows an example of a unit test I've written to validate that if a burst is longer than 5 seconds and the temperature is high (higher than 70 degrees), two emissions are produced. In my test, I use NSubstitute (http://nsubstitute.github.io/) as a mocking framework and set the mock for the IConcurrencyProvider to return the TestScheduler from every member of the concurrency provider. In your tests, you can use whatever mocking framework you like (or none if you prefer).

NOTE In my implementation, I consider an emitted temperature to be valid until another temperature value is emitted.

> **Listing C.7 Validating that 2 alerts are produced if the burst is longer than 5 seconds**

```
[Fact]
public void BurstOverFiveSeconds_RiskyTemperature_TwoAlerts()
{
    var testScheduler = new TestScheduler();
    var oneSecond = TimeSpan.TicksPerSecond;

    var temperatures = testScheduler.CreateHotObservable<double>(
        OnNext(310, 500.0),
    );
    var proximities = testScheduler.CreateHotObservable<Unit>(
        OnNext(100, Unit.Default),
        OnNext(1 * oneSecond-1, Unit.Default),
        OnNext(2 * oneSecond - 1, Unit.Default),
        OnNext(3 * oneSecond - 1, Unit.Default),
        OnNext(4 * oneSecond - 1, Unit.Default),
        OnNext(5 * oneSecond-1, Unit.Default),
        OnNext(6 * oneSecond - 1, Unit.Default)
    );
    var concurrencyProvider = Substitute.For<IConcurrencyProvider>();
    concurrencyProvider.ReturnsForAll<IScheduler>(testScheduler);
```

An emission of a high temperature; should result in an alert

A sequence of proximity notifications that are close to each other, but over a period of time longer than 5 seconds. This should result in two alerts.

Configures the concurrency-provider mock to return the TestScheduler from each of its members

```
var tempSensor = Substitute.For<ITemperatureSensor>();
tempSensor.Readings.Returns(temperatures);
var proxSensor = Substitute.For<IProximitySensor>();
proxSensor.Readings.Returns(proximities);
```

Creates the mock of the temperature sensor and configures it to return the test observable with the temperature emissions

Creates the mock of the proximity sensor and configures it to return the test observable with the proximity emissions

```
var monitor=new MachineMonitor(concurrencyProvider, tempSensor,
  proxSensor);

var res = testScheduler.Start(() => monitor.ObserveAlerts(),
    0,
    0,
    long.MaxValue);
```

Configures TestScheduler to subscribe to the observable at time 0

Configures TestScheduler to start the test at time 0

Configures TestScheduler to dispose of the subscription at the latest time possible

```
res.Messages.AssertEqual(
    OnNext(310, (Alert a) => a.Time.Ticks == 310),
    OnNext(6*oneSecond - 1, (Alert a) => true)
);
}
```

Asserts that a second alert was produced

Asserts the first alert was emitted when the emitted alert was produced

As you can see, even though this is a complex scenario to test (which makes the test itself a bit complex), the test is still readable, and creating it was relatively easy thanks to the utilites provided by Rx.

C.3   Summary

- Testing Rx code is important, just like testing any other code. However, without the proper tools, testing Rx code can be cumbersome, which naturally results in fewer tests and in lower quality. Luckily, Rx provides excellent utilities to tackle this problem.
- To get access to Rx testing utilities, you need to add the `Microsoft.Reactive.Testing` NuGet package.
- Test classes that test Rx code should inherit from the `ReactiveTest` base class to simplify the test code.
- `TestScheduler` is a special scheduler that allows you to control its inner clock.
- For a cold observable with a predefined set of values that will be emitted relatively to the observer subscription, use the `TestScheduler.CreateColdObservable` method.
- For a hot observable with a predefined set of values that will be emitted at an absolute time, use the `TestScheduler.CreateHotObservable` method.
- To create an observer that records the notifications it observes and the time they were observed, use `TestScheduler.CreateObserver`.
- The `AssertEqual` extension method allows you to assert that the expected emissions were observed by the test observer.
- Use the `TestScheduler.Start` method to start its clock.

- Use the `TestScheduler.Start(Func<IObservable<T>>)` method overload to simplify the test. It'll create the observable with the provided factory method, subscribe to it, and return the collection of emissions that were observed.
- Make your Rx code testable by providing the schedulers that'll be used through dependency injection.

index

Get the eBook FREE!

(PDF, ePub, Kindle, and liveBook all included)

We believe that once you buy a book from us, you should be
able to read it in any format we have available. To get electronic
versions of this book at no additional cost to you, purchase and
then register this book at the Manning website.

Go to https://www.manning.com/freebook and follow the
instructions to complete your pBook registration.

That's it!
Thanks from Manning!